FIT TO TEACH

Fit to Teach

Same-Sex Desire, Gender, and School Work in the Twentieth Century

JACKIE M. BLOUNT

STATE UNIVERSITY OF NEW YORK PRESS

Published by
State University of New York Press, Albany

For information, address State University of New York Press,
194 Washington Avenue, Suite 305, Albany, NY 12210-2384

Production by Kelli Williams
Marketing by Anne M. Valentine

Cover photo from the private collection of Catherine A. Lugg. Used with
permission.

Library of Congress Cataloging-in-Publication Data

Blount, Jackie M., 1959–
    Fit to teach : same-sex desire, gender, and school work
in the twentieth century / Jackie M. Blount
        p.   cm.
    Includes bibliographical references and index.
    ISBN-13 978-0-7914-6267-6 (hc : alk. paper) —
978-0-7914-6268-3 (pbk : alk. paper)
    ISBN 0-7914-6267-6 (hc : alk. paper) — 0-7914-6268-4 (pbk : alk. paper)
    1. Homosexuality and education—United States—History—
20th century. 2. Gay teachers—United States—History—
20th century. I. Title.
LC192.6.B56 2004
371.1'0086'64'—dc22   2004041624

10 9 8 7 6 5 4 3 2 1

Contents

Acknowledgments

As I write the final words for this book, I realize how utterly indebted I am to countless people, both known and unknown, who in some manner have helped me with this project. In a very direct sense, the existence of lesbian and gay historical archives has made this work possible. The staff and volunteers of these organizations spend untold hours quietly gathering, cataloging, and displaying the isolated artifacts that together document a rich, emerging history. I have been fortunate enough to visit the Gerber/Hart Library (Chicago), Gay and Lesbian Historical Society of Northern California (San Francisco), One Institute and Archives (Los Angeles), Lesbian History Project (Los Angeles), James C. Hormel Gay and Lesbian Center (San Francisco), and June L. Mazer Lesbian Archives (Los Angeles). Three women in particular went to great lengths to assist me in tracking down many difficult-to-find resources: Jo Duffy and Sarah Wright (Mazer Collection), and Yolanda Retter (Lesbian History Project). They also made Los Angeles a warm and welcoming place for two women from Iowa.

My travel to these archives, as well as to several large research libraries, was made possible by an Iowa State University (ISU) Research Grant and an ISU College of Education Small Research Grant. I received these necessary funds in large part because of the kind support of college administrators who believed in the value of this work: Camilla Benbow, Dan Reschley, Larry Ebbers, Dick Zbaracki, and Ann Thompson. I also thank Ann Thompson and Walt Gmelch for allowing me some time for this research during my own subsequent administrative appointments.

Priscilla Ross, Director of SUNY Press, has earned my undying gratitude for having confidence in this project and for her patience as my unanticipated four years of administrative work necessitated that I write many more pages of extension requests than manuscript. I thank Lisa Chesnel as well for her patience and editorial assistance. Kelli Williams led this project skillfully through production and Anne Valentine coordinated its marketing. I thank them both for their talent and attention.

Finding many of the sources cited in this book has been difficult, time-consuming work. Amazingly, Eric Rofes, who has provided significant leadership for a wide range of LGBT organizations from the 1970s through the present, accumulated a personal archive of primary source documents describing the educators and students who together made a movement. He generously invited me and my partner to his apartment in the Castro to peruse this well-maintained collection and he expressed only confidence as BeJae and I carted armloads of these valuable documents down Market Street to the nearest copy center. Although Eric is singularly well-poised to recount a full, complex, and lively history of LGBT school workers, he did everything possible to help me with this book. For the time being, his scholarly interests lie elsewhere, but he strongly believes that these stories need to be told. I cannot thank Eric enough for his kindness, support, access to this treasure, and long-term leadership that has improved conditions for all LGBT persons.

A number of other friends and colleagues have encouraged me in pursuing this project as well. Penny Richards, Chris Ohana, and Sine Anahita sent me valuable leads and research contacts. Cathi Lugg not only e-mailed me a number of precious resources, but she also gave me the captivating photo of her school-teaching grandmother that graces the cover. Cathi Lugg, Karen Graves, Susan Talburt, Eric Rofes, Andi O'Connor, Glorianne Leck, Kate Rousmaniere, Sine Anahita, Kayt Sunwood, John D'Emilio, Dick Zbaracki, and BeJae Fleming have helped me sharpen my thinking about this work by challenging my assumptions, suggesting theories, quickly finding the weaknesses in my arguments, and generally being wonderfully supportive colleagues. I particularly thank Eric Rofes, Cathi Lugg, BeJae Fleming, Karen Graves, and Dick Zbaracki for reading drafts of this manuscript and offering stunningly insightful suggestions for improvement. They bear no responsibility for the weaknesses of my work, but much credit for its strengths. Karen Graves even assigned the manuscript to the talented students in her honors seminar on LGBT issues in schools offered at Denison University. Of these students, the following provided me with detailed comments that have assisted me greatly with revisions: Lauren Haas, Joanna McKenzie, Benjamin Rorrer, Nicole Weaver, Lara Ellinger, Brooke Bluestein, Jimmy McCloskey, and Leigh Stone.

Finally, preparing such a work as this requires much more than archive and library time, quiet processing, and uncounted hours at the computer. So much of this project has unfolded within the context of enriching friendships. In particular, I extend my deep appreciation to BeJae Fleming, Sine Anahita, and Kayt Sunwood, who shared southern-fried tofu with gravy or campfire-grilled salmon all those nights of pitched tents, flaming logs, and hooting owls at Squirrel Hollow Park. There, under the stars, we talked through much of this book, Sine and Kayt's dissertations, and so many of BeJae's songs. Sine and Kayt now follow the nightly display of northern lights from their cabin in Fairbanks, Alaska where I wish them warmth and only friendly bears. Above all, I give my greatest thanks to BeJae Fleming, whose inspired music forms the backdrop of my life, and whose love gives it meaning.

Introduction

Among the women and men in this country who have founded schools, inspired their students, administered their districts, and otherwise sustained these institutions of promise, there always have been those who have desired others of the same sex or wished to transgress traditional gender bounds. These school workers typically are not obvious as they engage each day in their professional calling. Some fool their colleagues by switching gendered pronouns in describing their significant relationships. Others fool no one, but by remaining quiet about this central feature of their lives, colleagues tacitly agree to leave them alone—especially if they are valued or popular members of the school community. A few make their primary relationships or gender identity as clear and seemingly everyday as those of their peers, but, in so doing, they risk ostracism, parental outrage, punishment, and even dismissal. School workers learn that to remain above reproach, they must modify any personal behavior, fashion, relationship, or other facet of their lives that might cast doubt on their sexual orientation or gender identity. Consequently, schools tend to be gender-polarized places.

Despite the relatively low profile of school workers who identify as lesbian, gay, bisexual, or transgender (LGBT), these individuals enjoy a rich legacy of contributions to the welfare of students and the nation's schools. For example, during the mid-1800s, Addie Brown sent romantically passionate letters to Rebecca Primus, who taught in a Maryland school for freed blacks. She wrote, "I gasp for you."[1] As Superintendent Ella Flagg Young guided the enormously complex Chicago schools from 1909 through 1915, she relied heavily on her longtime companion, Laura Brayton, for both professional and personal support. Similarly, while Mildred Doyle superintended the Knox County schools (TN) from 1946 to 1976, she readily acknowledged the importance of Mildred Patterson in her life, both in the office and at home.[2] John Gish brought his partner, John Hanna, to the 1972 Delegate Assembly of the National Education Association (NEA). At that historic meeting, Gish shattered convention by organizing the NEA's Gay Caucus.[3] More recently, the Broward County (Florida) Teacher of the Year in 2002 acknowledged and thanked her partner in accepting the award.[4] These are just a few of the school workers who have left some record of their sexual or emotional longing for persons of the same sex or of their nonconforming gender identities. Most others have provided exceedingly few clues.

Over the twentieth century, educational service has been difficult at best among those desiring persons of the same sex or defying gender norms. Same-sex desire, considered unspeakable in previous eras, became the focus of scientific, artistic, and scholarly interest during the late 1800s. Persons who possessed such desires, who engaged in same-sex sexual behaviors, or who crossed conventional gender bounds came to be known by terms such as "homosexual," "invert," "deviant," "lesbian," or "queer." By the mid-1900s such individuals began claiming homosexual or cross-gender identities for themselves as many simultaneously clustered in urban areas around the country.[5] And with the visible postwar rise of self-defined homosexual and cross-gender communities, a backlash movement emerged in which suspected homosexuals were purged from the military, government—and schools.

Consequently, school workers desiring others of the same sex have faced many challenges, each pressuring them to conceal their sexual orientation. In the early 1900s, teachers in same-sex boarding schools confronted parental fear that such institutions fostered unhealthy attachments among students, sometimes culminating in sexual activity. Teachers responded by punishing student displays of affection. They also increased surveillance of student activities. In the end, teachers may have deflected attention from questions about their own desires by focusing on those of students.

During the 1930s and 1940s, single women, who accounted for the overwhelming majority of all teachers, encountered criticism that they influenced girls to become spinster teachers. This drop-by-drop poison, as one writer expressed it, supposedly allowed such women to reproduce themselves.

Then, during the 1970s, Anita Bryant, John Briggs, and others warned that "militant homosexual teachers" intended to recruit schoolchildren into the "homosexual lifestyle." They portrayed gay and lesbian teachers as pedophiles eager to seduce students and corrupt their nascent gender identities. These arguments provoked Miami voters to overturn a civil rights ordinance protecting gay men and lesbians from employment and housing discrimination. Despite a lack of research demonstrating a linkage between same-sex desire and pedophilia, the pedophilia bugaboo has long haunted school workers desiring persons of the same sex and has proven at times to be a politically powerful weapon.

Arguments that "homosexual" adults might distort the gender identities of children gained credence in the 1950s and 1960s. In 1962, one prominent study proclaimed that mothers caused their sons to become homosexuals by coddling them and preventing them from developing normal friendships with other boys. Such women also might harbor latent homosexual tendencies, the author claimed.[6] In the 1980s, the conservative Christian psychologist, George Alan Rekers, explained that parents must offer correct gender role modeling for their children. Further, they must actively intervene if their children displayed behaviors or characteristics of the other sex. Otherwise, he maintained, such children might become homosexuals.[7] Rekers subsequently developed therapies that purportedly "cured" homosexuals. He also helped create a national Christian organization that continues trying to make gay men and lesbians "straight."

These researchers provide only two examples of how fear of homosexuality, or homophobia, has compelled the reinforcement of strict, polarized gender behaviors and characteristics among youth—and adults. Through much of the century, conventional wisdom has dictated that cross-gender behaviors and characteristics are tantamount to homosexuality. Essentially, the argument goes like this: An important part of one's gender concerns one's attraction to the other sex. If one is attracted to one's own sex, obviously gender is reversed. The logic concludes that homosexuality can be controlled if gender can be controlled. Obviously, associations between gender and sexual orientation are deeply intertwined. This book explores both with a primary concentration on sexual orientation—or desire.

Today, LGBT educators often face overwhelming resistance in their schools and communities. Few states or cities currently offer nondiscrimination policies that include sexual orientation or gender identity/presentation. Even in the fourteen states that ban discrimination based on sexual orientation (including four that also ban discrimination based on gender identity), job security, safety, and community support are often tenuous.[8] In 2000, a Beverly Hills superintendent claimed that his school board dismissed him because he is gay.[9] A year later, a gay teacher in Wisconsin sued his school district for tolerating antigay harassment by students. A federal court dismissed the case.[10] Untold other cases fail to make headlines as LGBT school workers quietly endure.

Why do so many LGBT school workers remain silent about harassment, job discrimination, intimidation, and ostracism on the job? Mainly they believe the risks to their chosen livelihood are too great. Indeed, LGBT school workers have faced a difficult dilemma over the past fifty years. An important means of ending discrimination against LGBT school workers is to stand up and confront it. However, by confronting the discrimination, they reveal their identities and therefore risk punishment. In the decades following World War II, teachers accused of homosexuality faced certain dismissal, if not permanent career ruin. They had no legal basis for defending themselves. Homophile organizations, where they existed, had few members and little political clout. However, after the Stonewall Rebellion in 1969, the gay liberation movement eventually produced a groundswell of support for LGBT school workers. In 1974, when an episode of the then-popular series, *Marcus Welby, M.D.*, depicted a gay teacher who raped a male student, gay activists successfully spearheaded a national boycott of episode advertisers. Gay liberation activists also assisted in 1977 when Anita Bryant raised the specter of militant homosexual teachers corrupting Miami youth. A year later, they mobilized with exceptional power and skill when California Senator John Briggs promoted an initiative to purge the state's teaching ranks of openly gay men and lesbians as well as their allies. They also fought vigorously and won when the Oklahoma legislature approved a similar act to rid the schools of LGBT workers and their allies. Essentially, gay liberation activists have championed the cause of LGBT school workers even when individual LGBT school workers have felt they could not fight for themselves.

During the 1970s, however, LGBT school workers began to form their own organizations to fight for their employment rights. Skillful lobbying and political activism among teachers in New York, the San Francisco Bay Area, Los Angeles, Boston, Denver, and other cities gave significant momentum to the cause of employment rights for LGBT school workers. Individual LGBT school workers began filing lawsuits when dismissed for status. During these years, the American Civil Liberties Union (ACLU), the National Gay Task Force (NGTF), the National Education Association (NEA), the American Federation of Teachers (AFT), and other organizations supported lawsuits on behalf of LGBT school workers that gradually improved the employment rights of others.

More recently, some LGBT school workers have merged their individual and collective efforts with the larger umbrella organization, Gay Lesbian Straight Education Network (GLSEN). This group, originally called the Gay Lesbian and Straight *Teachers* Network (GLSTN), shifted its attention from LGBT teachers to the general improvement of conditions for *all* LGBT and allied persons in schools, especially students. GLSEN has focused most on helping high school students organize gay–straight alliances in their schools and on mobilizing student activism for policies supporting LGBT and allied youth. Remarkably, GLSEN members mostly have avoided the pedophilia bugaboo thus far.[11] They have done so in part by enlisting large numbers of straight persons—adults and youth—in the fight to end discrimination against LGBT persons in schools.

This book explores the experiences of school workers who have sexually and/or emotionally desired persons of the same sex or transgressed gender norms. It encompasses the past 100 years to reveal some of the ways that the experiences of such school workers have shifted over time. It reveals how notions of acceptable sexual orientation and gender identity have changed. It explores how school workers have been summoned to provide models of normative sexual orientation and gender—as well as to regulate these among their students.

The book focuses on the notion of "same-sex desire." The use of this flexible term is important. Over the past century, a variety of terms have been used to describe same-sex desire or the persons who manifest it. Some terms have scientific origins; others are slang used among persons desiring those of the same sex; and still other terms are intended as disparagement. Some of these expressions have crossed all of these boundaries. For example, because of the work of sexologists, the word "homosexual" mainly carried the aura of science during the early decades of the century. At mid-century, the term enjoyed common use among self-described homosexuals. During the closing decades of the century, though, the word "homosexual" often is used by those who refuse to adopt the language of LGBT activists; therefore it is regarded by many LGBT persons as denigrating.

Terms also have a way of changing meaning. Early in the century, the term "homosexual" described *behavior*. However, over time the term came to connote an *individual* who might engage in sexual activity with persons of the same sex. This change in usage signaled a critical shift from a behavior to an identity. Theoretically, it became possible to have a homosexual identity without ever engaging in same-sex sexual activity.

Admittedly, this is contentious terrain. Could one be gay or lesbian simply by desiring persons of the same sex or even centering one's life on members of the same sex—without having sexual relations? Arguably, a number of early twentieth-century women educators centered their lives on other women. They lived together, often sharing the same bed. They dined, socialized, and agitated for political change together. In many cases, friends and acquaintances recognized such pairs of women as companions. These women expressed their romantic desire for one another; however, sexual activity between them rarely can be ascertained. Most certainly, many of them would have resisted the label "lesbian." However, these women clearly centered their lives on women—and some such relationships included sexual activities. They refrained from marriage or intimate relationships with men. In the end, they lived outside the bounds of conventional heterosexuality.

Then there is the case of Joseph Acanfora. In 1971, Acanfora's district transferred him out of the classroom and into a central office administrative job when the *New York Times* published a story about his difficulty in getting a teaching license because of his sexual orientation. Acanfora considered himself gay even though he never had engaged in same-sex sexual activities. His district essentially punished him for an identity rather than a behavior. Similarly, James Gaylord lost his teaching position in Tacoma, Washington, the same year. His district never produced any evidence that he had engaged in same-sex sexual activity or that his sexual orientation affected his notable teaching ability. He, too, though, was dismissed for status. The term "same-sex desire" includes cases such as these where same-sex sexual activity does not necessarily exist (or cannot be proven, anyway), but the desire for it or the romantic longing for one of the same sex does.

The term "same-sex desire" also encompasses many historically contingent terms used over the past century. Naming, or labeling, is powerful because it effectively draws boundaries around groups of persons, setting them up for particular life chances or oppression. A spinster or bachelor woman teacher may have engaged in sexual activity with women, but until she was labeled "homosexual" or "lesbian," her activities, if discreet, raised little ire. During the mid-1950s, though, schools throughout the state of Florida hunted for homosexual teachers. Unmarried women, those who wore masculine clothing, cropped their hair a bit too short, or socialized mainly with other women ran the risk of such labeling and subsequent dismissal. The terms "homosexual" and "lesbian" became associated with women who transgressed the bounds of acceptable sexual orientation—and gender.

Adding to the complexity of terminology is the notion that boundaries between terms often are murky. A label to one person may mean something different to someone else. Also, labeling oneself differs from labeling others. Some persons may use the word "queer" as an insult. However, many now have reclaimed the term to describe themselves in a positive manner. "Queer," as it is often used in current practice, embraces the full complexity and fluidity of human sexuality and gender. It eschews the boundaries inflicted by such words as "gay" (men), "lesbian" (women), and "transgender" (persons whose identities defy conventional gender bounds). Because labels have shifted over the past century, because bounds between terms often are unclear at best, and because labels may create both new identity groups and forms of oppression, I use the more encompassing term "same-sex desire" in the title of this book. However, in the chapters that follow, I employ more specific terms in their historically appropriate contexts.

Finally, this book focuses on school workers, including teachers, administrators, and others involved in the work of schools. As I argued in *Destined to Rule the Schools: Women and the Superintendency, 1873–1995*, school work in the United States largely has been gender-polarized from the time women began teaching in significant numbers. In short, women have taught and men have administered. However, the fear of same-sex desire or gender nonconformity among school workers has contributed to this ongoing gender division between teaching and administration. Over the twentieth century, men, in what has been perceived largely as a woman's profession, have worked diligently to prove their masculinity—as well as their heterosexuality. And after World War II, spinster women teachers, who dominated the profession numerically and who had begun moving into administrative positions in significant numbers, increasingly needed to prove their heterosexuality as well. They did so by marrying and refraining from administrative work. To better see the full sweep of gendered employment patterns, the analysis in this volume includes teachers *and* administrators.

I became interested in the experiences of LGBT school workers during my final years of teaching at a high school in North Carolina. In 1988, I learned that a local religious group had implored school board members in the surrounding county district to eliminate all homosexual influences in the schools. The letter read:

> Greetings,
>   In the name of our Lord Jesus Christ, We the Citizenry of the Christian Faith greet you.
>   It is with great concern that we write to you, a member of the Davidson County School Board.
>   We are sure that you relize [*sic*] the need to clean up our County, starting with our schools of all "IMMORALITY", [*sic*] as do the County Commissioners of our Great County.
>   We have with great effort drafted a standard for you to use in your decisions concerning our Children.
>   1. No books, or reading material, will be purchased for use in our schools with out the approval of a board of Baptist Ministers.
>   2. All teachers will be subject to spot check, to determine if they are using drugs or not. All teachers found to be using drugs will be fired.

3. We have been informed by God fearing Baptist students that some teachers in our county are homosexual. This "MUST BE STOPED"! [sic]

4. All teachers will take the A.I.D.S. test before returning to teach in our schools this coming 88/89 school year.

5. All teachers male, or female, will be tested to see if they have any homosexual way about them. If so they will be fired.

6. All teachers will sign a form showing that they are of the Christian Faith before they are allowed to teach our children next year.

7. Male teachers will not be allowed to teach female students.

8. Female teachers will not be allowed to teach male students.

9. No teacher will be allowed to teach sex in our schools, unless they have been approved by a board of Baptist Ministers.

10. A female student who becomes pregnant while she is a student in our school system will be expelled from school for acts of immorality.

11. A male student who is found to be having sexual conduct with the female students of our schools will be expelled for having immoral conduct with other students.

12. All teachers must give a written report on their marital standing every 30 days so that their state of mind, as well as their sexual conduct may be determined by a board of Baptist Ministers.

IN GOS'S [sic] LOVE
CONCERNED PIEDMONT BAPTISTS OF DAVIDSON COUNTY

I may never know if there was a direct connection or not, but during the next school year, teachers throughout my district who were thought to be gay or lesbian or who displayed gender nonconformance were demoted, transferred, fired for different reasons, or reprimanded for things that would not have been considered problematic in the past. Our local NEA unit successfully defended these educators, even though the explicit charges did not concern sexual orientation or gender. Even if the charges had, though, North Carolina had no laws to protect school workers—or anyone else—from discrimination based on sexual orientation or gender identity. As a lesbian, I believed that my turn would come, too.

At that point, I began full-time doctoral studies. I read whatever I could find concerning the experiences of LGBT educators in schools—but, in the early 1990s, few such publications existed. There were notable exceptions, though. First, there was Karen Harbeck's groundbreaking dissertation on the history of LGBT educators (1987), later published as *Gay and Lesbian Educators: Personal Freedoms, Public Constraints* (1997).[12] Then there was Eric Rofes's moving autobiographical account of his first teaching job in *Plato, Socrates, and Guys Like Me: Confessions of a Gay Schoolteacher* (1985). I found both works quite compelling. They also convinced me that scholarship could be conducted on the experiences of LGBT school workers. As important, both Rofes and Harbeck have worked tirelessly since the publication of these works on behalf of LGBT students, school workers, and the larger LGBT movement.

During my final year of doctoral studies, I enjoyed the amazing opportunity to enroll in a graduate course on gay history—taught by the eminent historian, John D'Emilio. I had read two of D'Emilio's books, *Sexual Politics, Sexual Communities: The Making of a Homosexual Minority in the United States, 1940–1970* (1983), and *Intimate Matters: A History of Sexuality in America* (co-written with the remarkable historian Estelle Freedman). Both works deeply altered my thinking, revealing with linguistic grace the complexities and historical contingencies of human sexuality. D'Emilio, the professor, demonstrated instructional gifts at least as great as his vast scholarly talent. Toward the end of that expansive semester, my partner and I, like a number of others in the class, participated in the 1993 Gay and Lesbian March on Washington. Then I finished my research paper for the course on the historical experiences of lesbian and gay teachers in the United States. Over the ten years since, that small project has expanded into this book.

As I began researching this topic, I quickly discovered a problem. Historical evidence about the experiences of LGBT school workers truly is difficult to find. One professor in my doctoral program even warned that I would never be able to obtain enough data to piece together a respectable article, much less a book. Several factors contributed to this problem. First, until the 1960s, very little was published to describe homosexuality or cross-gender characteristics/behaviors among school workers. A powerful taboo prevented face-to-face discussion of the topic, much less coverage in relevant journals or books. Making matters even more complicated, much of the historical primary source material concerning same-sex desire ignores persons of color. Essentially, the experiences of persons of color who have defied gender conventions or desired others of the same sex have remained far more invisible than those of persons with white privilege.

Second, vandals have exacted a serious toll on the scanty material that has been published. Initially, through published bibliographies, I learned of a few books and articles describing topics connected with LGBT persons. However, when I traveled to libraries at various large research institutions to find these works, I discovered that many were missing, shredded, torn up, or defaced beyond use. For example, a 1964 *Life* magazine article that profiled the underground world of urban male homosexuals was neatly trimmed out of a volume at one library.[13] At another, the article had been ripped out, with ragged edges leaving clear evidence of theft. In yet another, about half of the pages were missing. In an entirely different region of the country, the article had been covered with black marker scrawls, its photos and some sections of text carefully removed. I finally tracked down a nearly intact copy of the article. Unfortunately, I found that this problem afflicted a number of other books and magazine articles that discussed homosexuality during the early and middle decades of the century. Eventually, I found many of the missing pieces I had sought by working extensively at the Library of Congress.

Third, much of the literature available in research libraries concerning school workers who desire persons of the same sex has been written by persons who do not identify this way themselves. Consequently, many of these works have pathologized or demeaned such school workers. In piecing together this historical account, I have wanted to include the perspectives of school workers who have desired persons of the same sex as much as possible. To accomplish this, I have visited a number of LGBT historical archives. During the 1970s, several LGBT archives began collecting and protecting documents that described emerging sexual subcultures around the country. By the mid-1990s, when I began this project in earnest, at least a dozen such archives had established extensive, well-organized collections. I traveled to as many as I could.[14]

The first LGBT historical collection that I visited demonstrated clearly the difficulties such organizations face. Before I journeyed halfway across the continent to use this facility, I called well ahead of time to assure my access. I was told which days and hours I could visit. However, I would not be given the address until I arrived in town. When I called for directions, the archivist asked me several questions to ascertain my legitimate research credentials. The building, he told me, offered no external markings. Once there, I would need to go around back, ring the buzzer, and wait. Eventually, after I rang the buzzer at the appointed time, the still-chained door opened. Again, I verified my identity, purpose, and credentials. The archivist instructed me to leave my backpack in the car and said I could use only the pencils and paper he would provide for me. Furthermore, the archives would only be open for two hours that day and two more hours later in the week. I had to work quickly and well, but the vastness of the collection cried out for extensive digging. Eventually, the archivist softened when he came to trust me. He then explained that archivists at the collection had to maintain extraordinary vigilance because theft and vandalism were constant dangers. The collection already had suffered.

The archivists at all of the LGBT collections I visited have been kind and helpful to me in my work. Not only have volunteers and shockingly few paid employees kept these collections rich, full, and well organized, but they have also been eager to help me find the most relevant evidence for my work. They also patiently indulged my penchant for browsing through as much of the general material as possible. Indeed, these institutions are gems that play an increasingly important role in preserving LGBT culture and history.[15]

And finally, I have been helped repeatedly by the kindness of friends who have sent me leads on relevant articles, books, or other documents. Most never would have come to my attention otherwise—and many have proven invaluable. Eric Rofes even allowed me to access his personal collection of lesbian and gay teacher association newsletters, clippings, personal writings, and other materials that he had accumulated over the course of his career as an activist gay teacher. These rare documents are centrally important to the story I have pieced together.

Aside from the great difficulties involved in finding relevant documentary evidence about the history of LGBT educators, other problems have kept scholars from the undertaking. A number of persons interested in starting such research have struggled to secure or retain academic positions because the topic is viewed as too controversial. And there has been strong societal agreement with policies aimed at limiting the employment of school workers who desire persons of the same sex. As a result, the practice hardly was problematized until the late 1970s. Of the education research that is emerging, little is historical in nature.

I argue that historical research is critically necessary to counter the prevalent assumption that intolerance of LGBT school workers has always existed. Instead, in this volume I examine how current conditions have developed in specific historical contexts; thus our conditions are open to question and critical analysis. And finally, in this volume I describe some of the powerful ways that school workers who desire persons of the same sex or manifest unconventional gender have resisted intolerance and demonstrated breathtaking power in pursuing their chosen profession.

CHAPTER 1

The Gender and Sexual Transformation of School Work

In 1911, tensions between men and women ran high in the New York City schools. Women headed most classrooms in the system and some even had become high-ranking administrators. Grace Strachan, a feisty district superintendent in the city, dared to lead a campaign demanding equal wages for women and men teachers. In turn, male educators despaired about losing their already diminished places in the schools. They resisted equal pay by sex, arguing that if women received the same salaries as men, the few remaining male teachers would leave in disgust.[1]

A headline from the *New York Times* captured the male teachers' concerns: "Appeal for Men Teachers—Boys Too Effeminate, Say Principals, When They Haven't Male Instructors." The article explained that "principals and men teachers are making an urgent appeal for more men teachers in the elementary schools, saying the lack of supervision and instruction by male teachers is a distinct loss to the boys." Worse still, the male educators interviewed in the piece contended that "under the present order of things, such boys end their school days without ever having had instruction from a man teacher. This . . . is a distinct discrimination against boys at an age when they most need instruction by men."[2] Male teachers had forwarded other arguments earlier in the equal pay campaign, ones that largely focused on the needs of men in the classroom. Such rhetoric did not sway public sentiment. This time, however, male teachers appealed not to their own welfare, but rather to that of their students. The tactical shift generated a positive response. Over the remainder of the twentieth century, many others would make similar appeals to the welfare of students as they promoted their own gender- and sexual orientation-specific policies in schools.

Despite the pleas of male educators and the effectiveness of this new rhetorical maneuver, however, Strachan and her supporters eventually won the battle for equal pay. And as the male educators had predicted, men's already scanty representation among schoolteachers continued declining. Men avoided school work in part because of poor pay. For some, the harrowing, increasingly regimented conditions of the work served as a powerful disincentive. Undoubtedly for most, however, the work also repelled those who wished to maintain a conventional middle-class masculinity in which men earned enough to support families, they exerted clear authority over women, and their work granted them independence. These men did not just fear that *boys* were becoming effeminate, but also, at a more fundamental level, they worried that the public regarded *male educators* as effeminate because they practiced a profession thoroughly reconfigured as women's work.

Before the invention of homosexuality and heterosexuality as distinct categories in the late 1800s, it is difficult to pinpoint precisely what is queer in the history of school workers in the United States. The categories employed before then vary substantially from those understood today. However, what is clear is that during the 1800s, profound changes occurred in the gender association of school work as well as in the range of sexual behaviors allowed of female and male school workers. To place developments over the twentieth century in context, a brief examination of nineteenth-century shifts in the expected sexuality and gender of school workers is necessary.

The protests of the New York male teachers effectively ended a remarkable century that had brought a fundamental change in the face and character of teaching. During the early 1800s, men performed virtually all paid teaching and tutoring work. Most did not view teaching as a lifelong mission, so schoolmasters usually taught for a few years to make ends meet following college. Then, after establishing reputations in their communities through teaching, men commenced their intended professions in law, commerce, medicine, or the ministry.

Even with the long-standing tradition of male schoolmasters, however, thousands of women began teaching during the mid-1800s, quickly outnumbering men. By 1900, women accounted for over two-thirds of all teachers. The upward trend continued into the 1920s when women claimed five of every six public school positions.[3] In this dramatic demographic shift, not only did women choose the toils of the classroom, but men also actively avoided it, eschewing any connection with "women's" work.

On one level, when teaching shifted from work done by men to that done by women, the change was simply demographic. At a deeper level, however, fundamental changes in the gendered nature of the work also occurred in parallel with this demographic shift. Teaching, although never well paid, once had allowed men opportunities for independence, to recruit students and manage school business, create curricula, expand scholarship begun in college, and associate with other respected men of the community. However, as women filled the ranks, a new class of school personnel emerged—male administrators—who, in turn, took on the duties of running schools requiring independent thought and action. Teachers lost independence and authority to the same degree that administrators gained it. Teaching became "feminized" in other respects as well. While early male teachers desired salaries allowing them to support families, though modestly, female teachers received a fraction of the meager pay of their male counterparts. Moreover, school boards generally expected female teachers to remain single—or to resign immediately upon marriage. While early male teachers had pursued liberal studies in college, female teachers, with limited college-level opportunities available, typically enrolled in normal schools. In these institutions they pursued a curriculum emphasizing pedagogical studies and only enough content knowledge to stay ahead of their students. As the 1800s began, men taught, but not women. By the end of the century, women taught, but few men remained. Within 100 years, the gender identification of teaching had reversed.

Had some inherent quality of the work caused this shift in gender association? And what is gender? While sex concerns one's anatomy and physiology, gender is a set of stories that people tell themselves and each other about what it means to be men and women. These stories are as varied as the individuals and the cultures in which they live. Sex-related anatomy and physiology can vary substantially; therefore a person's sex is not always as clearly drawn as the polarized female/male model might indicate. Also, in recent decades, transsexuals and the doctors who have assisted them in transitioning to the other sex have done much to shift and complicate cultural thinking about the meaning of sex (as well as gender and sexual orientation).[4] Gender has always carried the complexity inherent in any socially created quality. Individuals negotiate gender throughout their lives. Despite—or perhaps because of—this, some societies create uniform visions of gender, and then maintain them through promotion and sanction, through individual and group action, through what we tell each other and ourselves over and over again.[5]

Sexual orientation, in contrast with gender, concerns sexual desire. Gendered behaviors, characteristics, or identities assist individuals in navigating sexual choices within their cultures, helping them find others with whom sexual activity may be a possibility. Sexual orientation, like gender, has socially constructed components, and so is not a completely fixed quality. It can change depending on social contexts. For example, although mainstream media during the 1950s portrayed mainly one sexual orientation—exclusively heterosexual (as well as monogamous, with someone of a similar race/ethnicity and social/economic class)—a range existed at the same time, spanning a continuum of desire from exclusively heterosexual to exclusively homosexual. These divergent sexualities did not receive the same public endorsement, however. Sexual orientation has varied substantially across subcultures and through historical epochs as well.[6] Sexual orientation and gender are thus intimately intertwined, though separate concepts.

Although gender and sexual desire/orientation are fluid to some degree rather than fixed and essential, elaborate social mechanisms have been created in most cultures to perpetuate norms for both. Religious institutions, communities, and families traditionally have held much of this responsibility. However, as tax-supported schooling spread around the country and eventually became compulsory, schools assumed a greater share of the work of imparting "correct" gendered behaviors and characteristics in the United States. These responsibilities expanded as family and community structures shifted with the industrial-era realignment of the economy. Schools not only assumed much of the work of shaping students' gender, but they also tacitly aided in defining and regulating sexual orientation.

An important means that schools employed to influence students' gender was through the selection of school workers who might provide gender-appropriate modeling. As girls and boys began studying together in tax-supported schools during the mid-1800s, school work came to be divided into realms of work performed by men—administration, and that done by women—teaching. By so segregating the work, schools themselves came to resemble traditional male-head-of-household families whose services they had come to supplement. Administrative work, by definition, became what was manly or fitting work for men. Conversely, school teaching became work that was feminine, or fitting for women. Students confronted this unspoken lesson daily.

As with gender, school workers also modeled acceptable mainstream sexual orientation. School districts hired women teachers thought to be chaste and pure guardians of virtue. Not surprisingly, these women were single. Schools typically required women teachers to resign if they married, thus avoiding conflicts in their primary allegiances. Conversely, schools preferred hiring married men—who headed traditional, heterosexual households. Communities viewed unmarried men in school work as suspicious, lacking manliness, irresponsible, possessing poor character, or prone to womanizing. The marital expectations of men and women thus were inversely related. By hiring individuals who demonstrated conventional sexual desires appropriate for their sex, schools assured that proper models would influence young people. Later, schools would supplement modeling with curricula overtly intended to shape young people into properly heterosexual women and men well-versed in middle-class courtship rituals.

Although schools attempted to regulate the gender and sexual orientation of their workers—and by extension students—they also provided fascinating opportunities for supporting unconventional sexualities and gender behaviors, characteristics, and identities. For example, by the early twentieth century, so few men taught that districts hired nearly any man who demonstrated interest or possessed even modest prerequisite skills. So desperate were schools to employ male teachers that they hired those who did not fit conventional notions of masculinity. Women challenged mainstream identities, too. Because most school districts required that women teachers refrain from marriage, and because teaching allowed women to earn enough to support themselves humbly, large numbers of women chose to remain single. Some even decided to live with other women or otherwise to center their lives on communities of women without raising suspicion. This represented a radical departure from the tradition requiring middle-class women to structure their lives around men—either husbands or other male relatives.

Initially, opportunities for unconventional gender or sexual orientation among school workers were not widely discussed. In time, however, public concern mounted. Some critics worried that spinster teachers might compel girls to scorn marriage. Others contended that effeminate male teachers brought sexual abnormalities into the schools. In response to such concerns, schools scrutinized the gender and sexual orientation of their workers even more closely. Schools, then, have both nurtured transgressive gender and sexual orientation, and, just as surely, endeavored to contain such transgressions.

Mainstream notions of gender changed over the nineteenth century along with the economic, political, and cultural contexts of the nation. Early in the 1800s, white male-headed families formed centers of economic productivity, engaging in farming, craftwork, or other small commerce. Women often partnered in running family businesses, but typically their duties aligned with gendered expectations of the time, including domestic responsibilities. Men represented the public interests of the family, serving in community governance and controlling family capital. Men earned respect by the degree to which they preserved community welfare and brought honor to the family name. Meanwhile, the slavery-driven economy of the South disrupted family structures. Plantation owners often bought and sold African American slaves without regard for keeping families intact.[7] Similarly, Native American families also faced profound interference because of geographical displacement, genocide, and, later, forced boarding schooling. Consequently, notions of gender roles within families are bounded by historical conditions of racial oppression.

As the economy shifted toward industrialism with its attendant expansion of the working and middle classes, notions of exemplary white manhood changed. Anthony Rotundo argues that this shift fostered the rise of "self-made manhood," an idealized notion of masculinity based on individual hard work and achievement rather than on family name and the accomplishments of others. Masculine identity would no longer be contingent on a man's heritage alone, but also by his personal success and works.[8]

To achieve self-made manhood, white men increasingly required independence in their actions and social relations. They needed freedom from the constraints of strong mutual obligation that existed in small communities. They also required relaxed religious oversight. Rotundo describes this as a shift allowing men more freedom to indulge their passions. Their desire to rise above their station of birth and their willingness to compete aggressively fueled what became a system of rugged individualism. In this system, men learned to channel their passions rather than to deny or suppress them. Reason provided one important mechanism with which they directed these passions. At a time when the economy increasingly rewarded individual initiative and competitiveness, the virtue of independence grew more important. White men were expected to guard their autonomy and resist being controlled by others. In a society in which men competed vigorously with one another, those who sought to dominate others were regarded as virtuous.[9]

As the 1900s approached, Rotundo argues that combativeness and ambition became even more important virtues for men, and that tough, aggressive competitiveness was accepted and tenderness derided. He contends that prevailing notions of men's sexuality changed as well. Where sexual desire previously had been regarded as a passion over which men had limited control, the early 1900s brought increased acceptance of men's sexual desires. Indeed, men's bodies became symbols of manhood in which muscular build, proven strength, and sporting ability mattered greatly.[10]

Before the rise of "self-made manhood," men's public roles in small communities had helped ensure strong mutual bonds. Individual men regulated communities, but, in turn, communities regulated them. Where neighbors and townspeople failed to control men's behavior, religious groups exerted tremendous influence, urging men toward virtue and a sense of community obligation. However, as townships grew and public sector work intensified, community regulatory functions waned. Instead, moral regulation increasingly took place in the home—and became part of women's duties. While the new manhood encompassed gradually more independence, competitiveness, strength, and expression of sexual desire, women supposedly became moderating influences tasked with reining in the excesses of these qualities.[11] Consequently, women's roles changed along with men's. Women came to be regarded as the moral exemplars of the household, as upholders of virtue. As such, women's supposedly "natural" moral sense was thought much stronger than men's; thus women were to control men's immoderation, essentially stepping into the regulatory void formerly occupied by communities and religious institutions.

A significant implication of this gender redefinition is that women were accorded a separate place alongside men. This separate-spheres ideology not only indicated a sharp delineation between acceptable gender identities for women and men, but it also resulted in different physical spaces that they inhabited. Men spent much of their working and social time in places occupied primarily by other men. Women devoted much of their time to activities with other women or to solitary endeavors in their homes. Social groups of women clustered in other's houses or socially approved extensions such as schools, churches, or community organizations. Through the ideology of separate spheres, women and men not only assumed different gender identities and kinds of service, but they occupied different spaces and otherwise maintained homosocial worlds—men with men and women with women.[12]

Family size and structure shifted during the 1800s along with approved gender identities and socially assigned spaces. The rapid growth of urban centers and the industrial economy spelled the decline of family farms and some small businesses. Families no longer needed to bear as many children to support these domestic enterprises. Consequently, married couples found ways to reduce their family sizes. They employed new contraceptive devices and practices they had seen in catalogs, read in books, or otherwise heard about from friends and family members. Young married women commonly received contraceptive information in the mail—until the 1873 Comstock Law prohibited the distribution of such information through the postal system. Euphemistic labeling in published media and informal, word-of-mouth networks filled the gap afterwards.[13] Doctors and others who performed abortions offered their services, but some abortion methods did not work or carried extreme risk. A number of women died as a result of botched procedures. Taken together, these practices contributed to a decline in the size of families in the United States.[14]

As the birthrate dropped, conventional sexual activity became associated more with sexual desire and less with procreation. Romance assumed greater significance in intimate relationships. When men and women chose marriage partners, they increasingly valued romantic love—expecting to love someone before deciding to marry them, rather than the reverse: marrying someone deemed suitable and then learning to love them. Choosing a partner became a matter of finding a person about whom one could feel passionate. And sexual expression was often an important component of that passion.

Shifting gendered identities affected how such intimate relationships unfolded. Men, who valued independence and autonomy, felt freer than women to engage in a variety of sexual experiences. They sought to satisfy their strong passions. Women, however, were expected to confine their sexual activity to fiancés or husbands. Those whose sexual expression ventured beyond these bounds risked ostracism, a drop in social status, or impoverishment. Such sanctions carried different risks for women depending on their social class. Because women of privilege had much to lose, they tended to limit their sexual activity. Working-class and poor women, however, sometimes felt more at ease about pursuing their sexual passions outside marriage. Generally, though, communities expected women to constrain men's desire for relatively free sexual expression and help control their "baser instincts."[15]

Women were to restrain not only men's sexual behavior, but communities also expected them—as mothers—to teach their children proper sexual mores. However, over the second half of the 1800s as tax-supported education spread, teachers assumed growing responsibility for assuring both the proper gender and sexual development of children. Communities ensured this by carefully selecting school workers who might serve as exemplars for children. The kinds of women and men hired to work in schools indicated much about how communities defined acceptable gender and sexual desire.

Before women taught in appreciable numbers, male schoolmasters earned grudging respect only after years of exemplary service. Cultivating that respect was difficult because some schoolmasters, struggling with poor wages and difficult conditions, remained in the classroom only because they could find no other gainful employment. These pedagogues occasionally drank heavily, inflicted cruel discipline, or maintained slovenly grooming habits, all of which contributed to unflattering stereotypes. In Walt Whitman's 1841 story, "Death in the School-Room," a sadistic schoolmaster brutally flogged a student who, it turned out, was already dead.[16] Washington Irving's schoolmaster in *The Legend of Sleepy Hollow* (1819), Ichabod Crane, lacked the cruelty of Whitman's character, but instead demonstrated a clown-like ineptitude:

> He was tall, but exceedingly lank, with narrow shoulders, long arms and legs, hands that dangled a mile out of his sleeves, feet that might have served for shovels, and his whole frame most loosely hung together. His head was small, and flat at top, with huge ears, large green glassy eyes, and a long snipe nose, so that it looked like a weather-cock perched upon his spindle neck to tell which way the wind blew. To see him striding along the profile of a hill on a windy day, with his clothes bagging and fluttering about him, one might have mistaken him for the genius of famine descending upon the earth, or some scarecrow eloped from a cornfield.[17]

Subsequent writers capitalized on this stereotype.[18] One scholar, in his 1928 dissertation on male teachers, contended: "The common assumption was that anybody could teach school, and all too frequently the schoolmaster was very inadequately prepared for his work. . . . Failures, and even town charges, were given the post of schoolmaster so that they might earn their keep. In the middle states bond-servants were frequently chosen as instructors to the youth, and . . . in early Georgia the schoolmaster was little better than a vagrant wandering from community to community."[19]

A number of young men entered teaching only for the short term, hoping to earn a modest sum of money before pursuing their chosen careers. As such, teaching was regarded as youth's work in a number of states and territories.[20] While W. E. B. DuBois attended Fisk University as an undergraduate, he spent two summers teaching in a nearby rural Tennessee school. He described the sight of his students: "There they sat, nearly thirty of them, on the rough benches, their faces shading from a pale cream to a deep brown, the little feet bare and swinging, their eyes full of expectation, with here and there a twinkle of mischief, and the hands grasping Webster's blue-back spelling-book." The schoolhouse itself was a "log hut where Colonel Wheeler used to shelter his corn," rather than a prim building with the usual neat rows of seats that nearby white children attended. And the young DuBois boarded with the families of the children he taught, some meticulous in their housekeeping and others where "untamed bedbugs wandered."[21] Many school districts could ill afford to pay teachers wages allowing them to live independently. Thus, the work failed to attract many men past their early adult years.

Not surprisingly, those who became schoolmasters sometimes suffered barbs and their neighbor's wariness at first. Many wondered why men would seek such daunting, unremunerative work that ill afforded them essentials like clothing and shelter. Making matters worse, few schools recruited or hired teachers in a systematic way. Rarely was there adequate assurance that schoolmasters had prepared in a manner fitting them for service. Despite these significant challenges, some schoolmasters pursued their work with vigor and every intention of teaching students well. These individuals had prepared for the work first by studying in European or New England colleges. Eventually, those who proved to be gifted pedagogues earned community esteem second only to ministers.[22]

Even in the cases of the most well-respected schoolmasters, though, contradictions in the gender appropriateness of the work abounded. Americans popularly regarded scholars and schoolmasters as effete. In a rugged young nation, men who had devoted much of their lives to study—especially in Europe, men from socially prominent families, and men who had cultivated a sense of refinement seemed peculiarly out of place.[23] During a time when Manifest Destiny compelled young men to carve out niches in rustic territories, practical rather than academic knowledge was prized. And despite the fact that school teaching required much ingenuity, independence, and entrepreneurial skill, the work still involved close association with children. Many regarded nurturing and working with children as duties fitting for women, not men. As separate-spheres ideology gained credence, the association of children with women's work deepened. Male schoolmasters found themselves in the uncomfortable position of performing most school teaching before the Civil War, even though the work failed to accord them a strong, unambiguous sense of manliness. In his classic novel, *The Hoosier Schoolmaster,* Edward Eggleston describes the experiences of one such young man, fresh with his college education, who settled into an Indiana community to teach during the 1850s. Immediately, the schoolmaster faced a challenge from a grizzled man standing nearby: "Want to be a school-master, do you? . . . Well, what would you do in Flat Crick deestrick, I'd like to know? Why, the boys have driv off the last two, and licked the one afore them like blazes. . . . You see . . . we a'n't none of your saft sort in these diggin's. It takes a man to boss this deestrick. . . . But if you git licked, don't come on us." During the remainder of the novel, the clever schoolmaster found ways to teach well, endear himself to the community, and avoid the violence and corporal punishment typically expected from male teachers. Even with his education—which made him a "saft sort"—he proved his manliness and worth to the community.[24]

Around the mid-1800s, however, women began entering teaching in breathtaking numbers. Hundreds, then thousands enrolled in newly established women's seminaries and academies, pursuing some of the earliest formal educational opportunities allowed young women beyond primary instruction. With diplomas in hand, they eagerly sought teaching positions, one of the few avenues open to women for which their studies were necessary. Their services were urgently needed too, as common schooling spread across the continent. Educated young men could not be enticed into the work in sufficient numbers to satisfy the growing demand. Moreover, early women teachers quickly proved that they could handle the challenges of setting up and running rural schoolhouses and teaching their motley students. After these early demonstrations, communities eagerly sought motivated and pioneering women teachers. Because they could be hired at a fraction of the cost of male teachers, a number of communities expressly sought out women teachers without first attempting to locate willing men. This practice spread quickly in the end because many women simply wanted to teach, to work outside the home, to earn their own money, and to live independently.[25]

The shift of women into the ranks of schoolteachers did not proceed trouble-free, however. For some, the work involved tricky changes in social standing. Before teaching was available as a job for women, the only socially approved work outside the home involved domestic service in other homes. As such, only women of humble means engaged in paid labor. Women of greater means looked after their own households, supervising domestic servants. For these women, entering the realm of work outside the home entailed a loss of social status and implied that male heads of households could not provide well enough to cover their needs. By convention, men, not women, worked outside the home. Law dictated that men control household property, including that possessed by any female family members. Separate-spheres legal ideology of the time supported these practices.

And besides, married women who ventured into salaried employment discovered that they were required to submit to the authority of their superiors. However, women already needed to submit to male family members in the home. Theoretically, then, working married women had to obey the wishes of two different authorities: their employers and their male heads of household. Such a conflict was thought untenable. Catherine Beecher, a staunch supporter of women teachers, offered a clever way to resolve this tricky problem. Beecher, herself a single woman, strongly recommended that single, rather than married women should teach. The conflict of authority could thus be avoided because single women only owed allegiance to their superiors at work. Beecher further convinced skeptics when she argued that teaching prepared single women for marriage and motherhood. Their preparation and teaching experience would therefore not be wasted. When women married, they could step down and be replaced by other eligible single women. There would be plenty waiting to do so.[26]

For some skeptics, the greatest problem with women teachers concerned their supposed inability to manage students, especially older boys. Reflecting a common sentiment of the time, one superintendent maintained that "while I believe that women when they possess the scholarship and the necessary training can instruct as well as men, I doubt whether they can properly govern school or exert the proper educational influence over large boys and girls. We can not close our eyes to this condition of things. There are certain things which women, because of their sex, can not do and should not be made to do. I, for one, have always considered it cruel to place an innocent girl all by herself in a country school there to watch over the large boys."[27]

Despite this fear of women's supposed frailty in the classroom, women teachers proved to be more than a match for the challenges posed by young male students. Typically they used persuasion and other nonviolent means of maintaining discipline. Experts eventually conceded that women generally seemed to have as good, if not better, results with their disciplinary practices than many men who resorted to corporal punishment and intimidation. Word quickly spread that women teachers governed their classrooms effectively. Within a few years, even the most hardened critics of women teachers had to concede that the experiment was succeeding.[28]

Single women teachers faced a final significant hurdle in their quest for acceptance and appointments. As women accounted for greater portions of the teaching force, earning wages, living independently, and exerting authority in a public space, their detractors worried that they were becoming too independent, that they may not need men, or, perhaps worse, without the gender-regulating presence of men, women might assume traits customarily more desirable for men. School district officials assuaged these concerns by hiring male supervisors to oversee women teachers. These men initially traveled to district schoolhouses and performed maintenance tasks as needed. They also paid bills and observed the women teachers. Most of these early "superintendents" knew little about school work.[29] However, as men they seemed natural authority figures to whom women teachers would report. The presence of male superintendents averted the potential crisis of women teachers overstepping their gender-appropriate bounds—even as they inched beyond the domestic sphere.

In the years following the Civil War, women quickly dominated the work of school teaching numerically.[30] New England women's academies and seminaries continued graduating women who pursued teaching. Due to the efforts of common school advocates Horace Mann, Catherine Beecher, and others, these institutions were joined by a variety of others in preparing teachers. Northern, midwestern, and some southern states established normal schools to meet their growing needs. These institutions offered women formal education beyond the primary level. More important, they provided women with a means to an acceptable career outside the home. Many women reasoned that, by teaching, they could earn enough to support themselves without depending on their families. This financial security would free them from pressure to marry men they found unacceptable. Teaching also offered women career justification for pursuing formal education. They could answer incredulous skeptics who asked why they needed an education. And a few young women wanted to teach so they could carry on in the spirit of their own beloved and admired teachers, emulating them to the extent possible.

By the late 1800s, the trend toward hiring women teachers accelerated with the growth of graded schools in cities and townships. These schools, customarily built with multiple classrooms lining long hallways, typically employed one male supervisor or principal to oversee the work of many women teachers. Because of women's lower wages and the need for only one male, personnel costs remained relatively low—which satisfied local taxpayers. This arrangement also pleased those who believed that schools needed the gender-regulating presence of men—and that women needed to be supervised by them.[31]

The gender shift of teaching after the Civil War was caused not only by women streaming into the work, but also by men's active rejection of it. When the national economy slumped after the war, communities could pay the wages commanded by schoolmasters only with the greatest difficulty. These wages generally fell far short of what young men could earn in many other endeavors that offered greater social standing as well. Also, as more women moved into teaching, districts and states simultaneously mandated greater preparation and certification. Men reasoned that poor teaching wages did not adequately cover this costly additional study. Then there was the matter of authority and autonomy. Teaching increasingly had become work subject to supervision. The new class of administrators hired by schools assumed greater authority over teachers, demanding obedience, and gradually stripping teachers of their decision-making power in schools. Young men willing to endure these shifts discovered that perceptions of their masculinity had eroded. Finally, male teachers found themselves surrounded by women rather than by other men.[32] Gender scholar Michael Kimmel argues that it is men—and not women— who confer a sense of masculinity on each other. If he is correct, then male teachers no longer could enjoy validation of their manhood as they worked in schools filled with women and children.[33] In the final analysis, male teachers decided to leave the work in droves.

For the few men who continued teaching, the gender shifts of the work grew even more uncomfortable. They found themselves supervised closely by male administrators, hired in part to oversee women teachers. Male teachers disdained this patronizing treatment. One particularly frustrated former schoolmaster, C. W. Bardeen, argued that teaching had become "a hireling occupation" that kept teachers "in a state of dependency." He insisted that other professions typically pursued by men afforded much greater autonomy and control. Further, he contended that teaching, as it increasingly had been configured, effectively robbed men of their masculinity.[34]

Ultimately, as women took up the work of teaching, communities shifted the conditions of the classroom to align more closely with societal expectations for women rather than men. These conditions ran afoul of men's expectations, however. To resolve this seemingly unbridgeable gap, most male teachers simply opted to leave the work. Bardeen captured this prevailing sentiment when he explained that "teaching usually belittles a man. . . . His daily dealing is with petty things, of interest only to his children and a few women assistants, and under regulations laid down by outside authority, so that large questions seldom come to him for consideration."[35] Essentially, as teaching became "women's work," men wanted little part of it. As women rushed into the work, the exodus of men accelerated, especially in urban areas. In 1912, an article in the *Atlantic Monthly* summarized the situation: "In cities, the women fill nearly all teaching positions. New York City has 89 percent of women in its force; Boston, 89 percent; Philadelphia, 91.4 percent; Chicago, 93.3 percent . . . and in forty-six towns of 4,000 to 8,000 inhabitants there is no man on the force. . . . In half the cities of the United States there are virtually no men teaching."[36]

By the early 1900s, when the male teachers of New York City campaigned against equal pay for men and women teachers, the gendered transformation of the work was nearly complete. Few would come to the defense of male teachers—especially when they appeared weak and unsympathetic by battling women teachers. However, male teachers soon learned to shift attention away from themselves and toward male students. In 1903, a team of visitors from England had studied urban schooling in the United States and concluded that women teachers made boys effeminate.[37] New York City principals and male teachers played on these findings to build support for recruiting more men into school work. Because men generally found the work so repugnant by this time, the remaining male teachers thought that significantly higher wages were necessary. By 1911, when women teachers won the equal pay battle in New York City, this tactic no longer was possible. Besides, school districts scarcely could afford to pay significant numbers of men the salaries that would entice them. In the end, male educators' most effective strategy involved the creation of niches within schoolwork that remained exclusively male. These areas included athletics, manual trades, high school subjects—especially mathematics and natural sciences—and administration.[38]

Of all these niches, administrative work clearly held the greatest masculine appeal. From the start, schools had structured the work to align with gendered expectations for men. Administrative positions only appeared in schools when women began teaching. Early superintendent duties closely matched those expected of men in their households, including structural repair, financial control, and serving in authority over women.[39] Administrators received significantly higher salaries than did teachers, allowing them to support families as heads of household. Male administrators essentially could cultivate and maintain a sense of masculinity. For this reason Bardeen admired male administrators, but not male teachers. In describing superintendents, he explained that "the kinds of men chosen for these places are those who are least subject to . . . defects. . . . But the rank and file of men teachers are still seriously deficient."[40] The New York school board president in 1916 made clear the kind of men suited to the highest positions in schools: "Let him first be a man. . . . Red blood, hard muscle, virile speech, manly manners seem to me indispensable in the head of a school system. The traditional pattern with spectacles, with the scholar's stoop, the parchment skin, the painfully proper speech chastely devoid of slang and expletive—the type strictly devoid of variation from the conventional—has had its day."[41]

In the early decades of the twentieth century, men who remained in school work often aspired to the superintendency. Superintendents possessed increasing power as part-time, nonprofessional school board members granted them greater authority for running schools. Simultaneously, school district sizes increased, and along with them the tax bases from which superintendent salaries could be drawn. Higher salaries meant a great deal when economic attainment conferred manliness. A growing administrative hierarchy also allowed male superintendents to direct the labors of many others. Finally, as school districts grew larger, superintendents served in central offices somewhat removed from schools, but near municipal power centers. With proximity to government and business leaders, superintendents could socialize more easily with influential men of the community. School administration, then, particularly the superintendency, became at times a separate male space physically removed from women's realm of the classroom.[42]

When school principalships and superintendencies first appeared, school boards did not hire women for them. If they had, women administrators might have exerted authority over men, generally a prohibited condition. If any woman's promotion meant that even one man would become subservient to her, then she would be denied advancement. He would advance instead. However, because the pool of available male teachers had shrunk so dramatically by the early 1900s, many schools employed female school workers exclusively. Midwestern and western states found it particularly difficult to find men—even those without educational qualifications—who were willing to take on the work of the superintendency. To alleviate the shortage, districts in these regions hired women supervisors and superintendents on an experimental basis. As with teaching, women quickly proved that they were, as a class, exceedingly capable in their new duties.[43]

Hiring women school administrators prevailed only when willing men were unavailable, the demands of the position extreme, the pay relatively low, and lucrative opportunities lay elsewhere. Men consistently commanded higher salaries for the work. Women, however, had few avenues for professional promotion. Some women eagerly sought supervisory or superintendent positions to advance their careers, prove themselves, and demonstrate the civic contributions that women as a class could make. When school districts hired women administrators, they did so because of enthusiastic service at a bargain—and because men chose not to serve.

Arguably, when women entered school administration, they crossed a socially created boundary separating feminine and masculine realms. Some communities found this permissible as long as men's status in schools was not compromised and there was some economic or practical benefit to the district. If, however, women's supervisory work challenged the status of men—perhaps by giving them power over men—then districts deemed this gender transgression as outweighing the benefits women could bring to their positions.

In the end, Grace Strachan and the legions of women and men she inspired to join the campaign for equal pay successfully challenged the long-standing practice of paying women teachers substantially less than men. Her leadership in this battle as well as her position as a district superintendent in New York City required that she maintain a delicate balance of gender and sexuality. As a woman, she had risen to a position of administrative leadership in a large and complex district within the city, a position generally reserved for men. She had fought on behalf of all the women teachers of the city for better wages—in opposition to the wishes of many of her male colleagues. Women educators at the time were single. She was married, though, as were her male administrative colleagues. However, from her vantage as a female superintendent, she maintained the seemingly contradictory position that women teachers should remain single. She explained, "A woman teacher who marries and who retains her position as teacher, assumes obligations to two masters, and I agree with St. Luke's gospel, which says: 'No servant can serve two masters: for he will hate the one and love the other; or else he will hold the one and despise the other.'"[44] Was Strachan a master or a servant? As a woman, was it proper for her to remain in school work after her marriage, given her views on the matter? Into which set of gendered expectations should she fit—those for men or women? Although rules sometimes were easy to make, the realities of the sharply gender-polarized world of school work often were much messier and more difficult to navigate.

In the years ahead, a large number of women and some men in school work would choose to resolve these and a variety of new and equally vexing questions by centering their lives on members of their own sex. Eventually, the public would grow more aware of the existence of such school workers. It also would come to conflate same-sex desire with gender nonconformity. In response, the public would strictly regulate the proper gender roles of school employees and students. An important means of regulation involved hiring only those persons who exemplified acceptable gender qualities and apparent sexual desire, and excluding persons who did not.

CHAPTER 2

Passing Through That Phase of Homosexuality

With the approach of the twentieth century, the gender norms expected of school workers—as well as the range of their acceptable sexual behaviors—underwent rapid change. Although male teachers were thought to need salaries sufficient for supporting families, communities understood that the relatively low wages of teaching necessitated some prolonged periods of bachelorhood. Also, any man was thought capable of engaging in same-sex sexual activity. It was his discipline and uprightness that kept him from such "sinfulness." Soon after the introduction of the term "homosexual" in the late 1800s, however, England criminalized same-sex sexual activity among men. Awareness on both sides of the Atlantic of this new criminal transgression led to heightened scrutiny of men who gravitated too exclusively to the company of other men. The sense that any man could engage in same-sex sexual activity shifted to a perception that certain men were predisposed to such conduct—and further, that homosexual "habits" could be learned. Critics quickly turned their gaze to same-sex boarding schools in the United States and England, which were widely regarded as breeding grounds of homosexual practices. A number of the men who served as schoolmasters in the United States had studied in such institutions. Some carried the possible taint of such association.

On the other hand, the prospect of women engaging in same-sex sexual activity either was not taken seriously or was regarded as unlikely, if not out of the question. As large numbers of unmarried women taught in public and private schools throughout the country, few deduced that some of these women might choose to engage in same-sex sexual activity. When a number of unmarried women educators formed life partnerships with other women, most assumed that such arrangements reduced loneliness, increased standards of living, or otherwise made practical sense. And when it became common knowledge that girls at same-sex boarding schools in the United States and England frequently developed passionate emotional, if not sexual attachments to their peers, most considered this as part of an inevitable phase through which girls passed. Some girls, however, aspired to become like the unmarried women teachers they had long admired. By the turn of the twentieth century, teaching had become work that allowed women to remain unmarried and possibly to live in partnership with other women.

Over the mid-1800s, many of the individuals who became teachers had studied in privately funded academies, seminaries, and colleges. Of these varied institutions, most upheld strong allegiance to religious principles. Nearly all maintained single-sex enrollments. Faculty and youth studied, dined, played, and slept in campus buildings. Over time, these institutions built rich cultural traditions centering in large degree on gender identity. In contrast, tax-supported or common schools tended to be co-educational. Coeducation almost universally characterized rural schools and those in small townships during the late 1800s. Only a small number of urban schools separated the sexes even part of the time.[1] Among all private and public educational institutions, though, single-sex boarding schools provided the greatest degree of segregation by sex.

Sex segregation in schools mirrored larger patterns across a society governed by separate-spheres ideology. Men sought professional and social association with men, as did women with women. Not surprisingly, many families typically believed that their daughters and sons would benefit from schooling that prepared them for their places in a sex-segregated future. At single-sex boarding schools, peers and faculty members of the same sex surrounded students. These sex–identified school communities presumably reinforced gender-appropriate behaviors and characteristics. Sex-segregated schools had the added advantage of limiting contact between females and males, thus minimizing chances for heterosexual relationships that might scandalize parents.

Although such arrangements assured parents that their children would develop acceptable gender characteristics, in fact, single-sex schools allowed and possibly nurtured cultures of gender transgression as well as sexual and/or emotional relationships among students. For example, parents and faculty members regarded intense romantic relationships between girls as socially acceptable, even understandable, given the lack of opportunities to socialize with boys. Girls developed crushes or smashes on older, admired female students. They courted each other. They wrote each other letters pledging undying love. They demonstrated their passion for one another by giving extravagant gifts. Often girls outgrew these crushes, but, even so, they usually maintained lifelong commitments to close women friends.2 Occasionally, however, these intense relationships extended into adulthood, and some included sexual activity.3

Martha Vicinus has written extensively about such attachments among females in British boarding schools around the turn of the twentieth century. Because of similarities between British and American single-sex boarding schools of the time, her scholarship provides keen insight into the social environment of such institutions in the United States. She argues that boarding schools offered uniquely nurturing conditions in which passionate or homoerotic friendships could grow. The experience of living in these schools freed young women somewhat from family responsibilities while they studied. Other young women as well as admired teachers surrounded them in a web of relationships that did not raise suspicion. And at a time when women forged ahead into public, professional roles including teaching and social work, young women came to idolize the older, successful women who taught them and governed the schools. As such, these schools crackled with the passion and purpose of women who loved and respected each other greatly.4

In some ways, these boarding schools resembled the private domestic spaces that women governed in homes; yet the institutions were unmistakably public. As such, boarding school faculty encouraged girls to demonstrate greater independence and individualism than they might if they lived at home with their families. Faculty expected girls to display maturity by taking responsibility for their actions and accepting consequences. Vicinus further explains that girls learned to become autonomous and controlled within the school as a way of preparing for their roles in the larger social realm. Girls redefined and expanded their roles to include working for the greater public good.5

Vicinus contends that girls who matured in female boarding schools enjoyed a greater sense of freedom and independence than did girls raised at home. However, they also desired close, intense friendships. "If one's daily life demanded a public mask, a carefully cultivated sense of duty toward the group, then one found refuge—and an assertion of selfhood—through personal friendships." In this rarefied setting, romantic friendships between girls thrived. However, because girls were expected to demonstrate restraint and self-control, they often directed their passionate energies toward older girls or women whom they believed to be somewhat safer. Vicinus argues that these "erotically charged crushes" were often "a girl's most significant emotional experience."6

"Smashing" was common among the young women at these institutions. Several unique conditions converged in ways that fostered such smashes, crushes, or "raves." A strong reform ethic imbued these women's institutions with a sense of common purpose. Vicinus argues that the women who governed these schools wanted both to provide strong role models for students and to demonstrate the viability of the institutions. Their students in turn wished to demonstrate their worthiness to attend the schools. These complex tensions played out in relationships. Vicinus explains: "A rave simultaneously satisfied the desire for intimacy and individuality, independence and loyalty. . . . The emotions were concentrated on a distant, inaccessible, but admired student or teacher; differences in age and authority encouraged and intensified desire."[7]

The younger woman might not recognize any sexual elements of her feelings for an older, admired student or teacher. The recipient of such admiration probably understood these elements to some degree, though. However, the older rave recipient knew that such passionate love must be controlled—and channeled into a higher cause. She might encourage the younger woman to aspire to greater religious virtue, to the betterment of the school, or to improving conditions for all women. When the older rave shared the same feelings, she might lead the two in devoting themselves together toward such higher aspirations.[8]

The head of a British school in 1907 explained the important role of these romantic friendships in girls' schools: "[Such passions] should be recognized, allowed for, regulated, controlled, and made a help and not a hindrance to moral development. . . . A woman's life is, moreover, largely concerned with emotion; to suppress this will be injurious, to allow it to develop slowly and harmlessly, in respect or even reverence for someone who is older and presumably wiser than the girl herself, is not injurious and may be helpful."[9] Another woman who had been a part the world of college raves and smashes described her experiences:

> Girls between the ages of fourteen and eighteen at college or girls' schools often fall in love with the same sex. This is not friendship. The loved one is older, more advanced, more charming or beautiful. When I was a freshman in college I knew at least thirty girls who were in love with a senior. Some sought her because it was the fashion, but I knew that my own homage and that of many others was sincere and passionate. I loved her because she was brilliant and utterly indifferent to the love shown her. She was not pretty, though at the time we thought her beautiful. One of her adorers, on being slighted, was ill for two weeks. On her return she was speaking to me when the object of our admiration came into the room. The shock was too great, and she fainted. When I reached the senior year I was the recipient of languishing glances, original verses, roses, and passionate letters written at midnight and three in the morning.[10]

Unquestionably, raves among young women in colleges and teacher seminaries in the United States were common as well. A study published in *Pedagogical Seminary* in 1897 described the emotional lives of over 800 teachers and students in the United States. Although the survey did not explicitly solicit information about romantic friendships or same-sex love, participants volunteered many fond stories about passionate same-sex friendships. The author of the study concluded that such relationships must have happened frequently.[11]

Young women who studied in female institutions and the older women who taught in or governed them together created powerful communities committed to social reform. The effects of school communities such as Emma Willard's Troy Female Seminary (NY) rippled outward to touch larger circles of women, as graduates became teachers or community figures who, in turn, influenced others.[12] These educated women pushed beyond the traditionally prescribed domestic sphere and— through a missionary commitment to community good—achieved very public ends. Through service, women blurred the sharp lines between their domestic, private world and men's more public sphere.

However, once women entered the public sphere, their critics emerged. Groups of reform-minded women who organized women's clubs, political associations, settlement houses, or especially single-sex schools faced attack by those who feared shifts in gender-associated social roles. A highly effective means of punishing these women involved stigmatizing their romantic friendships, especially those so rampant at women's schools. As women became better educated and as the suffrage movement gained strength, critics disparaged single women teachers, accusing them of being poor models for female students and influencing them to lives of celibacy—and possibly to careers as teachers. Essentially, passion between women escaped notice until they were perceived to have transgressed their gender-appropriate boundaries and entered the public realm.[13]

Women's romantic friendships became suspect as women in general attained some degree of power in the public sphere. At first, little public concern greeted the phenomenon of young women falling in love with each other in women's schools. Many regarded these relationships as of little consequence, or, if anything, perhaps as good for the healthy development of young women.[14] But then around the turn of the century, matters shifted. Parents worried about these passionate friendships and considered them a waste of girls' love. They feared that such relationships might cause girls to refuse marriageable men in their later years.

Justification for these fears soon would be expressed in scientific language. In 1895, the pioneering British sex researcher, Havelock Ellis, published *Sexual Inversion of Women* in which he exhaustively documented cases of same-sex love among females. He argued that girls' boarding schools and women's colleges fostered "ardent attachments" between students. In these contexts, "kissing and . . . sleeping with the friend" were common, and one or both girls might experience "sexual emotion." Ellis believed that such attachments were more common among females than males because "the girl has a stronger need of affection and self-devotion to another person." Although females were supposed to keep a proper distance from males, they were permitted to enjoy "a considerable degree of physical intimacy" among themselves. This acceptance of physical intimacy between females, he contended, masked evidence of "homosexuality," a term that had entered the lexicon only recently. And homosexuality quickly became a purportedly new threat to the welfare of young women.[15]

Ellis and other sex researchers named this passion between women. They warned that romantic friendships among females involving sexual contact were harmful, deviant, and damaging in the long run. Advice books on sexual hygiene of the time cautioned that masturbation was wicked enough, but "when practised between girls . . . is a most pernicious habit which should be vigorously fought against."[16] They admonished young women to shun physical demonstrativeness among peers. They urged parents to watch for signs of deviance in their daughters' close friendships that might degenerate into unsavory, unhealthy, long-term attachments.[17] Echoing this concern, physicians in the United States declared, "Female boarding schools and colleges are the great breeding grounds of artificial [acquired] homosexuality."[18] An 1899 report of the American Medical Association warned that in women's schools, "The young girls, thus thrown together manifest an increasing affection by the usual tokens. They kiss each other fondly on every occasion. They embrace each other with mutual satisfaction. It is most natural, in the interchange of visits for them to sleep together. They learn the pleasure of direct contact, and in the course of their fondling they resort to cunni-linguistic practices . . . after this the normal sex act fails to satisfy her."[19]

Some of the women who taught in same-sex institutions lived with other women in committed, long-term relationships. Mary Woolley, president of Mount Holyoke College from 1901 to 1937 and Jeannette Marks, chair of the English Department, pledged their undying love in 1900 and then lived together until Woolley died in 1947. During the few times they were apart, they exchanged letters revealing the painfulness of separation. Woolley wrote: "It is just like having an unremitting pain, this having you away. There is a dull ache all the time, and I long, long for you . . . I think that you do not know, Dearie, how my real life is just bound up in you. Everything, my work, my happiness, has you at its center."[20]

Some Wellesley faculty members who maintained companionate relationships with other women described these as "Wellesley marriages."[21] Female faculty at many women's colleges during this time generally expressed their fondness for one another openly. They kissed, embraced, and held hands. They commonly shared beds as well.[22]

Consequently, when public scrutiny of young women's school friendships escalated, women faculty members were vulnerable. In part to deflect attention from their own relationships, some teachers restricted the relationships of their students. They shunned hugging, kissing, and other demonstrative behaviors as unhealthy. Faculty members in women's institutions became instrumental in thwarting budding romantic relationships among their charges.[23]

Intense emotional and sexual relationships existed among males as well. Anthony Rotundo explains how males commonly enjoyed close friendships during the mid-1800s. What began as warm friendships sometimes grew more intimate, intense, and romantic. For example, as a young man, Abraham Lincoln met Joshua Speed, with whom he developed a tender, abiding friendship. The two shared a bed for four years, not an uncommon practice among men at the time. They camped together on weekend trips, shared meals, and otherwise remained inseparable. Carl Sandburg noted in 1926 that the relationship between the two men had a "streak of lavender and spots soft as May violets." When Lincoln later married Mary Todd, he maintained a loyal correspondence with his beloved friend.[24] Though no numerical data substantiates the frequency of such friendships, documentary evidence indicates that many existed. Diaries and other personal documents filled with personal testimonials to a beloved bear this out. The openness of the expression suggests that romantic friendships among males may have been somewhat acceptable at the time.[25]

The sex-segregated worlds of boys' boarding schools and men's colleges offered environments where such mutual affection could flourish. As with female institutions, male students abandoned the security and comfort of their families to live in relatively more impersonal school settings with hundreds of other students. Boys typically sought solace in each other as they coped with their new lives.

Close attachments among boys in English boarding schools occurred so frequently that they were accepted as part of the school culture. Younger boys developed crushes on older, more admired boys who in turn provided mentoring, adoration, and sometimes protection. The British writer, Edward Carpenter, explained the experience in his controversial 1912 volume championing same-sex love, *The Intermediate Sex:*

> School friendships . . . filled a large place in the outlook of [a boy's] early years. . . . It is evident that the first unfolding of a strong attachment in boyhood or girlhood must have a profound influence. . . . They are genuine attractions, free as a rule, and at their inception, from secondary motives. They are not formed by the elder one for any personal ends. More often, indeed, I think they are begun by the younger, who naively allows his admiration of the elder one to become visible. But they are absorbing and intense, and on either side their influence is deeply felt and long remembered. . . . The younger boy looks on the other as a hero, loves to be with him, thrills with pleasure at his words of praise or kindness, imitates, and makes him his pattern and standard, learns exercises and games, contracts habits, or picks up information from him. The elder one, touched, becomes protector and helper; the unselfish side of his nature is drawn out, and he develops a real affection and tenderness towards the younger. He takes all sorts of trouble to initiate his protégé in field sports or studies; is proud of the latter's success; and leads him on perhaps later to share his own ideals of life and thought and work.26

These intense friendships often inspired boys to noble values and behaviors. In time, however, such relationships would trigger withering public attacks that would transform the conduct of activities at boys' schools. J. R. de S. Honey details this shift in *Tom Brown's Universe,* his remarkable history of elite British boarding schools in the 1800s. He describes how a headmaster leveled one of the first such public attacks in 1881 in a speech to the Education Society. The headmaster explained that he would "lay bare the cancer of upper-class education" by describing the supposedly shocking sexual practices among schoolboys. The behaviors he then recounted outraged members of the audience who wanted these hidden vices stopped. When the *Journal of Education* later published his speech, a public firestorm ensued.27

Parents and community members immediately pressured schoolmasters to control sexual behavior among their charges. Confronted by the accusation that boys' schools fostered sexual immorality among students whose families had paid substantial sums for their enrollment, schoolmasters instituted extraordinary measures. First, they eliminated or closed spaces on campus where boys might practice "the solitary vice." Shared dormitory rooms gave way to large, open barracks with lights left on at all times. Second, schoolmasters filled boys' schedules to capacity so that little free time remained during which they might choose their own activities. Third, schoolmasters supervised vigorous exercises and games designed to leave boys exhausted and unable to think about masturbation.

Schoolmasters made great efforts to prevent not just masturbation, but also "mutual masturbation," or sex between older and younger students.

By tradition at some schools, younger students sometimes impersonated females and assumed girls' nicknames. These boys cultivated relationships with older and stronger boys who then protected them in return for favors. However, in the face of increased public scrutiny, schoolmasters quickly forbade these activities. They enacted even more severe regulations. They prohibited friendships between older and younger boys. If schoolmasters saw older and younger boys conversing, they sometimes assumed it signaled a sexual relationship. In addition to minimizing opportunities for sex, schoolmasters urged boys instead to value emotional self-control. Simultaneously, they stigmatized any spontaneous emotional expression as unmanly. A properly masculine boy would refrain from hugging his friends, opting instead to maintain his composure.[28] In sum, English schoolmasters initially held somewhat dispassionate views about boys' romantic or sexual interests in each other, but in the face of public criticism, they quickly shifted to outright antagonism and active campaigns to make such affections taboo.[29]

Beyond instituting strenuous conditions designed to make sexual activity difficult, and encouraging boys to repress emotional expression among their peers, schoolmasters curbed homosexual activity among boys by persuading them to direct their emotional attachments not to other individual boys, but rather to the larger school community. They implored boys to excel and bring honor to the school, not to impress another boy.[30]

The momentum for scrutinizing boys' behavior at British boarding schools accelerated with the 1885 enactment of the Criminal Law Amendment, which outlawed homosexual behavior. The much-publicized trial of Oscar Wilde heightened public awareness of homosexual activities in general, as did the publication of works by Havelock Ellis and Edward Carpenter.[31] Some even regarded homosexuality as the vice of the owning class because elite boys' boarding schools supposedly nurtured it. Thus schools were seen as complicit in the problem.

Schoolmasters in particular needed to deflect any sexual scrutiny directed at them—even as they clamped down on emotional and sexual relationships among boys. With the criminalization of homosexuality, schoolmasters could ill afford to be charged with this new villainy. However, many men who taught in single-sex schools reputedly felt strong emotional and/or sexual connections with males. One writer joked, "Most good schoolmasters are homosexual by inclination—how else could they endure their work?—but their interest is diffuse and unacknowledged."[32] Edward Carpenter maintained that men who chose to teach were given to intimate relationships with their own sex. He explained this perceived connection:

> Another direction along which the temperament [uranianism, or attraction to one's own sex] very naturally finds an outlet is the important social work of Education. The capacity that a man has, in cases, of devoting himself to the welfare of boys or youths, is clearly a thing which ought not to go wasted—and which may be most precious and valuable. It is incontestable that a great number of men (and women) are drawn into the teaching profession by this sentiment—and the work they do is, in many cases, beyond estimation.[33]

With public criticism reaching new heights, however, schoolmasters needed to demonstrate their vigorous commitment to eliminating all same-sex attachments in their schools. They had much to lose if they failed. Rather than simply being men who centered their lives on men, schoolmasters could be tarred with a new, troublesome, and criminal identity: homosexual.[34]

To parents, the most terrifying prospect of all was that supposedly homosexual teachers might seduce their students into lives of degradation and depravity. A few teachers apparently did seek emotional and physical intimacy with students; however, such inclinations were the exception rather than the rule among schoolmasters.[35] Nonetheless, ever fearful of backlash from parents and the community, schoolmasters took careful steps to assure that inappropriate relationships did not develop. In 1910, for example, the staff of one school passed a resolution forbidding any master from having a boy in his room for longer than ten minutes, and, further, that no master should be alone with any boy behind closed doors.[36]

Boys' boarding schools and men's colleges in the United States dealt with the same issues because many American schools closely followed the British boarding school model. During the mid-1800s, several reformers contended that sexual activity among boys in U.S. boarding schools threatened to poison students' physical, mental, and emotional health as well as that of their progeny. Sylvester Graham, William Alcott, O. S. Fowler, and others wrote treatises urging young male students to refrain from all sexual indulgence, solitary or mutual.[37] In his book, *The Young Man's Guide*, William Alcott warned of the dangers that awaited unrepentant masturbators:

> When a young man, who is pursuing an unhappy course of solitary vice, threatened as we have seen by the severest penalties earth or heaven can impose,—begins to perceive a loss or irregularity of his appetite; acute pains in his stomach, especially during digestion, and constant vomitings;—when to this is added a weakness of the lungs, often attended by a dry cough, hoarse weak voice, and hurried or difficult breathing after using considerable exertion, with a general relaxation of the nervous system;—when these

appearance, or symptoms, as physicians call them, take place—let him beware! For punishment of a severer kind cannot be distant.[38]

Moral reformers warned that male boarding schools posed the greatest danger in developing such habits of vice. O. S. Fowler explained that
these institutions "are the most infected . . . first, because their boys are
highly organized, and as such experience proportionally greater pleasure
and injury; and secondly, this vice pre-eminently is catching especially as
they commingle thus freely with each other." He summarized: "This
sending children to school, however select, is a most grievous evil; because, as children are imitative creatures, all the bad habits of all the
scholars are adopted by all the others. Schools are complete nuisances,
propagating vice; nor can the evil be remedied till parents educate their
own children."[39] Evidence suggests that these male moral reformers may
have employed "the solitary vice" as code for homosexuality. They described masturbators as losing their masculinity. Furthermore, masturbation supposedly led to homosexuality because male students frequently
taught others these practices—and some then became sexual partners.[40]

One writer, using the pseudonym Edward Stevenson, explained in
1908 that students in U.S. schools were particularly prone to homosexual
relationships. "A special observer of youthful homosexuality in America
has stated that the practices of uranian boys [those who seek intimacy
with other males] in school are . . . 'nowhere quite so general' as in the
United States." He further contended: "Universities, the world around,
are centers of similisexual attraction [Stevenson's term for homosexual-
ity] and of 'relations' between fine-natured young collegemen." Generally,
he regarded the charged, sex-segregated environments of American
schools and colleges as supportive and nurturing for same-sex intimate
relationships among students.[41] Until the late 1800s—when the public
began scrutinizing the sexual desire of schoolmasters and students—they
also seemed to be modestly safe places for teachers who desired persons
of the same sex.

As the existence of homosexual behavior in boys' and men's educational institutions became generally known, however, school administrators clamped down vigorously. In 1920, the president of Harvard University convened a secret court to investigate a network of homosexual
activity among students, faculty, alumni, and others not connected with
the university. The investigation began when Cyril Wilcox, a student,
committed suicide and his brother brought information about Cyril's
homosexual acquaintances to a ranking university administrator. As the
secret court gathered information, it learned from a classmate how Cyril
had linked with the homosexual network: "While in his Freshman year

he met in college some boys, mostly members of his own class, who committed upon him and induced him to commit on them 'Unnatural Acts' which habit so grew on him that realizing he did not have strength of character enough to brake [sic] away from it concluded suicide the only course open to him." Another student indicated that he first engaged in homosexual behaviors in school at the age of twelve. He claimed that the boarding school he subsequently attended was "permeated with homosexuality" and "mutual masturbation." Other students told similar stories. The "habits" they learned while studying in boarding schools continued when they enrolled at Harvard. Eventually, the court handed down fourteen guilty verdicts. The students, faculty, and staff not only were dismissed, but also told to leave Cambridge immediately.[42]

Some youth who had studied in sex-segregated high schools and colleges later became teachers. The passion they had felt for their peers, which they tended to sublimate into their commitment to their schools or to larger social reforms, continued to burn in those who felt that their highest calling might be the work of the classroom. Indeed, a deep attachment to a respected teacher or schoolmaster often inspired students to pursue teaching careers themselves. Consequently, some continued to center their lives on persons of their own sex, a pattern sometimes lasting throughout adulthood.

In her pioneering work, *Gay and Lesbian Educators: Personal Freedoms, Public Constraints* (1997), Karen Harbeck describes a number of persons who taught schoolchildren and also maintained same-sex, romantic, and passionate relationships at some point in their lives. She lists the writers and activists Ralph Waldo Emerson, Margaret Fuller, Elizabeth Peabody, Amos Bronson Alcott, Henry David Thoreau, Henry Longfellow, Herman Melville, and Walt Whitman, among others. Some of these individuals taught only briefly before assuming the careers for which they would become famous. Fuller and Peabody, for example, worked together at the Temple School in Boston and developed a romantic friendship. Fuller maintained other such relationships with women, though she eventually married. Young men generally attracted Whitman. One of his biographers, David Reynolds, contends that angry townsfolk ran Whitman out of town after he had commenced a sexual relationship with one of his male students. But first, they reputedly tarred and feathered him and beat him so severely that it took a full month for recovery. Reynolds speculates that the trauma of this event may have led directly to Whitman's decision to abandon teaching.[43] Similarly, the Reverend Horatio Alger, author of such rags-to-riches stories as *Ragged Dick,* taught only briefly while preparing for the ministry. Then early in his ministerial career, his parish investigated his frequent social engagements with local boys, reporting that Alger has been "charged with gross immorality and a most heinous crime, a crime of no less magnitude than the abominable and revolting crime of unnatural familiarity with boys." Alger left town that night and subsequently became a writer.[44]

Similarly, Sherwood Anderson portrayed such a teacher in "Hands," part of his widely read and renowned novel, *Winesburg, Ohio* (1919). In the story, Wing Biddlebaum, a town eccentric with large, remarkable, fluttering hands that he struggles to hide, befriends only a young male journalist. Anderson eventually reveals that Biddlebaum, who formerly had taught in another state, had been much beloved by his male students and

> was meant by nature to be a teacher of youth. He was one of those rare, little-understood men who rule by a power so gentle that it passes as a lovable weakness. In their feelings for the boys under their charge such men are not unlike the finer sort of women in their love of men.
>
> And yet that is but crudely stated. It needs the poet there. With the boys of his school, [the teacher] had walked in the evening or had sat talking until dusk upon the schoolhouse steps lost in a kind of dream. Here and there went his hands, caressing the shoulders of the boys, playing about the tousled heads. As he talked his voice became soft and musical. There was a caress in that also. In a way the voice and the hands, the stroking of the shoulders and the touching of the hair were a part of the schoolmaster's effort to carry a dream into the young minds. By the caress that was in his fingers he expressed himself. He was one of those men in whom the force that creates life is diffused, not centralized. Under the caress of his hands doubt and disbelief went out of the minds of the boys and they began also to dream.

However, when one student, described as "half-witted," spread rumors that the teacher had done "unspeakable things" with him, townsfolk beat the teacher brutally and chased him out of town. In the story, Biddlebaum never was quite certain of what he had done to incur such wrath.[45]

Through the nineteenth century, countless men and women who desired intimacy with members of their own sex taught in obscurity compared with the luminaries and Anderson's fictional character previously mentioned. These humble teachers likely had studied for some time in sex-segregated schools, experienced intense, sometimes romantic and/or sexual friendships, idolized their teachers, centered their lives on persons of their own sex, and eventually entered teaching. Many held a deep commitment to their work, with a sense of mission cultivated in their earlier schooling experiences. Most found that their attraction to others of their own sex was greeted with some degree of acceptance, especially in more urban and formally educated communities—that is, until the late 1800s.

Then around the turn of the century, public awareness of romantic and/or sexual relationships among men occurred. Initially, few took seriously the possibility that women might engage in sexual relationships with each other. Consequently, the word "homosexual" applied mainly to men. As women grew more powerful in society, however, critics implicated their attachments to other women as well. Homosexual and spinster teachers eventually became the focus of critical attention.

Parents increasingly worried about the proper sexual and gender development of youths who studied with this large phalanx of unmarried teachers. Would boys become effeminate or lacking in manly qualities if their male teachers desired other men? Would young boys who idolized their teachers be influenced to pursue same-sex intimate relationships? Would girls, under the influence of their admired single women teachers, decide to emulate them by pursuing teaching, remaining single, and perhaps living with other women?

By the turn of the century, tax-supported common schools long had enrolled both girls and boys together. However, a small number of public high schools remained essentially sex-segregated. In coeducational public high schools, girls far outnumbered boys. Adolescent males tended to drop out to pursue jobs—or because they found that high schools did not meet their needs. David Tyack and Elisabeth Hansot have described this "boy problem" as one in which girls apparently outperformed boys in academic pursuits and persisted until graduation in much greater numbers. In response, much early twentieth-century public school reform concerned changing schools so boys would choose to continue their studies and succeed academically.[46]

Meanwhile, private schools, academies, and colleges continued with their traditional sex-segregated enrollments. However, the practice soon would endure scrutiny. First, some reformers simply argued that the time for coeducation had come. Public schools had been coeducational for the previous half-century. Females and males seemed to be learning successfully while studying in the same classes. Second, women's activists championed coeducation as a way to bring equitable educational opportunities to girls. Elite male schools and colleges, they argued, needed to admit females who showed just as much academic promise as males.

Finally, a few contended that coeducation would help children become properly heterosexual and develop gender-appropriate behaviors and characteristics. They argued that if youth attended only sex-segregated schools, they were more likely to develop emotional and/or sexual relationships with members of their own sex than if they attended coeducational schools. Coeducational schools offered girls and boys opportunities to be comfortable around each other—especially when they began experiencing sexual desire. This argument was employed as early as 1854 when a Pennsylvania school committee investigated the merits of co-education, finding that

> It is a fact, lamented by teachers, but existing despite their efforts, that in schools for boys, the college and academy, the state of morals is more loose than in society in general; that young men confined with others of their own sex will habitually engage in improprieties if not vices of which they would not dare to be guilty in other circumstances. . . . The same is true of schools for females, if not to the same extent. . . . In society at large, much good is owing to female influence . . . and if the admission of both sexes into our schools will have a tendency to produce this effect, it seems to us a strong argument in its favor.[47]

Then, in 1919, the noted psychologist, Dr. Constance Long, argued strenuously for co-education because it allowed girls to get used to having boys be attracted to them

> in order not to get her likings too strongly fastened to the qualities and attractions of the other girls. I happen to be an old maid, and I will tell you part of the reason. I lived with my grandmother. . . . There were no men, no boys in the household. I have an adopted daughter. She has been mine since she was eight months old. There has been no man, no boy in the household. This daughter of mine since she was fifteen, sixteen, seventeen, began to get crushes on girls of her own age, and while she was at Stanford, she had a terrible crush on a girl of her own age. She said to me: "Why, you have so-and-so," my best friend, a woman. I said: "Yes, but don't you see I am an old maid?" I wanted that daughter of mine to see that to be an old maid is not a thing desirable, that it is not the end and aim of a woman's life; and that to care too much for these girl friends of hers, to show them all of the devotion that would normally express itself in other directions might inhibit the preferable development. She was not abnormal but simply passing through that phase of homosexuality, and I said just that to her. She went horseback riding with a young girl chum the day a lieutenant in the army came one hundred miles to see her, left him waiting while she went riding with a girl college chum, which was an awful mistake. I had one school teacher under my care. She had a neurosis which expressed itself in all sorts of symptoms. She was a very decided homosexual. . . . She was a principal. She loved her pupils and she was splendid in the handling of her teachers; but she had one chum with whom her relations were more intimate than they should have been. This was the cause of the hyper-sex tension that revealed itself as asthma and anxiety and neurosis and a few more things.[48]

Long contended that women needed to grow comfortable with the affections of males. She held the then-common belief that homosexual relationships characterized a phase of youth, something routine and unremarkable. However, should such relationships continue into adulthood, she argued that women likely would suffer physical and emotional maladies. Finally, she explained that coeducation offered an important means of minimizing sexual maladjustment among students—helping them to pass through to the other side of the homosexual phase.

Finally, in 1932, the prominent sociologist of American education, Willard Waller, appealed to research revealing that many, if not all, girls passed through a homosexual period: "Sometimes a homosexual adjustment is made during [adolescence], especially if there is a severe inhibition of the normal flow of affection or a failure of the heterosexual outgo to find an object." Same-sex boarding schools theoretically kept students from finding a "normal" heterosexual outlet. He continued, "The homosexual adjustment is much more evident among girls than among boys; it probably appears in a larger number of cases and its character is less masked. Some writers maintain that all girls pass though such a period." The social structure of schools would need to shift, he argued, if adolescents were to "divert these interests into other channels."[49]

Although concern about same-sex attachments at private, single-sex boarding schools increased toward the end of the 1800s, tax-supported schools largely escaped this same oversight. For one thing, students returned home each school day to live under the direction of their parents. For another, females and males usually attended them together even though patterns of sex-segregation may have existed *within* some schools.[50] Finally, female common and public school teachers, many of whom had attended single-sex schools as youth, remained relatively free of criticism of their sexual desire as long as they provided an important service to the community at a relatively inexpensive cost and behaved within generally agreed-upon gender bounds for their sex. Some time would pass before single women teachers in public schools would raise eyebrows. By the late 1800s, however, male teachers faced greater scrutiny of their marital status, their behavior toward male students, and, increasingly, their very presence in work that had come to be associated with women.

CHAPTER 3

A Spinster's Profession

O nce women began teaching in the mid-1800s, they quickly filled schools around the country. Relatively few other jobs for women existed that required formal education at the high school level and beyond. By the turn of the century, the sheer numbers of such positions around the country ensured that hundreds of thousands of women could teach at any given time, making school work the most significant form of employment available to educated women. And to retain their teaching positions, women generally needed to remain unmarried. By 1900, women accounted for around 70 percent of all teachers. Of these, single, widowed, or divorced women accounted for well over 90 percent.[1]

Many young women entered teaching fully intending to find suitable fiancés and then to resign upon marriage. However, a sizeable number remained single throughout their lives. Accordingly, single women performed so much of the work of teaching that the profession quickly became associated with them. A "spinster" likely taught. A teacher became an "old maid" if she passed through her youth without marrying. This stereotype pervaded popular media and conversation of the time.

As single women began pursuing their first public profession, however, changes in several social and economic conditions were necessary. First, single women required acceptable housing. Second, they needed a variety of other services such as meal preparation, laundry, and reasonably priced clothing. Third, they desired social support for their pioneering lives. These prerequisites gradually materialized, and, along with them, recognizable sub-cultures of single women teachers emerged that sometimes served as surrogate families. By the 1930s, communities of single women teachers could be found in a variety of configurations around the country.

Communities of women teachers often included those who bonded in long-term companionate relationships with other women. Cherished, close friendships between women allowed them to share professional and social passions, deep emotional commitments, and the benefits of family without the associated burdens of heterosexual marriages. In many cases, women's romantic and/or sexual relationships with other women were essential for the establishment of women's social communities as well as for the welfare of the larger women's movement. Such passionate relationships often were common knowledge; however, they were not discussed publicly. As long as women in these relationships remained discreet, they may have been thought a bit odd, but neighbors and acquaintances readily accepted them.

Unmarried women have long been fixtures of American culture. During the nation's early years, women who remained single throughout their lives typically were demeaned as pathetic, unmarriageable females who lived off of the good graces of their families or of community members willing to take them in or employ them as domestic workers. In part, such women essentially had no other respectable means of supporting themselves outside the home. Popular sentiment gradually softened and allowed spinsters pity for their supposedly wretched condition, acknowledging that perhaps their unattractiveness to suitable men was not their fault.[2]

However, single women enjoyed new opportunities for independence and respect when they began teaching in appreciable numbers, especially after the Civil War. They could teach while searching for suitable husbands, resigning upon matrimony. Alternatively, they could remain unmarried throughout their lives and support themselves outside the home, however modestly. No longer did they necessarily burden family members or the community. Largely because of teaching, the place of the unmarried woman in American culture shifted from one of scorn or pity to one that sometimes accorded genuine admiration. At last, women who remained single could retain a female identity, demonstrate strength and independence, and earn respect for their contributions.[3]

Through teaching, even women of modest means could support themselves in lives apart from husbands or families. Consequently, the number of women who remained single during the late 1800s increased substantially. Harriett Elizabeth Paine, writing under the pseudonym "Eliza Chester," published *The Unmarried Woman* in 1892, a book describing the lives of the new class of single women emerging in the United States. Far from seeing spinsterhood as a curse as previous generations had, Paine articulated what she regarded as the virtues of living single. Chief among these was the privilege of actively choosing the course of one's own life. In making this point, she described the views of a man she regarded as unenlightened:

A facetious old gentleman, addressing a girls' school, once made the following atrocious joke: "Young ladies," he said, "you learn many things at school,—mathematics and history and music. You learn to decline many nouns; but there is one noun no young lady ever learned to decline,—that is, *matrimony*." A hush fell on the school, and after the departure of the old gentleman, the principal—an extremely shrewd widow lady, who read her fellow-beings like an open book—made her own speech. "Young ladies," she said, "I suppose that of all the interesting and valuable things our visitor told us this morning, nothing has excited so much comment, and is so likely to be remembered, as his unfortunately foolish remark about matrimony. For the sake of a joke, he has made a completely false statement. The truth is that probably no woman, rich or poor, beautiful or plain, ever yet reached the age of thirty without having some opportunity to marry. . . . But every sensible woman would rather lead a single life than to bind herself to any man whom she does not both respect and love."[4]

Paine argued that women's lives had improved considerably since spinsterhood had become a viable option. She contended that women could choose to marry because they had found worthy partners—and not because they otherwise feared economic ruin. She maintained that although unmarried women might not be for "the immediate benefit of the world," they definitely have "an educative influence which seems likely finally to raise the standard of marriage among men as well as women."[5] An anonymous writer for the *Atlantic Monthly* concurred: "We spinsters would marry . . .—if anybody asked us—if we could see happiness in it . . . but as civilization advances, it becomes increasingly difficult to marry satisfyingly. . . . An intelligent woman demands a husband who will be a congenial companion, or she will have none at all; for it is no longer necessary to have someone to take care of her."[6]

Remaining single became an increasingly acceptable option for women. Women gradually viewed it more as a positive choice rather than as a pitiable, demeaning condition. Along with this shift, other circumstances for women improved generally during the late 1800s as property and divorce laws accorded them greater rights, educational opportunities expanded, and the suffrage movement gained momentum. These changes occurred as more women chose to remain single, some of them consciously revolting against marriage, which at that time typically restricted women's opportunities to earn income, work outside the home, exercise independent judgment, and live free of husbands' demands.[7]

Not surprisingly, negative images of single women persisted in the late 1800s as "old maids" sometimes continued to be depicted as prudish, homely, provincial, bitter, nosey, dull, tedious, poor, crone-like, and fruitless women.[8] However, the large numbers of single women who became teachers and, as such, performed important community service, gradually rehabilitated the image of the spinster. Paine described this change: "A plain little teacher, with queer, shy ways, a woman of the sort that novelists are continually punching upon, extricates herself in real life from the half good-natured, half contemptuous ridicule which attends such a personage in books, not only by her sweetness and gentleness, but by her genuine learning. Everybody is compelled to respect her."[9] Truly, teaching at the turn of the century fostered the rise of the spinster by providing her with an acceptable livelihood and place in society.

Though a great need for single women teachers existed around the country, a lack of suitable housing limited them initially. In earlier generations, women teachers who moved to remote communities typically boarded with the families of their students. This arrangement, however, presented several problems. First, families were burdened by relinquishing some of their precious space and food. For families on the edge of survival, this entailed significant sacrifice. Second, teachers experienced little privacy as community members monitored their activities, however well intended such scrutiny might be. Third, boarding around seemed more appropriate for youths rather than adults. Although teachers commonly began working in their mid-teens, growing numbers continued teaching through much of their adult lives. Longer careers meant that teachers needed more permanent forms of housing.

From the mid- to late-1800s, women teachers in rural areas and small towns occasionally lived in their schoolhouses to avoid the humiliation of boarding around. Some buildings contained basement space, small attics, or attached rooms where a bed and a few modest possessions could be stored. Such arrangements offered women some privacy after students left for the day. Advantages accrued to the community as well. Teachers who lived independently did not burden families who otherwise might have to provide room and board. Also, by living in the schoolhouse, teachers could maintain the buildings easily and start fires in the stove each morning well before students arrived.[10] In some French Canadian schools, women began living in schoolhouses when teaching became more professional work and less a "family matter." In 1881, over a third of women teachers in two such school districts lived by themselves in schoolhouses.[11] Anecdotal evidence indicates that women teachers commonly did this in the United States and its territories as well. However, local residents worried about the safety of women in these situations because rapes or other attacks reportedly occurred from time to time. To minimize this danger, teachers sometimes invited family members to live in the schoolhouse with them. Later, two or more teachers might live together instead.[12]

Beyond living in a schoolhouse, women teachers in western states and territories enjoyed another housing option unimaginable in the more settled eastern states: They could acquire land and build their own houses. The Homestead Act in 1862, signed by Lincoln, permitted women as well as men to stake claims of 160 undeveloped acres. The act was remarkable for its time in that it did not discriminate against women. Once homesteaders staked their claims, they needed to improve their land within five years to qualify for a patent, or outright ownership. Single women teachers perceived many advantages in acquiring and developing their own homesteads. Their teaching duties provided the modest capital needed for erecting fences, hiring help, and constructing farm buildings. A few of them profitably sold their properties later to local ranchers seeking to amass large contiguous parcels of land. However, for many others, teaching while farming offered a viable lifestyle. Women who undertook these rigors did not intend to develop their property as a dowry for future marriage, but instead because they enjoyed the lives they had created. For example, evidence suggests that most of the women homesteaders in Wyoming remained single. Land records for several counties from 1888 to 1943 show that nearly 69 percent of women homesteaders remained unmarried and that many of them taught in nearby schools.[13]

Bess Corey, one such homesteading woman teacher, chose to remain single throughout her life. Friends and family knew her as "Bachelor Bess," the moniker ending each of her letters. Corey grew up on a farm in Iowa, but then after her father died in 1905, she attended a nearby normal school and became a teacher. A few years later, as her brother describes, "Bess set out for South Dakota. She intended to stake out a claim, homestead the land, and teach school. She was twenty-one and on her own." There, she taught for many years and developed her claim into a productive farm with a cozy home. Despite many suitors who proposed to her, she repeatedly declined their offers, preferring instead her vigorous life of teaching and farming.[14]

Another enterprising woman teacher in the rural West created an entirely different housing arrangement. Permeal French quickly rose through the teaching ranks in Idaho to become state school superintendent, a position from which she garnered great respect. Among her projects, she championed a legislative appropriation of $25,000 to build a women's dormitory at the University of Idaho. Years later, she moved into the dorm and lived there for much of her life. Although French apparently attracted many suitors, she, like many other single women of the time, declined them all.[15]

Rural teachers commonly preferred to focus their efforts on their teaching duties, rather than on trying to maintain a farm or ranch by themselves at the same time, however. For them, school districts began constructing apartments or "teacherages" near schoolhouses, in some cases with corridors linking the two buildings.[16] Districts in Nebraska erected the first known teacherages in 1894, but then the movement spread quickly.[17] Perhaps the staunchest advocate of teacherages was Josephine Corliss Preston. Preston, who had boarded around with community families when she taught in Walla Walla, Washington, years earlier, understood that teachers needed privacy and comfortable accommodations so they could perform their duties well. When she became county superintendent, she worked to ensure that all women teachers in her district could live in teacherages if they wanted. Then, upon selection to the state superintendency in 1913, she launched a program to provide such housing across the entire state. Where state funding fell short, she enlisted the assistance of the National Federation of Women's Clubs, which then took up the cause nationwide. Preston understood that the existence of teacherages served as a powerful recruiting tool during teacher shortages. Districts that could afford to build quality teacher accommodations routinely attracted the most qualified single women teachers. During Preston's eventual term as president of the National Education Association (NEA), she explained: "Let it be known that a district furnishes a school cottage for the use of its teacher and that district may have its choice from among the best teachers that the state affords."[18]

Other states, eager to compete for qualified teachers, clearly took notice. The National Federation of Women's Clubs in Texas assisted in building "more 'teacherages' in one year than Washington did in ten."[19] In 1930, the Texas superintendent of education reported that his state led the nation in number and value of teacherages. An audit indicated that school districts operated 1,330 teacherages around the state.[20] In Arizona, communities provided their teachers with basic necessities such as simple furniture, a stove with wood, and water. One relatively luxurious schoolhouse even included electricity, steam heat, and a bath.[21] A 1935 study of single teachers' accommodations in New York showed that teachers required "steam or hot-water heat, a bathroom shared with other members of the household, a telephone in the house, [and] an automobile costing less than $1,000."[22] Eventually, the U.S. Commissioner of Education joined the effort by encouraging the construction of such facilities for teachers across the country.[23]

Usually, teacherages housed more than one teacher at a time; thus they mainly served consolidated districts rather than isolated one-room schoolhouses. Shared housing offered several advantages. Districts could accommodate several teachers together more cheaply than they could by providing separate houses for each. Teachers living together felt safer than those living alone.[24] And teachers enjoyed the companionship of other professional women with lively interests and activities.

Single women who taught in urban areas confronted different challenges in finding suitable accommodations than did their rural counterparts. In the mid-1800s, single women simply could not obtain accommodations by themselves without sacrificing community respect or safety.[25] However, as single women began teaching in significant numbers and as positions for women in the "needle trades," manufacturing, sales, and clerical work emerged, enterprising landlords established boardinghouses exclusively for single women that provided inexpensive, safe accommodations, reasonably priced meals, and laundry services.[26] Because urban schools typically contained multiple classrooms, teachers from the same school commonly lived in the same boardinghouses. Living in close proximity to so many others, though, meant that teachers enjoyed little privacy in these houses.

Rooming houses, which did not include meals, served single women seeking to save money by cooking for themselves or dining elsewhere. Such accommodations could be harrowing, however. One female instructor described the difficulties single women teachers faced in managing their lives in a rooming house. She noted that teachers' modest pay:

> usually forces the impecunious instructor to all sorts of makeshifts, neither dignified, restful, nor entirely nutritious. She usually takes a room and "goes out for meals"; she undoubtedly makes her own bed; she probably has to do whatever dusting is done day by day with a woman coming in once a week for "general cleaning." She frequently gets her own breakfast—shredded wheat in such cases forming the piece de resistance. And in many cases she washes her own shirtwaists, and perhaps other garments, in the bath tub and irons them on her study table with an electric iron which she owns in common with three or four other instructors. And she performs all these domestic tasks as a matter of course, along with her darning and pressing and sewing on of buttons and skirt braids and cleaning of gloves and running in of ribbons.[27]

Eventually, women's apartment houses appeared—which offered single women teachers private bathrooms, kitchens, and living spaces.[28] An anonymous writer in the *Atlantic Monthly* described why she had built some of these units: "The very conveniences of living at present make the single life more agreeable than it once was. The comfort of small apartments, as they are now designed and equipped,—I have designed and built some,—makes the assistance of a strong masculine hand or the protection of masculine presence unnecessary. The domestic-minded spinster is no longer driven to the deprivations of the boarding house or the small hotel."[29]

Although some women teachers desired even more independence through home ownership, exceedingly few could purchase such homes. Harriett Paine indicated that "there are few unmarried women who can afford a dwelling-place which is any index to their tastes. This is not because they are poorer than the majority of married women; but the expense of an adequate home for one person alone is far greater than the proportional share of each one in a family, and, of course, a woman does not often earn as much as a man."[30] Studies confirmed the lack of home ownership among single women. A 1932 NEA report describing home ownership among city teachers concluded that 14 percent of single women owned or were buying their own homes compared with over half of male teachers. At the same time, 23 percent of single women teachers rented houses; 56 percent rented rooms, boarded, or lived with family members; and seven percent lived with nonrelatives.[31]

Despite the variety of living arrangements possible for unmarried urban women teachers, one writer in 1915 argued that each was inadequate: "Each of these methods of living involves definite and serious diversions of time and of strength from her legitimate job; and they all present striking contrasts to the normal satisfactions secured by the professional man with a home and a family and a domestic regime which takes respectful account of the demands of his professional life."[32] Single women teachers faced day-to-day challenges that differed from those of their male colleagues. Consequently, they needed different forms of social support.

One way that single women teachers contended with the heavy responsibilities of working full time while managing the details of their daily lives was to share some household tasks with trusted friends. Pairs or small groups of single women rented or jointly owned homes. In her 1938 study of women teachers, *The School Ma'am*, Frances Donovan, explained, "Teachers with a taste for domesticity rent apartments. Often two form a partnership that lasts for years. They share the expenses of the home and divide its duties. Such housemates also usually attend places of amusement together and take vacation trips in each other's company. Their friends are likely to be other teachers."[33] In such pairs of women teachers, each reportedly shared cooking and other domestic duties. They consoled each other during difficult times and celebrated the good. They organized social activities, reading circles, lectures, concerts, community services, and, in the case of groups of women teachers, professional development activities. Though they did not enjoy the luxury of wives who managed their households—as did many of their male colleagues and most male administrators they could share these duties and collectively lighten the load. Beyond providing a little ease, pairs and groups of women teachers often grew into dynamic communities with rich traditions, relationships, and shared accomplishments. By the turn of the century, recognizable cultures of single women teachers had emerged around the country, in many cases centering on the houses or buildings in which they lived.[34]

The women teachers who formed communities often found them remarkably satisfying. These vibrant groups shared lively conversations and often grew close to one another. Harriett Paine described how such households typically functioned:

> Sometimes half-a-dozen teachers combine in one household. Many such schemes are brilliantly successful. This is surprising, when it is considered that every new element in a family is a possible element of discord. But many a woman who is a very disagreeable addition to her married sister's family is thoroughly in place in such a voluntary association,—probably because all the members have equal rights, and the code of the household is arranged with equal reference to all. I doubt, however, if so large a family would be successful if its members were women of leisure. The teachers, of course, spend the greater part of their day in absorbing work, and they have no time for jangling. When artists or authors or dressmakers or saleswomen combine with teachers, so that no two members of the household have exactly the same occupation, it is said that the experiment is still more satisfactory, because each brings something fresh into the life.[35]

In large urban areas such as Chicago, the settlement house movement reached a peak around the turn of the century. Settlement houses brought together women from across social strata who wanted to work together toward social reform. A number of settlements housed well-to-do women who volunteered for settlement activities along with recent immigrants and fully employed women such as teachers. Organizers planned a variety of educational programs in which women taught each other skills of mutual interest. Social, political, and volunteer activities swirled around these establishments as women collectively worked to ameliorate the social problems attendant with staggering population growth, economic change, and social displacement. In the end, however, settlement house workers and women from across the larger women's movement came to understand that their actions ultimately were limited unless they also could achieve real political power by winning suffrage.

Women who lived in shared housing, communities of women teachers, and other clusters of women typically joined the larger women's movement of the time. This movement encompassed a broad range of social, educational, and political organizations established to bring women together. In their *History of Woman Suffrage,* Susan B. Anthony and Ida Harper indicated that over four million women belonged to women's clubs in 1900, or over one-tenth of the nation's population of women.[36] Initially, the women in some of these organizations wished to avoid political involvement, believing that such matters rested beyond their appropriate sphere of influence. However, eventually most agreed that women needed the vote to enact long-range social reforms. Temperance activists, child labor reform advocates, club women, and women teachers alike joined forces in campaigning for women's suffrage.[37]

The active women who worked for social reforms during the turn-of-the-century women's movement built communities of women. In turn, women replenished their energy and commitment to the movement by engaging with like-minded, caring women. Through this process of forging ahead while supporting one another, women's networks grew strong and some became politically influential. Historian Estelle Freedman explains that during these years, women who worked for social reforms connected with one another, sometimes establishing loving, caring bonds that nourished their work. Together they created public institutions that served essentially as separate women's spaces. Because of such "separate female institutions," as Freedman calls them, women did not have to assimilate into the public, predominantly male realm to achieve their causes. Neither did they need to banish themselves exclusively to the home. Instead, with female institutions, women created public, though separate, networks through which to agitate.[38] This separatist strategy allowed women to bond in close friendships, maintain separate physical and social spaces from men, and raise their collective sights toward improving social conditions. Taken together, these factors in turn strengthened social cohesion. Freedman argues that such women's separate institutions were essential to feminist politics of the time.[39]

Women teachers provided much of the vitality and leadership of suffrage organizations, in part because suffrage connected directly with their working conditions. School boards and superintendents made decisions that affected teacher pay, employment rules, curriculum, and other matters of importance to teachers. Male teachers could vote and therefore exert some influence on their own working conditions. However, because most women could not vote on school-related matters, achieving suffrage gained added importance.[40] As women began running for the superintendency, one of the only political positions open to women at the time, suffrage-minded teachers understood that electing women offered symbolic as well as practical benefits.[41] Women teachers rallied in significant numbers at suffrage conventions. They edited most of the suffrage newspapers published from 1849 to 1920.[42] Leading suffrage strategists and activists such as Susan B. Anthony and Carrie Chapman Catt taught at some time during their lives.[43]

Women teachers also organized for professional improvement. Male education organizations, which long had exerted tremendous influence over the profession, historically excluded women teachers.[44] When groups such as the National Teachers Association and the American Institute of Instruction admitted women in the 1850s and 1860s, they accorded them limited roles.[45] By the 1900s, many local groups of male teachers existed. They endeavored to improve male teacher salaries, recruit more men to the work, and upgrade the status of male teachers. Because of this history of exclusion, as well as the momentum of the larger women's movement, women teachers similarly sought to create their own professional associations. The author of a 1910 study on teachers' voluntary associations described the phenomenon where "in city associations of teachers, the prominence of women immediately strikes an observer. . . . In nearly every city there is some association in which women either form a total membership or else monopolize the offices, boards of control, and advisory offices. The indications are that in at least half the cities of 30,000 and upwards, there is at least one organization of teachers, composed of women only." He listed a range of organizations from the Chicago Teachers Federation and Ella Flagg Young Clubs in Chicago to the Savannah Kindergarten Club in Georgia.[46] Typical among these groups, the California Federation of School Women's Clubs, which organized in 1908, declared as its purposes: "To cultivate professional spirit among the women teachers of the state, that they may have a broader outlook upon their work and conception of it. . . . To encourage women teachers to organize as a help toward the above, that they may work together and have opportunities to discuss professional problems. . . . To promote acquaintance and fellowship, in order that co-operation may enable women to make their work more effective and secure adequate recognition of its worth."[47]

Eventually women teachers labored for greater power by forming a national association. The NEA, long controlled by a small network of powerful male administrators and professors, consistently resisted women's inroads into the organization. When the Chicago Federation of Teachers, an organization of women elementary teachers led by the indomitable Margaret Haley, failed to compel the NEA to provide it with greater recognition, its members organized teachers from around the country to form an alternative association, the National Federation of Teachers, in 1899.[48] This organization of women elementary teachers met annually at the same time as NEA meetings were held. Members lobbied effectively for greater women's representation in the NEA, culminating in the election of Ella Flagg Young of Chicago as the NEA's first woman president.[49]

In these socially rarefied environments and organizations, women teachers who lived together, worked together, and labored for common causes developed deep relationships with one another.[50] Just as the well-educated women who lived and worked at female schools and colleges sometimes lived in "Boston marriages," or long-term, committed, romantic and/or sexual relationships, so too did women public school teachers. Such relationships made sense. Unmarried women teachers could split domestic responsibilities. Their mutual presence enhanced safety. They enjoyed greater household resources with two incomes than if they lived alone. They shared social and professional interests, joining richly in each other's lives. These relationships sometimes included passionate expressions of love for one another. Undoubtedly in some cases, these relationships also included sex. And for a time, discreet Boston marriages among women teachers did not provoke community consternation.[51]

Passionate relationships such as these existed among a number of women educators in the 1800s and early 1900s, including some particularly accomplished women. In 1868, Caroline Putnam established a school in Virginia that she named after her life companion and teaching colleague, Sally Holley. The two Oberlin-educated women taught there for the remainder of their lives, working to provide a curriculum for the school's African American students that would honor the "struggle for black freedom."[52] Ella Flagg Young, superintendent of Chicago schools from 1909 to 1915, maintained a longtime companionship with Laura Brayton, whom she met in 1883. That year, Brayton had just begun her career as an English teacher in the school in which Young served as principal. Shortly afterwards, Young advanced to one of the newly created assistant superintendent positions in the city. She then invited Brayton to live with her. Brayton relinquished her teaching position and instead served as Young's personal assistant. Beyond sharing a deep friendship and professional interests, the two traveled and socialized together and their friends recognized them as companions.[53] Brayton took care of Young when she returned from work each day, shielding her from outside obligations and making sure her needs were met. When Young fell ill, Brayton nursed her back to health. Young, who died in the great 1918 flu epidemic, left Brayton all of her property and most of her estate.[54] Young and Brayton enjoyed friendships with other women who maintained such close primary relationships as well. Among their friends was settlement house pioneer, Jane Addams, who lived with Mary Rozet Smith for decades.[55]

In Texas, Annie Webb Blanton developed passionate relationships with other women throughout her life as well. Blanton began her career as a teacher, and then in 1917 became president of the Texas teachers' association. A year later, she assumed the state superintendency. Blanton lived with Emma Mitchell, one of her colleagues, for a few years. They traveled abroad, together hosted events for friends, and shared their lives. When Blanton moved to Austin to serve as state superintendent, Mitchell left her teaching position to become Blanton's assistant state superintendent. The two shared a room in Austin and ate their meals together.[56] Blanton participated actively in a number of women's groups, including the Woman's Shakespeare Club and the City Federation of Women's Clubs. When she joined the faculty of North Texas State University, she bought a four-bedroom house and invited several single women teachers to live there with her. She particularly enjoyed preparing a large Sunday buffet each week for residents of her house and their friends, a meal that became a tradition. In many significant ways Blanton centered her life on women and in turn relied on them professionally and personally.[57]

In numerous respects, the single women who entered the realm of paid labor as teachers needed support systems. While men could count on finding acceptable housing, food, and other services—and married men enjoyed the benefits of wives who tended their needs—unmarried women teachers faced the double burden of working long hours at school and then caring for their personal affairs and emotional needs during the few exhausted hours remaining each day. At first, such women managed with wholly inadequate accommodations and services. Then, by the late 1800s, a range of housing options, dining arrangements, and other services emerged to meet their unique requirements. As single women teachers clustered together in teacherages, jointly owned or rented houses, settlement houses, and other accommodations, they established social, professional, and political networks that sometimes grew into communities. These communities served some of the functions of traditional families in that caring bonds linked members and provided systems of social support.

In some cases, single women teachers lived together in long-term, committed relationships with beloved friends. These relationships served practical needs such as allowing women to share resources and divide household responsibilities. More important, however, the women who engaged in them maintained deep emotional and/or sexual relationships with each other that undoubtedly fortified them in their pioneering work as teachers and social reform activists. In the years ahead, these enriching, supportive relationships would become the target of a larger contemptuous attack on women's social, political, and economic gains. Because many women in such relationships either taught or served as school administrators, unmarried women school workers soon would confront a blistering array of new assaults on their character and their very qualification to serve students.

CHAPTER 4

A Rising Threat

Women enjoyed unprecedented new opportunities during the early decades of the twentieth century. They enrolled in colleges and universities at record levels. Many even continued their studies in graduate or professional degree programs.[1] They joined with millions of other women from across racial and economic strata as the collective women's movement labored for a variety of social and political causes.[2] This larger movement culminated in the enactment of national suffrage in 1920, thus cementing a place for women in political affairs.

The economic freedom and independence that accompanied a teaching career allowed many single women to join fully in the activities of the women's movement. Truly, these women teachers not only joined, but also provided vitally important grassroots leadership for the movement. And because of teaching and a growing number of other professional opportunities, women everywhere experienced new freedom to choose marriage, to remain respectably single, or in some cases to center their romantic and/or sexual relationships on other women. Such relatively well-educated single women could pursue their teaching responsibilities and social activities somewhat free of traditional family obligations.

By 1920, women accounted for 86 percent of all teachers, and, of these, the census found 91 percent to be single, widowed, or divorced. Essentially, an overwhelming 78 percent of *all* teachers were single, widowed, or divorced women. Teaching not only was a spinster's profession but, arguably, it also provided the most important form of employment for educated, unmarried women during these years.[3]

Through teaching, single women won modest respect as they provided valuable service to their communities. Although some male teachers found the large number of unmarried women teachers shocking, by and large, schools everywhere benefited from the work of this motivated, well-prepared, relatively inexpensive, and abundant labor source. Generally, as long as women served public needs and did not encroach on men's privileges, few questioned the arrangement. However, all this changed as women won political power, organized and demanded salaries equal to those of men, and increasingly lived independently of men.

As women's collective fortunes improved, backlash brewed. The signs seemed benign at first. Around 1900, a publisher distributed "The Jolly Game of Old Maid" in the United States. In this game, players matched cards in pairs—but the person ending the game with the unmatched "old maid" lost.[4] Then periodicals ran articles bemoaning boys' low enrollments in high schools, falling far short of girls'. Critics wondered if cadres of spinster teachers "feminized" their schools. They blamed single women teachers for making boys effeminate, arguing that when faced with the prospect of studying under spinster teachers, any self-respecting boy would leave. By extension, critics questioned the femininity of the young women who remained in high school, often excelling in their studies. Detractors also worried about the gender and sexual influences of spinster teachers on female students, especially those who aspired to become teachers themselves. Some even charged that single women teachers sought to reproduce themselves in this strange manner. Such fears unfolded against the backdrop of larger social changes such as declining marriage rates, increasing divorce rates, and a drop in the birthrate. Critics particularly concerned themselves with these changes in conjunction with middle- and owning-class white women.

Around the same time, works of European sexologists began circulating in the United States. These scientific studies of sex and sexual orientation gradually gained credence among scholars and reinforced a trend toward identifying and pathologizing non-mainstream sexual orientations and genders. Some sexologists conflated non-mainstream sexualities with gender-nonconformance. By this logic, those who desired persons of the same sex also likely displayed cross-gender qualities. Other sexologists took care to separate gender and sexuality. Taken together, though, the ideas of sexologists generally interacted with a larger cultural trend toward naming and rebuking persons with nonconforming sexuality and/or gender. Single women suddenly found themselves scrutinized closely by critics eager to denounce not their supposedly pathetic or pitiable state, but rather their so-called sexual deviance and mannish behavior. In time, the term "spinster" became synonymous with "deviant."[5]

With this heightened scrutiny during the decades following suffrage, increasing numbers of women chose to marry. A 1929 article in *Harper's Monthly* summarized: "There was a period, which can be roughly calendared as a decade ago, when it was prophesied that the life of an unmarried woman in the world would give a richer yield than had been believed possible. It was as if a new vein in the mine of women's prospects had been discovered and there was the natural rush to share in its riches. A good many girls decided to remain single. . . . But now some of the old dubiousness about the spinster life seems to be surging back."[6]

Mere doubts about single women teachers soon became outright denunciation as public perception shifted from regarding spinster teachers as good, upstanding members of their communities to castigating them as sinister, deviant women who corrupted children. By this reasoning, single women teachers turned boys into mollycoddles and girls into unmarriageable, mannish freaks. Eventually these perceptions translated into personnel practices—and the percentage of single women teachers plummeted. During mid-century, teaching shifted from a profession of spinsters to one dominated by married women.

By the 1900s, women enjoyed significantly greater educational opportunities than those available only two or three generations earlier. From coast to coast, nearly every young girl attended primary grade school. Many also went to high school. A large number of young women who graduated from high school later enrolled in normal schools, women's institutions, colleges, or universities where they pursued teaching credentials. A small but growing percentage also entered other professions such as law, medicine, journalism, and academia.[7]

Although women received a fraction of men's customary pay, they earned enough money to live independently, perhaps even to accumulate some modest wealth. Because they increasingly regarded marriage as a choice rather than a financial imperative, passion and romance played important roles in their relationships. Women generally believed that to marry, they first needed to love their partner and find satisfaction in the quality of the relationship. Within marriages, women also became freer to limit family sizes. And when marriages soured, women increasingly regarded divorce as an option, though a difficult one.

Along with these changes, women won the vote in states around the country in a broad-based movement that culminated in national suffrage. As a result, women quickly became formidable political players. Women's groups rallied for social causes and like-minded candidates. Sometimes they also propelled women candidates into important political positions from which they could shape law or policy. For example, organized women often elected women school superintendents where they enjoyed suffrage. In 1893, Colorado granted women full suffrage. Within a year, groups of women voters around the state displaced many of the male county superintendents by electing females. For the next fifty years, women dominated the county superintendency in the state—as well as the state superintendency.[8] A similar pattern played out in California, Iowa, and other parts of the country.[9]

Taken together, women's greater educational opportunities, increased economic independence, and growing political power constituted an overall rise in women's clout. Each factor contributed to the other, effectively enhancing the larger trend. Some women articulated the connections among these changes. Those who campaigned against women's servile condition, domestic abuse, child poverty, and other causes contended that women's conscientious vote would ameliorate such problems.[10] Some British suffragettes of the time chose to remain single because they regarded it as politically necessary for the women's revolution, or as one writer expressed it, "women needed the passion they would otherwise use in sex to fight for the emancipation of women."[11]

In some cases, suffrage activists consciously chose to form intimate relationships with other women, to center their lives on women. Edward Carpenter, the early-twentieth-century British writer whose then-controversial work attributed positive qualities to same-sex desire, argued that the women's suffrage movement brought women together across social and economic classes in passionate bonds for women's emancipation. He explained this common trend among both British and U.S. suffrage activists:

> It is noticeable . . . in this deepest relation to politics that the movement among women towards their own liberation and emancipation, which is taking place all over the civilised world, has been accompanied by a marked development of the homogenic passion among the female sex. It may be said that a certain strain in the relations between the opposite sexes which has come about owing to a growing consciousness among women that they have been oppressed and unfairly treated by men, and a growing unwillingness to ally themselves unequally in marriage—that this strain has caused the womenkind to draw more closely together to cement alliances of their own. But whatever the cause may be it is pretty certain that such comrade-alliances—and of quite devoted kind—are becoming increasingly common, and especially perhaps among the more cultured classes of women, who are working out the great cause of their sex's liberation; nor is it difficult to see the importance of such alliances in such a campaign. In the United States where the battle of women's independence is also being fought, the tendency mentioned is as strongly marked.[12]

Clearly, unmarried women, some of whom experienced such homogenic passion, stood out as significant leaders of the suffrage movement. They also rose to prominence in the other organizations that composed the larger women's movement of the early 1900s. As described earlier, single women constituted the vast majority of all teachers, and some of them ascended into school leadership positions as well.[13] Among the women who pursued other professions such as medicine, journalism, or law, single women also typically provided important direction.[14] Single women, consequently, constituted a group to be reckoned with.

The increasingly distinguished accomplishments of single women crept into public awareness—and stimulated research. In one study, scholars analyzed the entries of nearly 2,000 women listed in the 1936 edition of *Who's Who in America*. They concluded that of the distinguished women profiled, many remained single. Furthermore, they deduced that greater proportions of older women refrained from marriage than did those of younger generations.[15]

Many such high achieving women attributed some of their success to their status as single women, deeming it an advantage. However, critics challenged the virtues of spinsterhood. They charged that such women harmed themselves because their high attainment made them undesirable marriage partners. The authors of a 1924 article in *School and Society* described the esteemed unmarried women listed in *Who's Who:* "Though the task of achieving eminence vocationally does not prevent marriage, it can not be denied that it lessens the likelihood of marriage. . . . Accordingly it would seem that to become eminent cuts down a woman's chances of marriage about 20 times in 100."[16] Women could achieve, but apparently at the expense of their marriagability.

The accomplishments not just of single women, but of women in general also caused misgivings. During the early decades of the 1900s, women college and university students earned respectable grades, and in many cases, superior average grades to those of men in the same classes. Did this mean that women inherently possessed greater intellectual capacity than men? One writer commented on women's high rate of induction into Phi Beta Kappa, the academic honorary society:

Are women mentally superior to men? The reason that it is being asked is, that women students in our colleges and universities seem to be attaining to higher scholarship than men students. This fact seems thoroughly established as a result of the figures made public in 1917 by the Phi Beta Kappa fraternity, a scholarship organization which is open equally to men and women. It seems that during the three years, 1914–17, women won an aggregate of 1,979 places in this honorary organization, to 2,202 for men. But the number of men students available in the competition was much greater than the number of women students, since while twenty-seven chapters admitted men only, there were but six that were restricted to women, fifty-three (the remaining chapters) being in co-educational institutions. There can be no question, therefore, concerning the superior scholarship grades of the women students. And this fact is concerning Phi Beta

Kappa immensely, fearing, as they do, that the organization will become overrun with women—and, by no means incidentally, feeling mortified that men are unable to cope with women in competition for an honor whose one basis is in scholarship.[17]

Despite the stunning deeds cited, the author concluded that men and women probably possessed equal mental abilities, but women seemingly applied themselves more than did men.[18]

Even the notoriously male-identified and male-dominated field of sports found female challengers ready to demonstrate their gifts. Babe Didrikson, an astonishingly talented athlete in a variety of sports, and by some accounts perhaps the greatest athlete of the century, captured national attention because of her unparalleled athletic accomplishments. Her frank talk earned even more copy. However, Pat Griffin recounts how reporters savaged her with adjectives such as "mannish, unfeminine, rude, rough, and unattractive." Initially, the press described her as something of a "gender curiosity." As her accomplishments mounted, however, some reporters portrayed her as a "muscle moll" or deviant. Griffin explains that "questions about her gender and sexual identity placed her outside the boundaries of 'normal' womanhood, and she became a lightning rod for social anxiety about women athletes and changing gender norms."[19]

On the heels of the women's movement, unmarried women and women in general entered realms to which they previously had been excluded. Some achieved distinction. However, as women's collective accomplishments accumulated, their detractors found ways to minimize such feats by disparaging high achieving women for their status as single women, their "masculinity," or their suspected sexual deviance.

With women's growing prominence, Victorian attitudes about gender and sexual desire shifted. Women could attend graduate school, pursue careers in an array of professions, campaign for public office, and, after 1920, they could vote. Because of their newfound independence they could choose to live by themselves, live with other women, or marry a desired man. Those who married could limit the size of their families; and if relationships with their husbands did not endure, increasingly they could pursue divorce.

In response to these profound shifts in women's acceptable gender roles and bounds on their sexual desire, a variety of forms of research and popular criticism took shape that significantly undermined the social position of unmarried women, and teachers in particular. Early detractors developed language that placed the gender of single women teachers outside of feminine conventions. Politicians and other public figures bemoaned studies linking spinsterhood with higher education and accused educated single women of committing "race suicide." Sexologists identified and eventually pathologized women who chronically, rather than episodically, desired other women sexually. Psychologists followed with psychosexual theories of how single women developed so-called deviant sexualities. And in educational settings, social and mental hygienists attempted to synthesize these various strands of thought and suggest practical means by which single women could avoid what had become a supposedly wretched condition. These forms of backlash effectively changed the image of unmarried women teachers from that of virtuous individuals to that of menacing deviants who should be kept from the classroom.

G. Stanley Hall, the prominent psychologist and educator, stood out among early vocal opponents of women's new social gains. In his widely read and influential 1904 work, *Adolescence,* he depicted single women of achievement as victims, explaining that they had overdrawn their "account with heredity."[20] He described such women as having been taken in by feminists and that they would grow embittered when they finally discovered the limits of their abilities in comparison with men. Hall characterized single women as neither male nor female, but as something else.[21] He blamed biology—explaining that such women constituted a deviant third sex. In the end, he claimed that evolution would take its course because single women did not tend to reproduce. In a seeming contradiction, however, he strongly contended that although biology produced this third sex, women could choose a different course. He argued that they should receive training compelling them to become mothers and preparing them for maternal duties. In this way, single women might be spared the plight of permanent spinsterhood. He recommended preparatory jobs like elementary school teaching, which he thought enhanced nurturing qualities, provided women did not teach to the exclusion of marriage and motherhood.[22] Otherwise, he blamed women who remained single for their supposedly miserable state.

During the late 1800s, many regarded single women as virtuous individuals who refrained from sexual activity. Their seeming sexual innocence kept them above slander. Their usefulness mitigated any resistance that otherwise might have greeted their widespread entrance into the male-associated realm of salaried employment. However, after the turn of the century, critics such as Hall reframed single women as a "third sex," neither feminine nor quite masculine, and not altogether heterosexual, either. The author of a 1914 article in the *Educational Review* similarly contended that high-minded single women constituted a different gender/ sexual order. He believed that three kinds of women sought suffrage. The first, he explained, needed suffrage for her economic welfare. The second enjoyed taking men on in "intellectual combat." The third, "the mannish women, are in reality women only by accident, and the push of their life-force is towards masculine restlessness rather than towards feminine serenity. . . . Just to the degree that women enter intellectual, specialized pursuits where they vie with men in the use of masculine weapons, will the type of mind resulting come to be homogeneous—and masculine. . . . Feminism and . . . woman suffrage do not promise heaven, but mutilation for the race."[23]

In fact, concerns about the existence of large numbers of spinsters, who somehow stood outside of conventional heterosexuality, became intertwined with unease among privileged classes of whites about their propagation. Eugenics, a racist interpretation of evolutionary theory that gained credence early in the century, maintained that the white race could be perfected through careful selection of reproductive partners. Socially and economically advantaged whites stood to gain by perpetuating a belief in their supposed genetic superiority, which they wished to guard carefully. The eugenics movement strengthened when immigration from around the world brought exceptional diversity to the nation's cities. Confronted with this multiplicity, some advantaged whites believed they had much to lose if well-educated white women chose not to marry and bear children.[24]

Three important and well-publicized studies emerged around this time supporting the notion that dwindling numbers of college-educated white women married and raised children. These influential studies, which generally voiced strong numerical agreement, explained that married women accounted for only about half of college-educated white women between the ages of thirty-two and fifty-two. Those who married tended to bear only around two children each as opposed to over 3.5 each for women in the general population.[25] President Theodore Roosevelt capitalized on the alarm generated by these studies. With characteristic bravado, he led the charge against so-called race suicide. He complained bitterly about college-educated white women who abandoned their responsibilities to bear children, and, further, that women's educational experiences contributed to the trend in important ways.[26] A Smith College faculty member responded by challenging the studies undergirding such protests: "The statistical tables . . . fail to establish any causal nexus between higher education and the frequency of marriage and maternity on the other. The first kind of table is entirely in the air, the second institutes comparisons between women who are clearly not comparable, and the third leads to a lame and impotent conclusion." He chastised the studies' authors, claiming, "The results at which some writers arrive can be reached only by reading into the statistical data the conclusions which they wish to show."[27] Such responses, though, received relatively little attention in comparison to publicly expressed fears of "race suicide," especially those articulated from the presidential pulpit.

Higher education did not bear the brunt of criticism alone for producing spinsters. Elementary and high schools also received blame. Admired single women teachers supposedly inspired their promising female students to remain single. Their tutelage also purportedly made boys effeminate.[28] Remarkably, critics held unmarried women teachers to account both for girls who seemed to stand outside conventional heterosexuality by choosing to become single teachers themselves and for boys who displayed cross-gender characteristics—or who simply failed to impress peers with their masculinity. Such unmarried female teachers apparently did not police the bounds of gender and sexuality well enough for some or model them well enough for others.

G. Stanley Hall maintained that schools needed reform so they could assist, rather than hinder, the proper gender development of girls and boys. He contended that "what our schools and other institutions should do is to push normal sex distinctions to their uttermost and not obliterate them, to make boys more manly and girls more womanly. We should respect the law of sexual differences, and not forget that motherhood is a very different thing from fatherhood. Neither sex should copy or set patterns to the other, but all parts should be played harmoniously and clearly in the great sex symphony."[29] Hall believed single women were inadequate in the task of shaping the correct "sex," or gender, of children. Not only did they in some way seem different, a third sex, or even mannish, but increasingly their detractors came to regard single women as possessing deviant sexualities.

During the early decades of the century, concern mounted that single women might not simply be asexual as some previously assumed, but rather that some might actively engage in sexual behaviors—and not necessarily with men. The gradual circulation in the United States of works by British and German sexologists stimulated this awareness in part. At first, scholars and doctors mainly drew from this new scientific literature; but then popular periodicals joined in the discussion, using careful, euphemistic language. Eventually the stigma attached to spinsterhood resembled that of lesbianism. One writer in 1929 hinted at the connection: "In two ways, at least, these women [spinsters] are all alike, both marked with one stamp. They do not have a normal social life, no matter how good a time they may be having, and they do not have a normal release for the deepest emotions in them, which may therefore, either atrophy or nurture them or find an unnatural and illicit outlet."[30] At the time, direct mention of same-sex sexual activities violated taboos against discussing the "unspeakable" in public media.

These years witnessed a major change in general understandings about passionate and/or sexual relationships between persons of the same sex. Before this time, men violated religious mores when they engaged in sexual activities with each other. Any man was thought capable of such transgression. On the other hand, many thought women to be incapable of having sexual experiences with other women, or perhaps if they possessed the capability, such experiences were believed inconsequential. However, a number of historians have suggested that from the late 1800s through the early decades of the twentieth century, same-sex sexual activity shifted in popular thinking from *behavior* in which *any* individual could engage to an *identity* by which a few persons might be known. Persons who consistently desired same-sex sexual activities came to be labeled as "homosexuals." Essentially, the word "homosexual" shifted from an adjective to a noun, from a kind of sexual activity to a category of persons. The research of sexologists contributed to this shift, but so too did other social forces such as awareness of same-sex sexual behavior as depicted in criminal logs, newspapers, books, plays, and eventually movies. And in time, sexologists as well as many others would begin to find not just men's, but women's same-sex sexual activity—and then identity—quite interesting.

Among the influential early European sexologists, William Krafft-Ebing and Havelock Ellis stood out for their work on the behaviors and characteristics of lesbians. In particular, Ellis's 1895 volume, *Sexual Inversion in Women,* inspired subsequent researchers to study homosexuality among women. Krafft-Ebing, Ellis, and other sexologists catalogued in detail the observable physical traits, sexual activities, behavioral tendencies, and other characteristics of women who engaged in sexual experiences with other women. These sexologists published volumes that contributed to a larger social trend toward identifying and pathologizing women who persistently desired sex with other women. Both Krafft-Ebing and Ellis maintained that environmental contexts sometimes played significant roles in sexual activity. They regarded sexual behavior between women as common in certain homosocial environments such as boarding schools or colleges, and that women might engage in same-sex sexual activity in such contexts without necessarily being homosexuals. Conversely, though, they contended that some women manifested true homosexuality with characteristic "symptoms."[31]

Krafft-Ebing and Ellis attempted to distinguish between "homosexuals" and those they deemed "gender deviant." They endeavored to differentiate sexual orientation from gender. Other sexologists conflated these and, in popular writing, terms such as "homosexual" and "sexual pervert" often connoted both persons who engaged in sexual activities with others of the same sex and those who failed to manifest "appropriate" gender qualities. Women who stepped outside gender-appropriate bounds, perhaps by joining the suffrage movement and campaigning for greater rights, faced accusations of these new maladies. One writer in 1901 charged, "The female possessed of masculine ideas of independence; the viragint who would sit in the public highways and lift up her pseudo-virile voice, proclaiming her sole right to decide questions of war or religion, or the value of celibacy and the curse of women's impurity, and that disgusting anti-social being, the female sexual pervert, are simply different degrees of the same class—degenerates."[32] Sheila Jeffries argues that this labeling and stigmatizing amounted to a propaganda campaign to undermine the successes achieved by the women's movement. She also contends that it was intended to eliminate spinsterhood as a viable life choice for women.[33]

Around the same time that works of early sexologists began circulating in the United States, the first translations of Freud's works also arrived. Freud's groundbreaking theories described relationships between repressed sexuality and neuroses. Much of his work engaged in extensive analysis of women's sexuality.[34] Together, sexology and new psychological theories inspired by Freud's work led to a series of studies of psychosexual phenomena.[35] Several that centered on women appeared from the late 1920s through the 1940s. In these studies, researchers surveyed large samples of women to determine which qualities or experiences affected their sexual development. They focused extensively on unmarried women. In response to this heightened scrutiny of the intimate lives of single women, an exasperated, self-described spinster explained in the *Atlantic Monthly* in 1934 that:

> The world has gone mad on sex. . . . No other reason for anything has a chance until sex has been hypothesized. Nerve doctors and psychologists say "sexual origin" before they even see their patients. There are doctors and psychiatrists who, if called in by a spinster, would diagnose a broken leg as sex starvation. . . . In fact, unmarried women are no more given to nervous troubles than matrons are. Speaking unstatistically, I should say far less so. The most of them are going healthily along, giving only casual thought to their deprivations, certainly not being ruined by ungratified longings.[36]

Not only had single women become the focus of study, stigma, and scorn—with every malady attributable in some manner to psychosexual origins—but also because teachers accounted for such a sizeable portion of single women, unmarried women teachers in particular endured extensive analysis of their sexuality. Increasingly, unmarried women teachers were suspected of sexually desiring other women.

Katharine Bement Davis, a noted social activist and researcher, documented this possibility well in her pioneering and influential study, *Factors in the Sex Life of Twenty-Two Hundred Women* (1929). Davis began her career as a high school chemistry teacher. During the ten years she spent in the classroom, she saved money to attend Vassar. She graduated in 1892 with honors and then enrolled in the doctoral program at the University of Chicago. There, she wrote her dissertation under the direction of the venerable Thorstein Veblen, graduating cum laude in 1900.[37] Davis remained single throughout her life. She also counted large numbers of other single professional women among her friends. She enjoyed such great respect for her work that a League of Women Voters poll in 1922 named her as one of the twelve greatest living American women.[38]

Davis conducted the study, *Factors in the Sex Life,* with the sponsorship of the Bureau of Social Hygiene, a Rockefeller-financed philanthropic organization. This organization devoted its efforts to the "study, amelioration and prevention of those social conditions, crimes and diseases which, adversely, affect the well being of society."[39] For the project, Davis surveyed 1,000 married and 1,200 unmarried college-educated women to deduce patterns in their sexual experiences and choices. Among the 1,200 single women in her sample, teachers and superintendents accounted for 52 percent, suggesting the importance of public school education in employing such women. Of these single women educators, *nearly half* reported having experienced either intense emotional relationships or sexual relationships with other women. Davis categorized these relationships in the following manner:

> *Emotional relationships:* "Intense emotional relations with women unassociated with consciousness of a sex experience and unaccompanied by physical expression other than hugging and kissing"   22%

> *Sexual relationships:* "Intense relationships accompanied by mutual masturbation, contact of genital organs, or other physical expressions recognized as sexual in character," or "intense relations recognized at the time as sexual in character, but without expression other than hugging and kissing"   25%

> *Neither:* Women who indicate they have not had "intense emotional relations with another girl or woman."[40]   53%

Davis categorized relationships between women as sexual if sexual intent existed—regardless of whether or not sexual activities ensued.

Davis generally couched her discussion of the sexual orientation of unmarried women in positive terms. However, others found her work disturbing because it revealed that homosexual desire occurred among more women than previously believed, particularly among educated, unmarried women.[41] One researcher concluded that Davis had "found a high relationship between homosexuality and high mental level plus educational attainment."[42] Indeed, although the study contained a great deal of data describing a full range of women's emotional lives and sexual behaviors, many readers focused on the findings regarding higher education, homosexual desire and behavior, and women's decisions to remain unmarried.

Another researcher reacted to Davis's study by clarifying: "It is not to be concluded that just because a girl goes to college she is more likely to indulge in homosexual behavior. It is rather that the close association of women in a college atmosphere and their relative isolation from heterosexual contacts afford more opportunity for homosexual reactions, in the sense that homosexual behavior is a 'learned reaction.'"[43] Essentially, some readers of Davis's study deduced that women learned to desire other women sexually. Davis even pointed out that early influences in childhood could contribute to women's homosexuality. She offered the example of

> An older woman who says she grew up with the sense that certain things were bad. She early learned to indulge in auto-erotic practices. She became morbid as she grew older, largely on this account. She blames her parents for lack of oversight, for not gaining her confidence, and for lack of proper instruction. She always preferred girls to boys. She sums up with a statement that very well expresses the attitude of many of the older women toward the type of "college crush" that is not carried to extremes. "In college, maturing, there was a constant finding of congenial spirits, with considerable expression of affection by kissing and embracing. It seemed of the spirit rather than of the flesh, and I remember being very much offended at a girl who said it was not love. I felt that marriage was not for me, because I might carry on to children the bad tendencies that had appeared in my own childhood. But of these things I never spoke to anyone. Men either did not attract me at all naturally, or I was so inhibited that all the tenderness in me went out to girls and women. In those days we had no knowledge of such matters, and while some things may be eternally and immutably sex manifestations, to the ones who found in them the natural expressions of love for others, they *were* such expressions, not sex perversions, it seems to me, however sentimental such a view may be called by the

scientific mind. I incline to wager that the future scientist will find some attributes *human,* belonging to both sexes, that are now gummed up with
Freudian terms."[44]

Some concluded from Davis's research that schooling or education contributed in some manner to the homosexuality of young women; therefore they believed that schools should find ways to guard against this supposedly dangerous tendency.

Finally, against the backdrop of the rising divorce rate, large numbers
of unmarried women in the general population, the declining birthrate,
the widespread availability of birth control, and public discussion of
problems such as venereal diseases and prostitution, the social and mental hygiene movements emerged to guide changing gender boundaries
and sexual mores back to their traditional middle-class forms. Social hygienists came from a variety of fields—including business, education,
and medicine—but they shared a commitment to preserving traditional
gendered relations and sexual orientation. They viewed their central task
as maintaining social order by constraining sexual behavior, by limiting
it to certain acts within marriage. As such, social hygienists championed
sex education programs, but not ones that discussed sexual desire, re-
production, or even birth control. Instead, they sought to train young
people to avoid *all* forms of sex outside of marriage.[45] Schools and colleges offered hygiene classes that reinforced traditional gender behaviors
and sexual practices. Capitalizing on the eugenics movement, they also
provided advice on how youth eventually might find healthy spouses
with whom they could produce physically fit children for the "betterment of the race." Some texts even counseled weak or physically "infe-
rior" men to refrain from fatherhood altogether to avoid passing on
their "flawed" genetic inheritance.[46]

Closely related to the social hygiene movement was the emerging mental hygiene movement, which drew more exclusively on psychological
theories. Mental hygienists advised single women to avoid the life of the
embittered spinster, and to choose instead the "better" adjustment of
well-developed, married heterosexuality. Because unmarried women constituted such an overwhelming portion of the nation's teaching force,
mental hygienists directed much effort toward spinster teachers. The author of *Mental Hygiene for the Classroom Teacher* (1939) described how

> Mental hygiene is interested in the adjustments which the woman teacher
> who does not marry . . . eventually makes to the thwarted love life. . . . Wit-
> ness . . . the tremendous amount of running away from reality, of retro-
> gression, of evasion of issues, of recoil, of introversion which burdens
> human beings who have failed to learn the great lesson of compensation

and substitution for their strong but untoward or unachievable ambitions. . . . There may linger in the subconscious wastes of her mind resentments that she does not consciously recognize, discontent and unrest that she either fails to identify, or perhaps wrongly blames on the wearing strain of the profession upon her. It would be interesting if we could analyze the specific contributions made by this particular conflict to the crabbedness and the "nerves" and the breakdowns that bestrew the pathways of many women teachers as they climb up the years of their service. They have repressed fundamental instincts to the point of extinction, instead of sublimating them and finding peace and satisfaction in other compensating and stimulating ways.[47]

The author of this work urged single women teachers instead to direct their sexual frustration in socially useful ways.

The mental and social hygiene movements, in conjunction with the work of sexologists, psychologists, and a larger public shift in attitudes toward unmarried women all contributed to a general deterioration in support for spinster teachers. In 1929, a writer for the *Atlantic Monthly* explained that the "'old maid school teacher' was the scarecrow in the educational field. The teaching profession turned out spinsters as well as educators. It limited opportunities for meeting men. It set teachers apart as a group."[48] And, increasingly, the public also believed that such teachers might not fall within the bounds of conventional gender or sexual orientation.

This growing wariness found voice in a variety of artistic works of the period. The popular play, "The Captive," which ran during 1926–1927, depicted the experience of a young woman who fell in love with another woman, but who married a male friend in part to hide from her father the real object of her affection. When the play ran, critics called it "objectionable and salacious," and police soon stepped in to investigate. For two weeks, the controversy captured the front page of the *New York Times*.[49] Katherine Davis described the impact of this production and how it "focused the attention of the public upon the problem of homosexuality which before that time had never been made a topic of conversation in polite society. Many adults, particularly women, claimed they did not know such a condition existed."[50]

Then, in 1928, Radclyffe Hall's novel, *The Well of Loneliness,* arrived in bookstores. This widely read and much-discussed British work centered on an ill-fated lesbian relationship. When the book reached the United States, police in New York seized it and charged the publisher with obscenity. The judge in the case convicted him, arguing, "The book can have no moral value, since it seeks to justify the right of a pervert to prey upon normal members of a community, and to uphold such relationship as noble and lofty. Although it pleads for tolerance on the part of society of those possessed of and inflicted with perverted traits and tendencies, it does not argue for repression or moderation of insidious impulses."[51] The judge's decision was later overturned and the book eventually became a bestseller. Arguably, its publication marked a watershed moment in lesbian history.[52]

A few years later, lesbian characters entered the cinema when the 1931 German movie, *Maedchen in Uniform,* came to the United States. The film portrayed a lonely girl's crush on her female teacher at a girl's boarding school during the rising Nazi regime. At the film's climax, the central character, Manuel, declares her undying affection for her beloved teacher. Though this film initially was banned in the United States because of newly instituted Hollywood production codes prohibiting homosexual characters and themes, Eleanor Roosevelt, who marveled at the film's powerful content, helped lift the ban. *Maedchen* then became the first film screened in the United States with clear lesbian content. Critics from the *New York Times* quickly called *Maedchen* the best film of the year and audiences around the country packed movie houses. Pauline Kael of the *New Yorker* wrote at the time: "The teacher is not viewed as decadent or naughty; she [is] on the side of the liberal, humanitarian angels, yet unmistakably lesbian." The immense box office success of *Maedchen* inspired other filmmakers to copy elements of its central theme.[53]

Popular representations of lesbians in plays, novels, and films demonstrated a growing awareness of women who sexually desired other women. The controversies that some of these works inspired kept the topic of women's same-sex desire focused in the public eye. For some, these depictions offered a healthy acknowledgment of a heretofore hidden population. The revelations scandalized many others, however, and provided vexing proof that single women, increasingly suspected of deviance, even lesbianism, were going too far with their newfound freedoms. If women wished to remain untainted by such doubts about their sexual orientation and gender, they would have to go to greater lengths than in the past to prove their heterosexuality and femininity.

Communities became increasingly uncomfortable with their large populations of unmarried women teachers. However, they continued employing them because unmarried women teachers offered several important benefits such as low cost, excellent availability, and relatively good professional preparation. Around the turn of the century, school officials *preferred* hiring single rather than married women teachers. Then during the Great Depression they *formalized* the practice by officially barring married women from the classroom. In short, administrators considered married women teachers selfish for denying jobs to men and needy single women while unemployment rates remained high. During this time, most city school systems adopted policies requiring women teachers to resign when they married.[54]

As generalized suspicion of unmarried women mounted, however, critics questioned the wisdom of hiring them to teach if they supposedly could not offer desirable gender or sexual characteristics for their students to emulate. Concurrently, scholars, policymakers, and educators began championing married women as potentially excellent teachers. One writer described the appeal of married women teachers: "The most desirable women for teachers are not only those who have a chance to marry but those who do marry. . . . Ask any superintendent which he would rather have for permanent teachers, the women who did marry during the first six years of teaching or the women who didn't. Unfortunately for teaching, the young men get the first choice, and they usually choose wisely. . . . It is not only that the more feminine have been selected out, but the tendency of those who settle down to teaching without hope of rescue is to lose the desire to be attractive."[55] Furthermore, he contended that women who made good teachers shared the same qualities as good wives: They were attractive to men, compliant, and dependent. Women with qualities likely to result in marriage would, in all probability, also succeed in educational work.

In 1934, David Peters released a detailed study, *The Status of the Married Woman Teacher,* which documented the prejudices directed against married women teachers, especially as school systems instituted policies prohibiting their employment. He concluded that while single and married women teachers offered similar effectiveness, "the measured mental growth of the pupils taught by the married women teachers exceeded the measured mental growth of the pupils taught by the single teachers."[56]

Around the same time, the NEA published a study describing the personnel policies of 1,500 city school systems. The study particularly explored policies concerning the employment of married women for teaching positions. The authors concluded that 77 percent of reporting districts refused to hire married women teachers. Only 37 percent of districts allowed women to continue teaching if they got married after being hired.[57] Rural and remote school districts were much more likely to hire and retain married women teachers than were their urban counterparts, mostly because rural districts faced a pressing shortage of qualified teachers. Also, they eagerly employed well-prepared persons willing to work for relatively low wages. Urban districts, however, hired single women teachers almost exclusively.

The NEA then began encouraging school systems to hire married women teachers. They argued that "marriage and parenthood are likely to enrich a teacher's understanding of childhood and family life and thus will help her to be a better teacher." The NEA strongly argued for the abolition of "the celibacy rule," a change that "would do much over a period of years to remove the 'old-maid school teacher' cliché which is so distasteful to many teachers and so injurious to the morale of many of the younger members of the profession."[58]

Eventually after World War II, districts around the country decided to eliminate their policies restricting the employment of married women teachers. One reason for this shift was that fewer single women wished to pursue teaching. During the war, large numbers of women teachers left the classroom to work in military-related industries. Not only did they assist in the war effort by doing this, but they also earned higher wages than they could by teaching. When the war ended, returning male veterans pushed women out of their industrial jobs. However, relatively few women wished to return to the classroom. Some of them entered the rapidly expanding realm of pink-collar jobs as secretaries and clerical support staff instead. Many others chose to marry during the postwar marriage boom, after which the baby boom quickly followed.

At the same time, millions of male war veterans returned home to compete for relatively few civilian jobs.[59] Although these men needed employment desperately, only some entered school teaching, which offered low wages and the stigma of women's work. Because schools urgently needed teachers, they vigorously recruited male veterans. And to circumvent policies requiring equal pay for male and female teachers, districts presented men with additional compensated duties and promises of rapid promotions.[60] Such incentives enticed a few men.[61]

These measures failed to attract enough teachers, though. As a result, school districts dropped their policies prohibiting employment of married women teachers. Some districts ended their bans immediately following the war. Most others delayed the change for a few years. Districts typically cited earlier arguments forwarded by the NEA—that married women offered efficient instruction and that they somehow understood children better than single women did. Educators everywhere also wished to purge teaching of its reputation as a spinsters' profession, which connoted possible deviance. One education professor in Kentucky even explained that it was important to do something to change the work that made so many women "queer."[62]

From 1940 to 1960, single women departed teaching rapidly. Meanwhile, married women, heretofore largely denied the opportunity to teach, flooded into the work. Some found that the teaching schedule matched their maternal duties better than did twelve-month, eight-to-five

Table 4.1. Percentage of Single, Widowed, Divorced, and Married Women in
Teaching and the U.S. Labor Force

Year	Married Women in U.S. Labor Force	Married Women Teachers	Single Women Teachers	Widowed or Divorced Women Teachers
1920	9[a]	10	86	5
1930	12[a]	18	77	5
1940	17[a]	25	69	7
1950	25[a]	47	43	9
1960	31[b]	59	29	13

Note: Statistics derived from Folger and Nam, *Education of the American Population,* p. 81, unless otherwise noted.

a. Lynn Weinner, *From Working Girl to Working Mother* (Chapel Hill, University of North Carolina Press, 1985), 89; cited in Nancy Cott, *The Grounding of Modern Feminism* (New Haven: Yale University Press, 1987), 183.

b. U.S. Department of Labor, Bureau of Labor Statistics, *Labor Force Statistics Derived from the Current Population Survey: A Data Book,* vol. 1 (September 1982), Bulletin 2096, table C-11; 1985: BLS News Release, USDL 85–381 (September 19, 1985), table 1; total from unpublished tabulations.

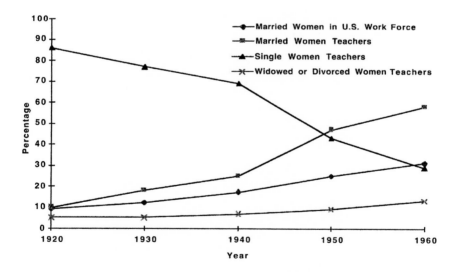

Figure 4.1 Single, Widowed, Divorced, and Married Women in Teaching and the U.S. Labor Force

Note: Table 4.1 and Figure 4.1 appeared in Jackie Blount, *Destined to Rule the Schools: Women and the Superintendency* (Albany, NY: SUNY Press, 1998), 104–05.

jobs. School districts argued that marriage and motherhood prepared women for the toils of the classroom.[63]

As districts lifted their marriage bans, the proportion of married women teachers soared. If the only causative factor were the elimination of marriage bans, then within a few years the proportion of married women in teaching should have *matched* the rate of married women in the general workforce. That did not happen, however. Instead, by 1960, the proportion of married women in teaching had *doubled* the proportion of married women in the general workforce. Conversely, from 1940 to 1960, the percentage of single women in teaching slid from 69 to less than 30 percent.[64] Although marriage rates rose after the war, the increase should have been reflected equally in the marriage rates of women in the general workforce and in teaching.

The elimination of marriage bans alone does not account for this stunning reversal in the demographics of school teaching at mid-century. Also at work was a widespread desire to rid teaching of its association with spinsters. Essentially, schools tolerated unmarried women teachers—in fact, preferred them—as long as they filled a compelling need that was unmet by other segments of the population. However, when the economic benefits of employing single women teachers no longer existed *and* spinsterhood became associated with deviance or even lesbianism, the makeup of the teaching profession changed as fundamentally as it had a century earlier when women supplanted men in the classroom.

By the early 1950s, ongoing headlines brought the topic of homosexuality into the home. School board members and administrators responded to the supposed threat by filling the ranks of educators with persons meeting culturally idealized representations of men and women. They sought, in part, to provide correct gender modeling for children. However, they also wished to provide modeling of monogamous, married heterosexuality. In particular, school administrators sought male personnel without any discernable traces of homosexuality. They regarded homosexual male teachers as dangerous to the development of male students' proper heterosexuality because as Willard Waller, the eminent sociologist, argued in his classic work, *The Sociology of Teaching* (1932), "nothing seems more certain than that homosexuality is contagious." Waller described several methods by which school administrators assessed job candidates' supposed homosexuality, such as by asking male applicants, "Do you like boys?" and then watching for overly enthusiastic, confused, emotional, or "unduly hurried" answers. He explained that a more sophisticated method involved carefully scrutinizing the candidates' "carriage, mannerisms, voice, speech."[65] And for women, unmarried status connoted possible deviance. Such women needed to prove their commitment to monogamous, married sexual relationships with men if they wished to avoid suspicion of lesbianism. Celibacy or seeming asexuality no longer sufficed.

All school employees increasingly needed to demonstrate not only their gender-conformity, but also their heterosexuality through marriage or obvious attraction to persons of the other sex. Because of the linkage in popular imagination between gender-nonconformity and homosexuality, school officials commonly assessed the likely heterosexuality of education job candidates by evaluating their gender presentation. During the decades following World War II, school administrators vigorously employed these and ever-more insidious methods of rooting out homosexuality among job candidates and current employees. The mere suspicion of homosexuality soon provided ample grounds for banishment from school work.

CHAPTER 5

The New Moral Menace to Our Youth

The decades following World War II brought profound changes in the gender identities and sexualities allowed of school workers around the country. Before the war, single women dominated the classroom, though mounting questions about their gender and sexual orientation made support for them tenuous at best. After the war, however, married women quickly outnumbered single women teachers, doubling the rate of married women in the general workforce by 1960.

Also, before the war, large numbers of women had moved into middle and upper levels of school administration, particularly elementary school principalships and county superintendencies. After the war, returning male veterans quickly displaced them, sending the percentage of women in these positions sharply downward. Then male school administrators and their advocates reshaped the field so that it became work reserved not just for men, but also for notably masculine men.[1]

A growing fear of homosexuality added to these shifts. Increasingly, school workers who defied gender norms or remained unmarried risked suspicion of homosexuality. During these years when experts touted homosexuality as a serious and contagious illness, schools became remarkably hostile places for suspected homosexuals. Political forces even would enlist school administrators and teachers in the front-line battle against this supposedly dangerous social scourge.

Indeed, during the decades immediately following the war, an intense new awareness of homosexuality fostered vigorous public discussions that previously had been censured or otherwise considered impolite, even unspeakable. In part, this heightened consciousness of same-sex desire followed the publication of Alfred Kinsey's landmark studies on human sexual behavior, which indicated a higher incidence of homosexual activity than previously had been understood. Though many welcomed this carefully researched news, others expressed alarm that homosexuality, like a cancer, would metastasize and devour the nation's youth.

Parents and school officials reacted to this alleged threat in several ways. Following the lead of Senator Joseph McCarthy and his much-publicized congressional hearings on communists and then homosexuals in government, state and local government officials launched investigations to ferret out homosexual school workers. Because homosexuals were thought to recruit aggressively among youth, school administrators screened candidates, eliminating any whose gender presentation strayed from polarized norms. They cast a dubious eye on those who remained unmarried. They reinforced niches in school employment for "manly" men, including high school coaching positions, vocational instruction, and especially supervisory positions. They deepened the association of women with areas such as elementary and home economics instruction. They regarded deviation from gender norms as connoting sexual abnormality because popular sentiment confused the two. Finally, state legislation required police in California to inform school officials about any school workers arrested on morals or sex-related charges. Clearly, concern mounted about the presence of educators who stood outside the bounds of conventional sexual desire or gender—either in their professional or personal lives.

Teachers, long expected to adhere to rigid and highly restrictive codes of acceptable moral behavior, found that during the middle of the century, school officials focused more narrowly and intensely on those thought to be homosexual and/or gender-nonconforming.[2] School workers who desired persons of the same sex deduced that they either needed to leave the profession or disguise their sexual orientation. Some self-identified gay men and lesbians arranged marriages of convenience to avoid the searing scrutiny associated with unmarried status. A few probably married heterosexual partners either to assimilate or cloak clandestine activities. Because many thought that homosexuals could be identified by cross-gender characteristics and behaviors, all school workers learned that to stand above reproach, they needed to accentuate the gender-appropriateness of their clothing, appearance, and actions. They could not aspire to cross-gender realms in school employment and expect to avoid scrutiny. And to prevent the further spread of this new public plague, schools implemented curricula intended to keep youth sexually straight. In effect, schools became fundamentally important agencies in the nationwide campaign to fight homosexuality.

Wartime social conditions in the United States fostered many eventual changes in acceptable sexualities and gender identities. Large-scale military operations created a variety of homosocial environments in which men lived and socialized almost exclusively with other men, and women with women. Military bases, battlefields, and warships alike employed men who shared bunkers, meals, tasks, and off-duty recreational activities. Meanwhile, women's military divisions, such as the WACs, WAVES, and SPARs, created similar environments for women. Women also filled ship-yards and other military industries, earning relatively high pay while aiding the nation's war effort. These women commonly lived together in dormitories, barracks, or other makeshift mass housing units. Within these single-sex communities, intense friendships developed that many nostalgically recall as the most significant in their lives—especially among male soldiers closest to combat.

The U.S. military traditionally resisted homosexual activity among male soldiers; however, during World War II it instituted for the first time a process intended to rid the ranks of exclusively homosexual individuals. The army and navy employed psychiatrists who, drawing on recent research on sexuality, assisted in identifying persons with homosexual histories. When men showed up at induction centers for screening, psychiatrists asked them questions and studied their behaviors to determine if they might be homosexual. Because these screening questions typically lacked subtlety, recruits found them easy to circumvent. Incentives for evading this categorization were high: Failure to fool the screeners resulted in rejection from armed service. Furthermore, the reason for rejection frequently became public knowledge and effectively barred young men from civilian employment as well. Consequently, recruits rarely admitted having previous homosexual experiences when asked during military induction.[3] Not surprisingly, military psychiatrists managed to identify only a relatively small number of supposed homosexuals, men whose behaviors and characteristics were deemed most effeminate. However, the screening itself alerted many to the existence of homosexuality, even as it perpetuated stereotyped and largely inaccurate images. The process also shifted resources and attention to homosexuality, and it increased interest among physicians and psychiatrists in better detecting and treating this purported malady.

Women who entered military services such as the Women's Army Corps (WAC) did not face the same overt screening for homosexuality as male inductees. Instead, a broad system of WAC policies attempted to govern all sexual activity in which women might engage. However, by definition, women who entered military service crossed into a masculine realm, symbolized in part by the required uniforms, which in the case of the WAC were modeled after men's and even sized for men. One WAC psychiatrist contended that any woman who voluntarily joined the military already had proven her masculine identification. At the time, such mannishness on the part of women typically connoted lesbian tendencies. WAC administrators, then, strictly monitored women for mannish behavior, expelling those who refused to hide their cross-gender qualities. Meanwhile, lesbians who adopted feminine dress and demeanor generally were ignored even when their same-sex sexual activities were well known.[4]

Despite military screening, men and women who sexually desired others of the same sex successfully entered and served in the military. The large homosocial communities of military bases and urban manufacturing centers created conditions in which same-sex activity might easily occur. Indeed, historian John D'Emilio argues that homosexual subcultures appeared in cities around the country during World War II. The free labor system that existed in these urban centers allowed large numbers of women and men who desired persons of the same sex to live in community and organize around emerging sexual identities.[5] In the war setting, young men and women who desired persons of the same sex unexpectedly found themselves among many others like them. They devised new ways of meeting each other and sustaining their relationships. Entrepreneurs established small businesses such as bars, cafés, and entertainment venues that catered to lesbians and gay men near military centers. And they joined in a newly thriving subculture that had not existed to the same degree earlier in the century. D'Emilio and Estelle Freedman, in their pioneering work on sexuality in U.S. history, *Intimate Matters* (1997), conclude that "truly, World War II was something of a nationwide 'coming out' experience."[6]

When the war ended, men and women who desired same-sex love often settled in urban areas, fostering the growth of identifiable lesbian and gay communities. Within these communities, they created patterns of meeting, socializing, dressing, speaking, romancing, and living that characterized new gay identities.[7] Men, generally granted freer access to public spaces than women, searched for partners in bars, parks, and other areas. Women, lacking men's freedom of movement or their economic resources, created more private spaces such as social networks. They hosted parties and events in which other lesbians could relax and feel part of a like-minded group. Gay bars offered both men and women safe spaces that further bolstered their emerging sense of homosexual identity.[8]

The years following the war brought dramatic shifts in the demographics of public school employment. With marriage bans lifted, married women quickly filled teaching positions as single women moved on. The authors of a best-selling book in 1947 even went so far as to argue "that all spinsters be barred by law from having anything to do with the teaching of children."[9] However, school administration, long the province of men, soon would require visibly higher standards of masculinity.

Before World War II, women had risen into a number of school administrative positions. They accounted for around 10 percent of all school superintendents serving between 1910 and 1950.[10] They also held the majority of elementary school principalships and a sizeable portion of other school administrative positions as well. After the war, however, school boards asked women to step down so men could assume the more desirable administrative positions. Women who had served long and well in elementary principalships, for example, were required to return to the classroom so that young men, fresh from the war, could serve in the principal's office. Adding to the insult, district officials often expected these women to train their male replacements. Indeed, women school administrators all but disappeared after the war.[11]

As school districts searched for men to lead their schools, they recruited not simply men, but men with readily apparent masculine qualities. Men with records of distinguished service in the military, athletic achievement, and seemingly obvious heterosexuality in the form of marriage were desirable in a profession eager to shed its long association with women, particularly single women. A 1946 article in the *American School Board Journal* described how one lucky district had snagged an ideal administrator: "The man selected could not be labeled as an effeminate being. He was a former collegiate athletic hero. His physique was comparable to any of the mythical Greek gods. He was truly the ultimate in manliness. The last, but not least in importance of his personal characteristics, was the fact that he was married."[12]

For administrative aspirants, marriage offered evidence of stability and success in upholding men's traditional responsibilities. It also removed any possible taint of homosexuality from questionable candidates. Conversely, unmarried male candidates raised doubts among school board members. The *American School Board Journal* printed an article in 1947 explaining that "the unmarried superintendent is an enigma to school boards. . . . A young bachelor will be tolerated, but an older man who stubbornly refuses to enter the conjugal state receives little sympathy or consideration. A bachelor is considered 'odd' or 'peculiar,' vain, selfish, and even a delinquent member of society."[13] At a time when the word "homosexual" rarely appeared in mainstream publications, code words such as "odd" and "peculiar," especially when used in this context, typically connoted homosexuality. Another article in 1963 summarized: "We would like to have a man who is married, with a family."[14] When the

American Association of School Administrators (AASA) released its 1952 report on the superintendency, it proudly noted that 97.3 percent of all male city superintendents were married, a rate significantly higher than that of the general population of men in 1950: 69 percent. School boards that sought superintendent candidates typically circulated job announcements with listed qualifications, including marriage. On the other hand, marriage seemed to reduce chances that women might ascend into superintendencies. The same 1952 AASA survey indicated that five single, widowed, or divorced women held such leadership positions for every one occupied by a married women.[15]

Although public awareness of homosexual activity had grown steadily during the first half of the century, in 1948 a fundamentally important event focused national attention on it. That year, Alfred Kinsey and his research team published the landmark study, *Sexual Behavior in the Human Male.* Over the previous decade, Kinsey and his colleagues had carefully interviewed and surveyed 12,000 men about their sexual activities. Kinsey, an entomologist by training, employed a taxonomic approach in analyzing the results. The study catalogued the range of men's sexual activities along a continuum. Kinsey and his team endeavored to describe the incidence of these activities without labeling or stigmatizing the persons who engaged in them. The book's carefully chosen title, *Sexual Behavior in the Human Male,* reflects this effort to describe behavior rather than to create or reinforce sexual identities.

The book's frank, careful analysis and its sometimes-surprising results catapulted it to second place on the national nonfiction bestsellers list. The publisher, anticipating the slow sales of a dry, scientific exposition, printed only 5,000 copies at first. However, with attention generated from an advance review in *Look* magazine, book sales soared. A variety of magazines and other media outlets then devoted extensive coverage to this study that many eagerly embraced. So much attention greeted *Sexual Behavior* that a Gallup poll indicated most Americans knew about it and considered it important.[16]

Among the fascinating revelations in the study, one of the most often discussed concerned the extent of men's same-sex sexual activities. Kinsey's team found that around half of all men admitted some erotic attraction to other men. Further, over one-third of all post-adolescent men had reached orgasm as a result of sexual activity with men. The study refrained from calling such men homosexuals, preferring instead to place their activities along a continuum of sexual experiences ranging from exclusively heterosexual to exclusively homosexual. The team explained this practice:

> The classification of sexual behavior as masturbatory, heterosexual, or homosexual is . . . unfortunate if it suggests that three different types of responses are involved, or suggests that only different types of persons seek out or accept each kind of sexual activity. There is nothing known in the anatomy or physiology of sexual response and orgasm which distinguishes masturbatory, heterosexual, or homosexual reactions. The terms are of value only because they describe the source of the sexual stimulation, and they should not be taken as descriptions of the individuals who respond to the various stimuli. . . . For the present, however, we shall have to use the term homosexual in something of its standard meaning, except that we shall use it primarily to describe sexual *relationships,* and shall prefer not to use it to describe the *individuals* who were involved in those relationships.[17]

The study's authors explained that around 4 percent of all men engaged exclusively in homosexual activities. These men could be found in every profession, each state and region, and across all social strata.

Additionally, Kinsey's team found that far larger numbers of men had engaged in sexual activity both with men and women than the 4 percent who exclusively preferred men. However, in the polarized Cold War climate that greeted Kinsey's work, popular convention increasingly labeled individuals (rather than behaviors) as either heterosexual or homosexual. Those who were known to experience same-sex desire or engage in same-sex sexual activities typically were regarded as homosexual, even if they also desired or engaged in opposite-sex sexual activities. The concept of bisexuality did not fit well in such popular analysis. Even though the Kinsey team cautioned readers to see the continuum rather than only polarized extremes, in conventional practice, such prudence was ignored.

Five years later, Kinsey's team published the companion volume, *Sexual Behavior in the Human Female.* This study, based on interviews and surveys of 8,000 women, catalogued the range of women's sexual activities. Readers quickly discovered that women engaged in sexual behaviors more actively than had been popularly believed. And, as with Katherine Davis's 1929 study, readers learned that homosexual behaviors among women were not uncommon. Not surprisingly, the study revealed that single women most often experienced sexual relationships with other women, though such experiences also occurred among divorced, separated, or widowed women. The report explained, "By age forty, 19 per cent of the females in the total sample had had some physical contact with other females which was deliberately and consciously, at least on the part of one of the partners, intended to be sexual." The rate reached 24 percent for women who had never married and 9 percent among divorced or widowed women. The reported incidence of same-sex activity among married women was lower, around 3 percent. Kinsey's team argued that marriage in essence kept women from engaging in sexual activities with other women.[18]

The study frankly acknowledged the public perception that better-educated women tended to have a greater incidence of homosexual experiences. Though the team offered no specific data on the matter, they hypothesized that

> Moral restraint on pre-marital heterosexual activity is the most important single factor contributing to the development of a homosexual history, and such restraint is probably most marked among the younger and teen-age girls of those social levels that send their daughters to college. In college, these girls are further restricted by administrators who are very conscious of parental concern over the heterosexual morality of their offspring. The prolongation of the years of schooling, and the consequent delay in marriage, interfere with any early heterosexual development of these girls. This is particularly true if they go on into graduate work. All of these factors contribute to the development of homosexual histories. There may also be a franker acceptance and a somewhat lesser social concern over homosexuality in the upper educational levels.[19]

The Kinsey team speculated that women whose experiences tended toward the homosexual end of the continuum often worked "in business, sometimes in high positions as business executives, [and] in teaching positions in schools and colleges." These women, many of them of an older generation, "were professionally trained women who had been preoccupied with their education or other matters in the day when social relations with males and marriage might have been available, and who in subsequent years had found homosexual contacts more readily available than heterosexual contacts."[20] Interestingly, the study's authors did not argue that women might choose homosexual activity even if they enjoyed ample opportunities for relationships with men.

In these two major studies on human sexuality, Kinsey's team argued that Americans seemed peculiarly distressed about homosexuality. "In our American culture there are no types of sexual activity which are as frequently condemned because they depart from the mores and the publicly pretended custom, as mouth-genital contacts and homosexual activities."[21] Furthermore, "there appears to be no other major culture in the world in which public opinion and the statue law so severely penalize homosexual relationships as they do in the United States today."[22] The volumes offered no explanation for this state of affairs. However, Kinsey soon would confront this hostility directly.

Though the Kinsey team's studies initially were greeted with tremendous interest and positive regard, an angry reaction brewed among conservative readers. Some charged that Kinsey's team *promoted,* rather than *described* sexual practices. In particular, they accused them of advocating homosexuality. They questioned the studies' research methods, though subsequent major studies conducted by other researchers reflected similar results. Critics even accused Kinsey of aiding communism. The furor over the Kinsey findings eventually led funding agencies to withdraw their support for his research, leaving Kinsey confused and bitterly disappointed in the way his work had been received.[23]

As knowledge of the incidence of homosexual behavior spread, conservative opponents found ways to convert awareness to fear. The military became one of the first postwar institutions to hunt for homosexuals. Officials, alert for opportunities to thin the ranks during peacetime, launched initiatives to identify and then purge homosexuals from all military branches.[24] During 1943–1944, the army had discharged homosexuals quietly with neither an "honorable" nor a "dishonorable" discharge. However, in 1947, the army and navy quickly changed this practice. Much more rigorous screenings for homosexuality and rapid discharges led to the exodus of thousands of soldiers. The screening process included scrutinizing effeminacy among men and masculinity among women, listening for use of supposedly homosexual slang words, and allegedly submitting soldiers to hormone tests to check estrogen or androgen levels.[25] Investigators forced those accused of homosexuality to name other names as well.

With little prodding, Senator Joseph McCarthy and his colleagues decided to probe civilian agencies to see if they, too, employed homosexuals. A 1950 senate committee investigated the purported existence of widespread homosexuality in government bureaus. In a report entitled, "Employment of Homosexuals and Other Sex Perverts in Government," committee members announced that homosexuals had infiltrated all levels of government employment. Like communists, homosexuals supposedly presented a serious threat to national security. The authors contended, "Psychiatric physicians generally agree that indulgence in sexually perverted practices indicates a personality which has failed to reach sexual maturity." They argued that homosexuals presented security risks because intense fear of exposure made them easy targets for blackmail. What congressional committee members feared most, however, was the alleged contagiousness of homosexuality. The committee's report explained that

> The presence of a sex pervert in a Government agency tends to have a corrosive influence upon his fellow employees. . . . This is particularly true in the case of young and impressionable people who might come under the influence of a pervert. . . . It is particularly important that the thousands of young men and women who are brought into Federal jobs not be subjected to that type of influence while in the service of the government. One homosexual can pollute a Government office.[26]

Thus homosexual experiences were thought to be so appealing that the uninitiated made easy prey. Only strong punitive measures could prevent the trend.

After the release of this report, McCarthy's committee launched a full investigation into homosexuality among federal employees. Using the same tactics employed in finding communists, investigators identified persons who supposedly engaged in homosexual behaviors. They questioned these individuals extensively and threatened them with expulsion or more severe punishments unless they provided names of other homosexuals. Eventually the *Congressional Record* listed numbers of homosexuals purportedly employed in each of the federal government agencies who then were forced to leave their jobs.[27]

After the military and federal government instituted homosexual purges, popular media soon investigated this allegedly growing problem, too. First, though, publishers needed to abandon the informal prohibition on using the word "homosexual" in mainstream venues. Practitioners of some religious traditions considered homosexual behavior literally an unspeakable sin. During the 1951 meeting of the American Association of Marriage Counselors, participants in one session discussed "the growing 'H' problem," unable to speak or print the word "homosexual."[28]

In 1950, however, editors of the popular magazine, *Coronet*, dutifully abolished such long-standing reticence. They published an unprecedented article aimed at demolishing "a long-standing taboo against a frank and factual discussion of homosexuality." Their brief introduction to the piece, "The New Moral Menace to Our Youth," claimed immodestly that it presented "a significant survey of the entire subject as it endangers the youth of America—the most comprehensive such survey ever to be published in a national magazine."[29]

The author of the article, Ralph Major, asserted "homosexuality is rapidly increasing throughout America today." Furthermore, unless parents acknowledged the problem and guarded against it, homosexuals would threaten their children. Major warned, "Behind a wall erected by apathy, ignorance, and a reluctance to face facts, a sinister threat to

American youth is fast developing." From statistics provided by the Kinsey studies, he extrapolated that homosexuals accounted for over eight million persons in the United States. Major suggested that a number of scientific studies revealed a wildly growing rate of homosexuality. Where did he gather this information? In great measure, he referenced Kinsey's work, lifting a passage from the volume on men to explain: "We ourselves were totally unprepared to find such data when this research was undertaken."[30] Major argued, however, "It took a bally-hooed Congressional investigation to put homosexuality in the headlines."[31]

Major offered the frightening prospect that homosexuals aggressively recruited young people. He quoted the California Special Assistant Attorney General who maintained: "All too often, we lose sight of the fact that the homosexual is an inveterate seducer of the young of both sexes, and that he presents a social problem because he is not content with being degenerate himself; he must have degenerate companions, and is ever seeking younger victims." Major summarized: "Therein lurks the hidden danger of homosexuality. No degenerate can indulge his unnatural practices alone. He demands a partner. And the partner, more often than not, must come from the ranks of the young and innocent."[32]

Major warned that not only did strangers or other members of the community pose potential danger to children, but so too did teachers. He urged parents to scrutinize their children's teachers carefully to avoid horrifying problems. He recounted the story of John T., a young student who had just finished his first year at a prep boarding school. Shortly after John returned home for the summer break, the police called his father:

> "Your boy's in trouble," he was told. "Come down right away!"
>
> John's mother and father were shocked by what they learned. Their son had been discovered in a warehouse with a delivery boy. Where had John picked up this abnormal habit? "One of the teachers at school taught me," he admitted shamefacedly.
>
> A shy lad, John had not made friends easily at school. When he failed to win membership in an exclusive school club, he ran tearfully to a faculty member. The instructor, as it turned out, was more than solicitous. He persuaded John to forget his disappointment in a whirl of new thrills—thrills which made John feel far superior to his untutored classmates.
>
> Fortunately, John's parents were able to rescue him in time to prevent his complete conversion to the unfortunate cult.[33]

Major cautioned that parents must keep homosexual teachers from corrupting their children. Because scientists allegedly regarded homosexuality as a learned behavior, he then argued, "More than anyone else, parents are responsible for erasing the treat of homosexuality." But how could parents determine which teachers were homosexual? Some, he contended, displayed rather obvious cross-gender behaviors or characteristics. Others could not be identified so readily and therefore presented the greatest risk. Nonetheless, he reiterated that parents must bear the burden of scrutinizing the adults in contact with their children.[34]

Major insisted that homosexuality was a learned characteristic and that parents played a critical role in preventing it. This reasoning reflected conventional wisdom of the time, as clearly illustrated in social guidance films screened in classrooms around the country during the 1950s and 1960s. One 1953 film, *Social-Sex Attitudes in Adolescence*, highlighted the sexual development of two teen-agers who eventually became supposedly well-adjusted, married adults. Early in the film, Mary, the film's female lead, spent a great deal of time with her female best friend. She also idolized female athletes and thought about admired women constantly—all of which concerned her mother. Mary's mother then provided a well-timed intervention that resulted in a redirection of Mary's affections toward male football players, much to her mother's relief. Mary had just gone through a phase, the film explained, and her mother had thwarted a dangerous sexual turn.[35]

The notion that children and youth possessed sexual innocence contrasted sharply with a growing fear of adolescent sexual desire after World War II. These years brought nearly universal high school attendance around the country as communities struggled to construct buildings to accommodate teeming teen-aged student populations. Police, social workers, and school workers alike fretted about the problems of so-called deviant youth, a broad category that included adolescents who broke the law, engaged in sanctioned sexual activities, or violated conventional expectations for gender presentation. The major motion picture, *The Blackboard Jungle* (1955), illustrated this palpable social discomfort with adolescent sexual desire. In the opening sequence, teenaged males wolf-whistled at a female teacher, commented on the sexual attractiveness of a male teacher, and apparently assaulted a sensitive male student in the bathroom. Education journals printed scores of articles on the exploding problems of deviance and juvenile delinquency.[36] This concern about deviance and delinquency among youth paralleled a more general postwar hysteria about sexual perverts or sexual psychopaths who supposedly preyed on children.[37]

Of all possible forms of youth delinquency, though, homosexuality inspired some of the greatest concern. Though parents generally were thought capable of preventing homosexuality in children, no agreement existed about its actual causes. Then-prevailing and often conflicting theories about the causes of homosexuality in women included fear of pregnancy or venereal diseases, heterosexual trauma or disappointment, satiation with males, society's heterosexual taboos, seeing parents in coitus, seduction by older females, masturbation that leads to homosexuality, endocrine imbalance, penis envy and castration complex, father-fixation or hatred toward mother, mother-fixation, continuation of a childhood "bisexual" phase, a fixation at or a regression to an early adolescent stage of psychosexual development, a defense against or a flight from incestuous desires, or constitutional congenital or inherited traits or tendencies.[38]

Regardless of the causes, however, concern escalated about how adult homosexuals could be identified so that their corrupting influence could be prevented. Major indicated that cross-gender characteristics offered one important clue, though not an infallible one. Many experts of the time regularly described homosexuals as persons with personalities and physical qualities commonly ascribed to those of the other sex. Because these differences could be subtle, expert assessment sometimes was necessary. Kinsey outlined these then-common beliefs about supposed links between gender and sexual orientation, even as he argued that they could not be verified scientifically:

> It is commonly believed, for instance, that homosexual males are rarely robust physically, are uncoordinated or delicate in their movements, or perhaps graceful enough but not strong and vigorous in their physical expression. Fine skins, high-pitched voices, obvious hand movement, a feminine carriage of the hips, and peculiarities of walking gait are supposed accompaniments of a preference for a male as a sexual partner. It is commonly believed that the homosexual male is artistically sensitive, emotionally unbalanced, temperamental to the point of being unpredictable, difficult to get along with, and undependable in meeting specific obligations. In physical characters there have been attempts to show that the homosexual male has a considerable crop of hair and less often becomes bald, has teeth which are more like those of the female, a broader pelvis, larger genitalia, and a tendency toward being fat, and that he lacks a linea alba [vertical line down the front of the abdomen]. The homosexual male is supposed to be less interested in athletics, more often interested in music and the arts, more often engaged in such occupations as bookkeeping, dress design, window display, hair-dressing, acting, radio work, nursing, religious service, and social work. The converse to all of these is supposed to represent the typical heterosexual male. Many a clinician attaches considerable weight to these things in diagnosing the basic heterosexuality or homosexuality of his patients. The characterizations are so distinct that they seem to leave little room for doubt that homosexual and heterosexual represent two very distinct types of males.[39]

Although, as he points out, "the implication is always present that an individual's choice of a sexual partner is closely related to the masculinity or femininity of his personality," Kinsey steadfastly maintained that such opinions were based only on impressions rather than on scientific evidence.[40]

Other researchers did not exercise the same degree of caution as Kinsey's team in linking cross-gender traits with homosexuality. A 1961 article printed in the *American Journal of Psychotherapy* reported a strong link between effeminacy in men and homosexuality. The author indicated, "These men [homosexuals] produce an aura of effeminacy so subtle that it is very difficult to describe." He argued that "the fact that it exists . . . accounts for the uncanny facility homosexual men have in recognizing each other, usually instantaneously, even though they may be total strangers." He elaborated: "It can be in the way they hold their heads. It may lie in the tone of voice or the inflection. It may reveal itself in the way a man throws a baseball, in his intonation, in his attitudes in general, in his interests, and in his particular value system. Even the experienced observer cannot always pinpoint explicitly the particular traits which convey the feeling of femininity."[41] Another volume listed several key characteristics including "1. Dressing in clothing that depicts the opposite sex; 2. A manner of speaking and behaving which is indicative of the opposite sex; 3. Employing actions and reactions which are usually interchanged between members of the opposite sexes; 4. Showing a noticeable attraction for members of the same sex at work as well as at leisure and usually relating more readily to members of the same sex." According to the author, these clues allowed homosexuals to identify each other.[42]

Kinsey's pleas to avoid linking gender traits with homosexuality largely went unheeded. When he cautioned that the causes of homosexuality needed to be determined by careful scientific research rather than simple conjecture, popular experts and writers did not pause. And perhaps his most central argument also appeared to be lost on those eager to arouse antihomosexual sentiments. Kinsey maintained that sexual orientation should not be viewed in polarized terms. He strongly asserted instead that human sexual desire, like gender—as indicated on the Terman-Miles masculinity/femininity scale—exists in subtle gradations. He argued that it was absurd to label persons as homosexual after they had engaged in a single same-sex experience, and, once labeled, to punish them severely.

Despite Kinsey's cautions, growing fears that adults might corrupt children led to stiff penalties for homosexual activities. And, in a remarkable shift that signaled a clear demarcation of a distinct homosexual identity apart from homosexual behavior, social penalties also increased for persons deemed homosexual, whether or not they actively engaged in same-sex sexual activities. Homosexual teachers presented a compelling problem because they supposedly could so easily influence children. Even worse, many believed teaching to be a profession that held particular appeal for homosexuals. The author of one of a growing number of popular books on the subject of homosexuality maintained that "denied, through lack of wife and family, the satisfaction of home life, the homosexual must look more and more to his work to bring him what might in some sort compensate him for this deprivation. . . . This may be a reason why some homosexuals, consciously or unconsciously, gravitate to professions that can give emotional satisfaction—teaching, social work, the ministry, and the like."[43] Lee Mortimer, a widely published tabloid journalist, ran sensational stories in the *New York Daily Mirror* charging that homosexual teachers actively recruited students.[44] Frank Caprio, author of *Female Homosexuality: A Psychodynamic Study of Lesbianism* (1954), advised that female students were not safe from homosexual influences. He argued that lesbian teachers regularly preyed on girls. He described how "a young girl, age fifteen, committed suicide. Upon investigation it was disclosed from evidence contained in personal letters, that a woman schoolteacher apparently had carried on an 'immoral' relationship with the young girl."[45]

At the same time, a series of sex-crime panics erupted around the country. In the mid-1950s, after the shocking rape and murder of two children in Sioux City, Iowa, police rounded up twenty men, mostly homosexual, and then incarcerated them in a mental hospital.[46] Estelle Freedman argues that during this time of widespread alarm over sexual crimes, the term "sexual psychopath" was often used synonymously with "pervert," "sex criminal," and "homosexual."[47] To many, homosexuality and psychopathology essentially were the same; thus incarcerating homosexuals seemed like an appropriate way to protect communities against child molestation.

Then, in 1955, *Time* magazine broke the story of an alleged secret homosexual network in Boise, Idaho. This ring purportedly had corrupted many of the town's teenaged boys. An investigator who had assisted with Senator McCarthy's homosexual purge of federal agencies traveled to Boise to use similar tactics in cracking the case. The town newspaper justified the investigation in an editorial:

> Confessions by homosexuals invariably bring out the stark fact that these
> victims of a puzzling physical or mental quirk were themselves infected as

young boys. There the die was cast. They grew into manhood to infect other boys who, in turn, unless effective intervention follows, will travel the same path and carry the identical threat to the next generation of youth. Tragically, the scourge multiplies since one adult homosexual usually infects several boys. . . . Homosexuals must be sought out before they do more damage to youth, either by investigation of their past records or by appeal to their unbalanced minds.[48]

Ten years later, John Gerassi wrote a book on the case, *The Boys from Boise.* Gerassi recounted the story of a teacher who left town in the middle of breakfast, right after he had read a newspaper editorial describing the investigation. The teacher immediately packed his belongings and headed for San Francisco, never to return. Friends discovered the open newspaper and his uneaten breakfast days later when checking to see why he had not shown up for work. Gerassi later interviewed the man:

> "Okay, so I'm gay," he told me in 1965, "but I've never hurt anyone, or let it affect my responsibilities. And then this thing breaks. Even before Moore got arrested, friends of mine warned me that a witch hunt was going on. I didn't believe it. But when they went after Moore, Christ, I saw the handwriting on the wall. And that editorial, too! First they say, 'Save the kids.' Then they say, 'Crush the homosexuals.' Enemies of society—that's what we were called. I remember very well. So I asked myself, where will this stop? I've never had any kind of relations except with consenting adults. But is Boise going to be calm enough to draw the difference? Will they *look* for the difference? No, I knew they'd go after anybody who wears a ring on their pinky. I wasn't going to take the chance and get swallowed up in a blind, raging witch-hunt. I got the hell out."[49]

Another informant told Gerassi about a teacher at the high school "who was probably queer." The man explained, "We all knew it. He was a nice guy, and some of us even kidded him about it. He used to come down to the locker room and play around—you know, snapping towels and stuff like that. So he liked to see us naked, so what? We laughed about it. He never tried anything that I know of, and I *would have known.* But boy, did he get scared when the scandal broke. He ran out of town."[50]

Reportedly, many people left town as the Boise investigation unfolded. An anonymous source explained: "I know hundreds of Gay people left the city, schoolteachers, people in every walk of life—Gay people who had never gotten involved in anything, who were just afraid."[51] Their fears were justified. Investigators publicly exposed and humiliated purported homosexuals. Many lost their jobs and families. Some entered the criminal justice system while others faced involuntary commitment to psychiatric treatment facilities.

Around the same time, the Florida legislature began investigating the incidence of homosexuality in the state as city vice squads reported supposedly rampant homosexual activity—even among teachers. In one incident, Hillsborough County school officials worked with local sheriffs to probe the extent of homosexuality among county teachers. Sheriffs watched suspected homosexual hang-outs such as lesbian and gay bars. On a tip, they staked out an Anna Maria Island apartment where fifty-four female teachers stayed one weekend. Some purportedly were seen engaging in sexual activities with each other. The investigation ended when the names of twenty-three to twenty-seven lesbian and gay teachers had been added to the list. State officials drew on such reports as they argued that greater and more centrally organized vigilance was necessary. Because some identified lesbian and gay teachers had attended the University of Florida or Florida State University, the legislature in turn probed these two institutions to determine the extent of homosexual infiltration.[52]

Merril Mushroom, recounting her adolescence, described the events and climate in the state during these investigations:

> In 1954 a teenage hustler murdered a gay man in Miami, and the case became sensational. Because of this, the extent of the gay subculture in Dade County was publicized as scandalous. The media demanded that something be done to purge the county of this pestilence. An anticrime commission was set up to investigate perversion and gambling, and two years later, the state legislature appointed the Johns Committee to investigate "freedom riders, communists, and homosexuals" throughout Florida. These investigations continued for the next eight years, and countless gay people had their lives destroyed as a result.[53]

By 1963, the Florida legislature formally established the Legislative Investigation Committee, otherwise called the "Johns Committee" after the representative who led its work. This committee was charged with the mandate to determine "the extent of infiltration into agencies supported by state funds by practicing homosexuals, the effect thereof on said agencies and the public, and the policies of various state agencies in dealing therewith."[54] The committee eventually proposed initiatives for dealing with homosexuality, an especially important project according to committee members because of a supposed "rise in homosexual activity" in the state. Their recommendations included mandatory psychiatric examinations, the creation of outpatient treatment centers, confidentiality for first arrests, felony convictions for second offenses, and the "creation of a central records repository for information on homosexuals arrested and convicted in Florida and provision that such records shall be open to public employing agencies."[55] The Johns Committee formed following rumors suggesting that many homosexuals had moved to Gainesville after the war and that some taught in its high schools. Committee members pursued suspected homosexual teachers, investigating them aggressively. Investigators then pressured suspected teachers to name other names or else face public exposure and court subpoena.[56]

Once the committee finished its work and presented the Superintendent of Public Instruction with a list of allegedly homosexual teachers, the superintendent instituted procedures for permanently revoking their teaching licenses. Three teachers fought this revocation on procedural grounds and eventually, in 1962, the Florida Supreme Court reinstated their lifetime teaching credentials. However, the material that the Johns Committee had gathered about those teachers to prove their homosexuality was still used as the basis for revoking their licenses once again.[57]

In its 1965 final report, the Johns Committee rationalized its work in rooting out homosexual teachers:

> Because of their constant contact with, and influence over the youth of the state, teachers have been a focal point of investigations and discussions of sexual deviation among state employees.
>
> It should be made abundantly clear that careful scrutiny by the Committee during this biennium has revealed: 1. That the number of deviates among the teachers of Florida is proportionately low, and that in this regard Florida is substantially better off than many of her sister states with less rigid certification procedures which are now facing up to a serious problem of moral misconduct among teaching personnel. 2. That the Teacher Certification Division of the State Department of Education, armed with new power granted it by the 1963 Legislature, has done, and is doing, a thorough and competent job of investigating reports of deviate behavior on the part of school personnel. In this effort the Department has received strong support from The Florida Education Association.[58]

John Sorenson, who headed the Miami vice squad during the Johns Committee investigation, explained why he thought it was important to focus on homosexual teachers. "Now, you take a young homosexual, say, at thirty, thirty-five. This person here is death on children. . . . He is the most dangerous person. I'd keep him in prison for twenty years till he was fifty-five. You wouldn't have as much of a problem then. The kids wouldn't bother with him in the first place. He wouldn't have the attraction." When the reporter asked him if it mattered if homosexuals only engaged in private sexual activities with other adults, he responded:

> I think it's just as much an abomination. . . . There are so many people that say, 'Well, if two men wanted to walk into another room and do something

by themselves, I couldn't care less.' Well, this is not my philosophy at all. I could care because those two have got to come out of that room again and they may be schoolteachers teaching my children and I don't want any sick person teaching my children and yet there are sick people in our schools right now teaching our children. And they are mentally ill. . . . And yet here they are teaching our children reading, writing, arithmetic, science and so forth. And their philosophies and their morals spill over.[59]

A writer for the Los Angeles based *Mattachine Review,* one of very few publications produced by and for homosexuals, argued that the Johns Committee had failed miserably in its task of proving the "infiltration" of homosexuals throughout Florida government. Instead, the piece indicated that the only state agency to forward names was the State Department of Education. The teachers cited, though, were charged on grounds of general moral turpitude—and there was no explicit count of the number of homosexual teachers after all. The author concluded: "One wonders how many were guilty of adultery, fornication, drunkenness, forgery, lewd and lascivious acts with women, etc. We know that two of these teachers, as the newspaper clipping reveals, were specifically charged with misconduct against six high school girls. What about the rest of them?"[60] Essentially, he argued that the committee was forced to name names, yet they barely could do so and their credibility had been severely impeached. Adverse reaction was not limited to the gay press, however. *The Nation* weighed in on the matter in 1964:

> The spirit of Joe McCarthy lives. . . . The staff director of the Florida legislative investigation committee, [told a group of] wide-eyed women that he knows the names of the 123 teachers who are suspected homosexuals and that homosexuality is being allowed to "flourish" in the teaching profession.
> In one foul swipe, he put Florida's 50,000 teachers under suspicion. Governor Farris Bryant, trying to down the specter of Florida's school children being molested in the cloakroom by their teachers, called for an immediate investigation. . . . Legislators in the Sunshine State have had a strange preoccupation with homosexuality for nearly five years. The legislative investigation committee was originally set up to look into the state's racial problems, but in 1959 it switched over to hunting for Communist infiltration of state government and the university system. As with McCarthy, the legislators frequently saw communism as synonymous with homosexuality, and by 1961 the committee had moved into the study of homosexuals altogether. What a perverse field day they have had . . . coaxing students to report "queer traits" in their teachers.[61]

Merril Mushroom, who at the time was an adolescent becoming aware of her own lesbian desires, described how the state investigations damaged the lives of teachers. "Of course no discussion of teachers by a lesbian would be complete without mentioning the gym teachers. I recall a succession of unmarried, butchy women throughout junior high and into high school, but every year we had new ones. I wonder now, in retrospect, if this rapid turnover was a consequence of the investigation. In any event, by 1956 unmarried women no longer were hired to teach girls' physical education, and two very safely married women were installed in those positions." Mushroom summed up the situation for Florida teachers at the time: "Being gay was not safe. . . . We knew there was an investigation going on. We knew that a few of our teachers had given notice or been terminated. We heard from the bar dykes that adult gays were being arrested, incarcerated, given electroshock treatments, and lobotomized; were losing their jobs and families and freedom; were committing suicide."[62]

California also confronted its own public fears of homosexual teachers. In San Francisco during the mid-1950s, police arrested Jose Sarria for sexual solicitation in a men's bar. Sarria had been studying to obtain his teaching credentials, but this arrest for a "sex crime" ensured that he never would face a class of students.[63] Long Beach and Los Angeles police reported teachers who were picked up on public morals charges. Legislation passed after World War II required police to notify both the state licensure board and local superintendents when homosexual sting operations netted teachers. Such teachers lost their jobs immediately, even if the charges later proved to be false or there was no evidence. California was the only state to have passed legislation requiring police to inform school officials of alleged teacher misconduct.[64]

The case of Thomas Sarac illustrates the process. During the summer of 1962, Sarac, a high school teacher, allegedly touched the genitals of an undercover policeman in a public bathroom. When the police reported the violation to the state board of education, it revoked his teaching license. The board reasoned that Sarac had committed "a homosexual act involving moral turpitude," which it believed proved his unfitness to teach. Sarac appealed this decision explaining that his activity in the public bathroom had no connection with his ability to teach effectively. The Court ruled, however, that because homosexuality long had violated community standards of decency, the board justifiably could revoke his teaching credential because of his unprofessional behavior. The Court maintained that Sarac could no longer influence his students with proper morality.[65]

Despite the disposition of the Sarac case and others that followed, some believed that teaching provided an important form of employment for gay men and lesbians in California. One minister explained matter-offactly, "If you removed all the homosexuals from the schools in the Bay Area, the schools would have to shut down."[66] Undoubtedly, lesbians and gay men taught in schools and some also participated in a growing homosexual community life. This carried great risk, however. During one community costume ball in San Francisco in 1965, the police burst in.

> The place was in chaos. . . . Some of the people were just terrified, especially the schoolteachers. And there were quite a few teachers at the ball. At that time, if a teacher were known to be homosexual, they'd move to yank their license, because, of course, he or she didn't have the proper moral standards. I remember a couple of women who were schoolteachers. They wanted to be sneaked out the back way because the police were taking pictures of people as they left. They were terrified that somehow the state Board of Education would get the pictures and move against them.[67]

One woman summarized the situation for lesbian and gay educators: "There was a list of about twenty-one things that you could lose your teaching certificate for. The first one was to be a card-carrying Communist, and the second was to be a homosexual. . . . The suspicion is it: You're convicted, hung, tied, and quartered. And not only would you never teach in California, you would never teach again in public schools anywhere."[68] Such stories usually were followed by investigations into identifying homosexual teachers—which inevitably ended with their firing or the revocation of their licenses. One woman recalled the case of a young lesbian teacher:

> By then you weren't only afraid just to be gay, [but you were also afraid] you would get called in or investigated or in some other way implicated. . . . One time, I remember, one of the group did lose her job, a teacher. You would never have suspected anything about her, I mean, she didn't "look" like a butch or anything. She was one of the nicest people around. Apparently someone had just gone with some rumor to the head of the school and that was enough to get her out. Actually, the guy who fired her gave her the chance to resign so her record wouldn't be completely ruined. But still there were blacklists and she knew she couldn't get a job in the state ever again. She was on the verge of killing herself. That job of hers meant everything to her. We spent a lot of time with her, keeping an eye out for her. Finally she decided that she'd be better off if she left the state.[69]

In many cases, substantiation of homosexuality was unnecessary. Mere rumor sufficed. A high school student in Oregon dropped by her teacher's house unannounced one day. The girl noticed that the two women who lived there shared only one bedroom. After the girl relayed this information to her mother, rumors spread. Eventually, the school board fired the teacher on the suspicion of lesbianism.[70]

The 1961 movie, *The Children's Hour,* illustrated for millions how the rumor of homosexuality could destroy teachers' lives. The film, based on Lillian Hellman's play of the same title, depicts the lives of two women, Karen Wright (Audrey Hepburn) and Martha Dobie (Shirley MacLaine), who run an elite girls' school. Their problems begin when a malicious girl tells her grandmother that the two women are lesbians. The grandmother spreads the rumor and the community is inflamed. The story ends when Dobie confesses her love to Wright, admitting that a grain of truth lay beneath the accusation. Dobie then hangs herself and Wright, in shock and mourning, forgoes marriage to her fiancé. This film was the first major Hollywood-produced motion picture with central lesbian or gay characters. Though its portrayal of the two women was somewhat sensitive for its time, it did offer what the director-producer called "a clean picture with a highly moral story," that is, one in which the lesbian character—as in so many other mainstream novels and stories—kills herself.[71]

Because of the severe censure that lesbian and gay teachers endured, and because rumor was enough, school workers who wished to keep their jobs understood that they needed to cloak seeming evidence of homosexuality. Women who taught physical education found that they were particularly vulnerable. One lesbian, who lost her physical education teaching position after confiding personal details to a friend, decided that she needed to overhaul her image. She married a gay man, wore skirts, dresses, and heels, and insisted that she be called "Mrs." She succeeded in getting and keeping another teaching job, but she admitted that, "I keep a low profile and I'm always on guard."[72] Maintaining a gender-appropriate wardrobe apparently constituted such a fundamental survival strategy for lesbians that a 1961 issue of *The Ladder,* one of the earliest lesbian periodicals in the country, printed a cartoon of a woman donning the look with the caption, "Oh, I always wear skirts and blouses in public so people won't suspect that I'm gay."[73] Many cities even enforced laws against cross-dressing, or otherwise dressing in a gender ambiguous manner. *The Ladder* later ran a story describing how Houston police had rounded up and arrested a group of lesbians. The arresting officer explained that the women "were dressed in men's pants, men's shirts and men's shoes. . . . This is a violation of the city ordinance that forbids wearing of the clothes of the opposite sex."[74] From the mid-1800s through early-1900s, dozens of cities around the country had passed laws prohibiting cross-dressing, in some cases, to rein in the freedoms demanded by suffragists. The ongoing association in popular thought between gender nonconformance and homosexuality, however, meant that such laws could be used to target homosexuals.[75]

In the charged atmosphere of the 1950s and 1960s, school workers across ranks understood that if they wished to keep their jobs, they needed to avoid any suspicion of homosexuality. To do this, they needed to maintain dress, appearance, movements, speech, and behaviors deemed appropriate for their gender because gender nonconformity connoted homosexuality in conventional thinking. Educators who pursued sexual or romantic relationships with persons of their own sex struggled to do so as discreetly as possible. Trips to gay bars or certain parks entailed a high level of risk. Generally, men could not live with other men.[76] Women could live with other women only when they kept separate bedrooms and obviously needed the additional household income, though this was not danger-free. Because postal inspectors were authorized to report individuals who received homosexually oriented materials or letters, personal information that traveled through the mail became a source of anxiety.[77] No longer could educators who centered their lives on members of their own sex find acceptance and respectability in the work. Schools had become terrifying places for lesbian and gay workers. The message was clear for everyone else, too. Maintain acceptable gender characteristics or risk the consequences.

Communities that wished to rid schools of homosexuals did so ostensibly to protect children from becoming homosexuals. As stories about sexual predators appeared in local papers and, increasingly, national publications, a sense of urgency hastened the drive to do something. This urgency intensified as readers worried that the supposed homosexual disease might spread out of control and threaten the traditional heterosexual institution of marriage. Still, however, few knew much about homosexuality because of the long-standing taboo in discussing it—but curiosity flourished. To satisfy this interest, in 1964 *Life* magazine featured a series of stories on homosexuality, explaining that homosexuals lived in a "secret world," but one that grew "open and bolder," forcing society "to look at it—and try to understand it." The lead article described figures in a dark, shadowy photo: "These brawny young men in their leather caps, shirts, jackets and pants are practicing homosexuals, men who turn to other men for affection and sexual satisfaction. They are part of what they call the 'gay world,' which is actually a sad and often sordid world." Homosexuality exists

> across the spectrum of American life—the professions, the arts, business and labor. It always has. But today, especially in big cities, homosexuals are discarding their furtive ways and openly admitting, even flaunting, their deviation. Homosexuals have their own drinking places, their special

assignation streets, even their own organizations. And for every obvious homosexual, there are probably nine nearly impossible to detect. This social disorder, which society tries to suppress, has forced itself into the public eye because it does present a problem—and parents especially are concerned. The myth and misconception with which homosexuality has so long been clothed must be cleared away, not to condone it but to cope with it.[78]

The author of this piece and others that followed in national magazines assured readers that they would uncover this emerging "social disorder" to aid public understanding. Presumably, the purported affliction could be prevented—if its origins could be understood.

In 1962, Dr. Irving Bieber released the results of his nine-year study of the causes of homosexuality, *Homosexuality: A Psychoanalytic Study of Male Homosexuals.*[79] He and his team supported by the Society of Medical Psychoanalysts had identified 106 male homosexuals and 100 heterosexual men, all of whom had undergone psychoanalysis.[80] Bieber's team concluded that a significant number of the homosexual men had been indulged by their mothers throughout their childhoods. These overprotective mothers supposedly coddled them. They also kept them from developing friendships with other boys and protected them from the interest of girls. Mothers, then, bore important responsibility for producing homosexuals, according to Bieber's team.[81]

Experts implored parents to take responsibility for assuring the heterosexuality of their children, or else suffer blame. In 1965, the *Ladies Home Journal*, echoing the conclusions of the Bieber study, cautioned that "the emotional climate of the home in which the male homosexual most often develops is one in which the mother is close to her son—too close—and the father is weak, cruel or absent." Essentially, "In every instance, the mother is the key person in the development of a male homosexual." Mothers who jealously guarded their sons' affections without allowing them to develop normal relationships with other boys and girls supposedly forced their sons to homosexuality. Worse still, "the woman who is unconsciously hostile to men—or, more particularly, to what is commonly thought of as the masculine quality of a man—frequently seeks safety (or revenge) by emasculating the men in her life, including her male children." But the mother was not completely alone in this process. "The weak father is the most common type in family relationships that result in a homosexual son. He is the sort of man who relegates most of the family authority to his wife. He takes little interest in assuming the role of leader of the family." The article suggests that because children are excellent imitators, it is crucial for parents to provide appropriate modeling, with parents responsibly assuming their assigned gender roles.[82]

A 1966 piece in *Good Housekeeping* offered similar advice. After pro-filing the shock one mother experienced when she discovered that her seventeen-year-old son might be homosexual, the author explained: "The deeply troubling truth is that male homosexuality is one of the most seri-ous problems confronting our society at the present time and a direct menace to impressionable and emotionally unsure young boys." The au-thor offered encouraging words to the distressed parent, though. Citing a recent study by the New York Academy of Medicine, he argued that a timely diagnosis of homosexuality increased the odds of a cure. After es-tablishing the seeming normality of the story's featured family, the author revealed the real cause of the son's homosexuality. "Bess, unaware of what she was doing, feminized her son almost from the beginning. She discouraged him from becoming interested and involved in masculine things and at the same time bound him so closely to her that he was un-able to become emotionally interested in other females. And Jack was not father enough to prevent this sad twisting of his son." Fortunately, the au-thor explained that the mother found the strength to seek help. She lo-cated a doctor who gave her a sedative and helped her understand how to help her son become heterosexual. Then the son received psychotherapy for two years. Happily, the author explained, the son became heterosex-ual. The mother later recalled: "When I understood at last, I had to fight to cure myself. You know, I felt like an addict of some kind, struggling to free himself from something—and when I explained this to my doctor he said that was exactly the kind of experience I was going through. . . . I had to fight with myself to stop smothering and coddling my son."[83]

Then, in 1968, Peter and Barbara Wyden published *Growing Up Straight: What Every Thoughtful Parent Should Know about Homosex-uality,* essentially a guide for raising heterosexual children. They con-tended that the Bieber study, the New York Academy of Medicine study, and several newer ones indicated that scientifically verified methods could reverse or prevent homosexuality. The Wydens compared homo-sexuality with cancer, explaining that although the two are quite similar, "a more significant difference is that while many forms of cancer are not readily preventable, most homosexuality—conceivably almost all—probably is."[84] They offered parents the encouraging words: "How could there be a better way to avoid the confusion and anguish that in-variably accompany homosexuality than to keep the condition from arising in the first place?"[85]

The Wydens explained that one impediment to helping parents under-stand these matters was that even though the times allowed more candid discussion of sex, parents still felt somewhat uncomfortable talking about homosexuality. They speculated that perhaps this was because "the one line in our culture that seems most clearly drawn and inviolable is the division between male and female; any violation of this division, so deeply ingrained in most of us, will make us feel uneasy." The Wydens assumed that if one were homosexual, one would have to transgress traditionally defined gender roles in some manner. They continued: "This feeling is bound to be reinforced by the fact that many of us have felt attracted to someone of the same sex at one time or another, at least during playful exploratory episodes in our own childhood. Many of us felt guilty about these perfectly innocent incidents at the time. Some of us still do. When we now contemplate homosexuality in others, these needless and pointless guilts may well be stirred."[86] In essence, the Wydens admitted that attraction to persons of one's own sex was common—but how one handled it was critical.

The Wydens summarized the findings of a number of experts when they explained that homosexuality resulted from three combined factors. First, children at risk included those who suffered impaired gender development—failing to manifest strong gendered characteristics in alignment with their sex. Second, the risk increased if youth came to fear intimate contact with persons of the other sex. Finally, the possibility of homosexuality escalated if youth came into contact mainly with members of their own sex. Instead, the Wydens argued that youth should not have "opportunities for sexual release with members of the same sex." Presumably, single-sex schools, especially boarding schools, posed a hazard. In the end, they argued that the key to preventing homosexuality was to reduce the possibility that any of these three triggers might develop. Most important, parents should watch for "any weakening of a child's sense of masculinity or femininity," the most significant evidence of a child sliding slowly toward homosexuality.[87]

Flying in the face of such widespread "expert" advice, the noted psychologist, Evelyn Hooker, disputed the contention that parents caused their children to become homosexuals, or that parents could prevent homosexuality. In a 1969 article published in the *Journal of Consulting and Clinical Psychology,* she presented her survey research demonstrating that there can be no causal connection assumed between poor child relationships with parents and later manifestation of homosexuality. "Serious questions are raised about the role of parent-child relations as necessary and sufficient conditions leading to adult male homosexuality."[88] Hooker's contentions, however, did not reach a broad audience of parents or educators.

Instead, popular media urged parents to assure the correct gender and sexual orientation of their charges. Schools, too, were pressed into service. In 1969, Dr. George Kriegman published an article in the *Journal of*

School Health outlining the roles that educators could play in eliminating homosexuality. He argued that boys are more likely to become homosexual when they are not able to develop a strong masculine identity. This identity could be thwarted in a number of ways, including attendance at single-sex schools. If students developed homosexual tendencies while attending single-sex institutions, he urged parents and teachers to transfer them immediately to coeducational schools. But in an even larger leap away from his data, Kriegman largely attributed homosexuality to a society in which "the feminine revolution, the emerging dominant tendencies of many American women, the rise of 'momism' and the diminishing importance of the parental role in the home, are other significant sociological factors that reverberate in intra-family relationships and hinder the development of healthy masculine identifications."[89]

Though educators could do little to arrest these larger problems, as Kriegman identified them, another viable option existed. They could recommend that homosexual students work with psychologists or counselors with professional training. Efforts to cure them, he assured the reader, lay beyond teachers' abilities. Trained professionals would explain to homosexual students that "satisfactions in living cannot be achieved by continuing to live in this manner. Basically, it results in frustrations, guilt and shame." He advised that teachers served students best simply by identifying which students needed sexual orientation counseling.[90]

Sex education programs, which had taken on greater importance in schools during the 1960s and 1970s, did not tend to focus on homosexuality except to disparage it. However, in a relatively innovative program offered in Anaheim, California, teachers presented the somewhat liberal family life and sex education curriculum (FLSE) in coeducational settings and in age-appropriate ways throughout the grades. In ninth grade, students learned that homosexuality had existed throughout history. Further, the teacher's guide explained that adolescents commonly experienced intense attractions for persons of the same sex without growing up to become homosexual. Teachers then typically showed the brief 1961 film, *Boys Beware,* which warned young males to avoid seduction by homosexual child molesters.[91] In the film, Jimmy befriends Ralph, an older, balding man with sunglasses and a neatly trimmed mustache. Ralph hangs out with Jimmy, buying him gifts, and treating him well. The segment closes as Jimmy and Ralph enter a hotel together as the narrator explains, "Payments were expected in return." During the second vignette, young Mike is murdered after hanging around men in a public restroom.[92] Although this film offered the then-stereotypical portrayal of homosexual men as inveterate child molesters, the FLSE curriculum guided teachers to explain that what was needed was "adequate sex education of both parents and children, so that the homosexual can understand himself better and the community can free itself of its punitive attitudes toward all sexuality."[93]

Although the years before World War II brought an increased awareness of same-sex desire as scientific studies, novels, plays, movies, and other popular treatments incorporated the theme, the years immediately following the war saw far greater recognition. Kinsey's groundbreaking research offered a general understanding that the incidence of homosexual activity was much greater than generally believed or acknowledged. However, a virulent backlash followed that revelation. The military, government agencies, and then schools purged their ranks of alleged homosexuals. Because homosexuality was regarded synonymously with child molestation and perversion, well-publicized sex crimes against children, including those perpetrated by men against girls, resulted in hyper-vigilance and stiff punishments against homosexual men. Experts warned that homosexuals could be identified by their cross-gender characteristics. Individuals who tested the bounds of their gender-appropriate behaviors and characteristics increasingly risked being labeled homosexual—with all the attendant social penalties. Parents were warned to be especially mindful of the threat posed by homosexual teachers who might recruit among their students or otherwise alter their gender identities. And then teams of scientific experts argued that indulgent mothering and effeminate fathers caused homosexuality. With proper parenting and attention from teachers, homosexuality could be prevented or even cured. Schools, then, had become sites both of potential homosexual corruption as well as agencies for prevention. Caught in the middle were school workers who understood that to avoid suspicion of homosexuality, they needed to demonstrate and enforce "correct" gender behavior and characteristics and otherwise seem as heterosexual as possible.

CHAPTER 6

Sometimes You Just Have
to Take a Stand

After World War II, school workers increasingly understood that if they wished to avoid trouble with school officials, they needed to navigate narrow bounds of acceptable sexual orientation and gender. Those educators who desired persons of the same sex in particular learned that they needed to hide any evidence that might trigger suspicion about their sexual orientation. Otherwise they risked their jobs, their good standing in the community, their families, and often their health. In Florida and California, lawmakers instigated conditions for well-publicized purges of allegedly homosexual school workers. In other localities, school administrators quietly told suspected homosexual employees to resign or face publicly humiliating terminations.

By the late 1960s, however, some persons who desired others of the same sex and/or defied gender conventions had reached the limit of their willingness to acquiesce quietly to these purges, large and small. Against the backdrop of significant civil rights movement advances and the sexual liberation movement that accompanied widespread availability of "the pill" and other contraceptives, some believed the time had come to instigate change. Just as a generation of disaffected youth had begun rejecting the mainstream values that prized economic competition, acquisitiveness, military superiority, and indifference to the oppression of whole classes of persons, so too would self-described lesbian, gay, bisexual, and transgender (LGBT) persons begin rejecting the conditions of their oppression. Submission gradually gave way to anger as LGBT persons reached their collective limit in enduring job loss, denial of housing, police raids on bars, mandatory gender-conforming clothing, enforced psychiatric exams, and other insults. A highly visible grassroots gay liberation movement would emerge soon. This larger movement would inspire LGBT school workers to join gay pride parades, organize, and fight back when school administrators dismissed them on account of their sexual orientation or gender presentation. And by the end of the 1970s, LGBT school workers would need the organizational might of the larger gay liberation movement to win battles that centered specifically on the rights of LGBT teachers.

In 1951, Donald Webster Cory's (pseudonym) *The Homosexual in America* appeared in bookstores around the country. This volume offered a remarkable first-person perspective to larger discussions of homosexuality swirling through print media of the time. In it, Cory wrote from his own decades of experience to articulate a vision of a positive homosexual identity. He described in detail the ongoing harassment that homosexuals had endured at the hands of police, employers, doctors, and the like. He departed sharply from other writing of the time in that he specifically argued for acceptance of homosexuality—rather than ways to hide or diminish it. He contended that most homosexuals lived in a trap where they feigned heterosexuality to avoid severe social sanction, but until they were willing to speak and identify openly as homosexuals, matters would be unlikely to improve.[1]

That same year, a group in the Los Angeles area essentially started a homosexual emancipation movement when it established the Mattachine Society. Initially, this group drew its leadership from homosexual men who had been active with the Communist Party or other left-wing political groups. As such, they possessed strong political organizing skills and a deep wisdom about clandestine strategies. For example, to protect members, the Mattachine Society functioned in secret cells. The group published a magazine, *One,* and the newsletter, *The Mattachine Review,* both of which enhanced common understanding among members and contributed to a sense of larger community.[2]

Similarly, in the fall of 1955, a group of eight lesbians in the San Francisco area founded the Daughters of Bilitis, which met regularly and printed *The Ladder,* a monthly newsletter eventually circulated around the country. President Del Martin explained in the first issue of *The Ladder* in 1956 that "the Lesbian is a very elusive creature. She burrows underground in her fear of identification. She is cautious in her associations. Current modes in hair style and casual attire have enabled her to camouflage her existence." However, even though Martin argued that such women often could take care of themselves in modest ways, "what will be the lot of the future Lesbian? Fear? Scorn? This need not be—IF lethargy is supplanted by an energized constructive program, if cowardice gives way to the solidarity of a cooperative front, if the 'let Georgia do it' attitude is replaced by the realization of individual responsibility in thwarting the evils of ignorance, superstition, prejudice, and bigotry."[3]

Martin urged lesbians to work together to understand themselves, to educate the public, to assist with relevant research, and to change laws affecting homosexuals.[4] For women too shy or fearful of attending meetings of lesbians, *The Ladder* served a vital role in linking a scattered and invisible community. Women who subscribed typically shared their copies with many others as readership far exceeded circulation.

One, The Mattachine Review, and *The Ladder* together fostered a sense of community and common identity among the gay men and lesbians with access to copies. For readers, these publications also countered many of the prevailing myths and stereotypes about homosexuality prevalent in mainstream media. For example, the October 1959 issue of *The Ladder* enthusiastically reported that the Mattachine Society had broken through the "conspiracy of silence" among newspapers when its annual convention in Denver attracted reporters from mainstream media who then posted seven stories "presenting, honestly and fairly, the aims of the Society and the homophile movement."[5]

Inexpensively copied organization newsletters eventually gave way to professionally published general magazines. The humble newsletter of one Los Angeles area homophile organization, PRIDE (Personal Rights in Defense and Education), metamorphosed into *The Advocate,* a magazine that eventually would become a major national source of news for, by, and about gay men and lesbians. Several gay men in the entertainment industry produced the first issue of *The Advocate,* which they secretly printed in the basement of the Los Angeles headquarters of ABC television in September 1967.[6] The editors modestly stated in the first issue:

> With few staff members and even fewer dollars, The Los Angeles *ADVOCATE*'s chances of survival would be rated by experienced journalists as somewhere around zero. Yet, we've decided to stumble ahead with this venture because, we feel, the *ADVOCATE* can perform a very important service as the newspaper of the homophile community—a service that should be delayed no longer. Homosexuals, more than ever before, are out to win their legal rights, to end the injustices against them, to experience their share of happiness in their own way. If the *ADVOCATE* can help in achieving these goals, all the time, sweat, and money that goes into it will be well spent.[7]

Over the coming years, *The Advocate* would chronicle many stories about LGBT school workers and their battles against job discrimination—as well as the larger and strengthening gay liberation movement that would trigger and then support those battles.

Arguably the most pivotal moment in the emergence of the full-blown national gay liberation movement occurred on June 28–29, 1969, at the

Stonewall Inn, a Greenwich Village gay bar. The bar's patrons had endured many raids by police intent on jailing them. At two in the morning, however, they had suffered enough. Police broke in for the usual roundup and then arrested several employees. This time, though, patrons gathered outside and began throwing coins, cans, and rocks. One transvestite reportedly ripped a parking meter out and threw it as well. The police retreated into the bar and called for backup, but then the bar began burning. Newly arriving officers found crowds outside growing in number and rebelliousness, chanting "Gay Power," and "Equality for Homosexuals." Soon, protesters filled the streets, blocking traffic, and shouting, "Christopher Street belongs to the queens!" Boys pasted "Equality for Homosexuals" bumper stickers on police cruisers and prisoner vans.[8] When the riot eventually died down a day later, several underground newspapers ran extensive stories on the new "gay power." And beat poet, Allen Ginsberg, surveyed the piles of rubble and reflected, "They no longer have that 'wounded' look . . . It's time we did something to assert ourselves."[9]

The Stonewall rebellion steadily grew in significance. On the first anniversary of the uprising, thousands of gay men and lesbians marched both in New York City and Los Angeles. The New York event attracted between 2,000–3,000 participants who marched from Greenwich Village to Central Park for "Gay Power." Marchers chanted, "Say it loud— Gay and proud." Over twenty-five different homophile organizations took part, including the Daughters of Bilitis, Mattachine Society of New York, Radicalesbians, Queens, and the Gay Activists Alliance (GAA). At the close of the day, a member of the GAA proclaimed to "every politician in the state and nation that homosexuals are not going to hide anymore. We are becoming militant, and we won't be harassed and degraded anymore." The Christopher Street Liberation Day Committee called the peaceful and flamboyant proceedings "the most important gay event in history."[10]

Meanwhile, the Los Angeles anniversary event offered not just a march, but also a parade on Hollywood Boulevard. *The Advocate* described the proceedings in which "flags and banners floated in the chill sunlight of late afternoon; a bright red sound truck blared martial music; drummers strutted; a horse pranced; clowns cavorted; 'vice cops' chased screaming 'fairies' with paper wings; the Metropolitan Community Church choir sang 'Onward Christian Soldiers'; a bronzed and muscular male model flaunted a 7-foot live python." Crowds of between 15,000 and 20,000 watched and cheered the procession. *The Advocate* concluded that "sensation-sated Hollywood had never seen anything like it. Probably the world had never seen anything like it since the gay days of Ancient Greece."[11]

Each year afterwards, activists organized gay pride parades in many other cities. These events became rallying points for disparate LGBT persons and the organizations that increasingly represented them. They combined grassroots organizing with festivity. In the spirit of the civil rights movement of the time, many community leaders used these events to raise awareness of gay political activism. Clusters of organizations formed, drawing together activists intent on winning basic rights for homosexuals. Crowded and theatrical gay pride parades effectively countered the dispiriting silence and isolation experienced by LGBT persons for so long. Mainstream media covered the events as fascinating spectacles, filing stories that generated extensive attention on the evening news. With the continued rise of a gay liberation movement, more LGBT persons found the strength and support to resist the varied oppressions that previously they had faced alone.

In the early 1960s, when lesbian and gay teachers ran afoul of school administrators on account of their sexual orientation, they typically resigned quietly. Legal challenges to school districts entailed costs far beyond what suspended school employees could afford. Although young homophile organizations supported the employment rights of lesbians and gay men, they scarcely possessed the resources necessary to assist with protracted court battles. Matters shifted substantially by the middle of the decade, however, when the American Civil Liberties Union (ACLU) joined the case of the fired California teacher, Mark Morrison.

In 1964, Morrison had engaged in sexual behaviors with a male teacher at his school who had been experiencing marital difficulties. These behaviors, which occurred over the course of one week, did not include either oral or anal sex and, as such, were legal in California. Some time later, Morrison's male colleague told district officials about the incidents. Morrison then resigned. Within a couple of years, he also lost his life teaching credentials because of his supposedly immoral behavior. Because of the legal support that he received from the ACLU, however, Morrison engaged in a lengthy legal battle to regain his teaching credentials. Eventually, the State Supreme Court ruled that Morrison's "homosexual character" per se did not interfere with his ability to teach; however, it held that the school district justifiably could keep him away from impressionable children. Because the district deemed his sexual behaviors immoral and because these behaviors had become public knowledge, the Court argued that the school district's decision was warranted.[12]

Although Morrison would not be allowed to resume his teaching career, his case did result in softening of the legal logic that homosexuality necessarily meant unfitness for educational service, a ruling celebrated in

The Advocate only months after the Stonewall riot.[13] Soon, professional and gay advocacy groups joined the ACLU in providing legal support for homosexual teachers filing lawsuits against school districts that fired them on account of their sexual orientation.[14]

Only a year after the Stonewall riot, a counselor at the American School for the Deaf in West Hartford lost his job immediately after he discussed gay rights on television. The young man, who had served as an officer of the Kalos Society: Gay Liberation, Hartford, had agreed to participate in a televised panel discussion on gay liberation and society. He would attempt to fight his dismissal.[15] However, around this time, the *Journal of the American Bar Association* released poll results indicating that respondents "considered homosexuality a crime second only to murder or to murder and armed robbery."[16] Despite this considerable public hostility, other educators besides the West Hartford counselor would begin standing up as well, even if termination were inevitable.

Peggy Burton, a rural Oregon high school teacher, needed the legal assistance of the ACLU in 1971. At school one afternoon, Burton's principal confronted her with rumors circulating about her suspected lesbianism. As she explained it, "There was no complaint. It was a rumor. Someone hinted to Principal Leonard Federico that I might be a homosexual."[17] Other teachers before her who had been confronted with a similar situation had taken one of two courses of action. Some simply denied that they were homosexual—and then they engaged in extensive damage control to assuage community fears. Others admitted their sexual desires and then entered treatment programs or stepped down from their positions.[18] Burton, however, would not be cowed. She replied to her principal, "So what." Several days later, despite high evaluations, she lost her job. This was not the first time the school had faced controversy, however. The previous spring, several male students had filed a suit against the school for suspending them for wearing their hair long. A male teacher also initiated legal proceedings claiming the school had failed to renew his contract because he wore a mustache.[19]

Burton decided to bring a lawsuit against the district. She explained, "I am bull-headed. I felt bad at first, and I cried for days. I still cry about it. It really did hurt. I never really could understand. I knew that I wasn't a bad person, and I decided to stand up for my rights. . . . Sometimes there are things you can't compromise with. Sometimes you can't live with yourself if you compromise. Sometimes you just have to take a stand."[20] The ACLU supported her case so it could establish the larger precedent that homosexuals as a class were entitled to civil rights. Over the years that the case unfolded, Burton struggled financially to support herself and pay her student loans while earning a meager salary in a fish cannery.[21] A year after filing her case, the U.S. District Court rendered its decision that the Oregon statute granting school districts power to dismiss teachers for immorality was too vague. The Court explained,

> This statute vests in the school board the power to dismiss teachers for immorality. However the statute does not define immorality. Immorality means different things to different people, and its definition depends on the idiosyncrasies of the individual school board members. It may be applied so broadly that every teacher in the state could be subject to discipline. The potential for arbitrary and discriminatory enforcement is inherent in such a statute. A statute so broad makes those charged with its enforcement the arbiters of morality for the entire community. In doing so, it subjects the livelihood of every teacher in the state to the irrationality and irregularity of such judgments. The statute is vague because it fails to give fair warning of what conduct is prohibited and because it permits erratic and prejudiced exercises of authority.[22]

Despite the positive ramifications of this decision, Burton's attorney pressed for full reinstatement. He explained, "What the judge did was to say that the school board had no right to fire her, but refused to protect her right to work there."[23] Burton eventually won some minor concessions like the remainder of her salary for the year she was fired, pay for an additional six months, a few hundred dollars for attorney fees, and the right to have the school district expunge records of her case from her employment file. However, she would not be allowed to resume her teaching duties in the district.[24]

Although Burton had not participated in the post-Stonewall gay liberation movement before her dismissal, she quickly came to see the value of organizing to fight discrimination. "I don't think any of us can stand up when we are all by ourselves. We need backing. We need to know that we can stand up and can do it. We need to get together in small groups wherever we are to offer each other support."[25] Undoubtedly, she also needed the backing of the ACLU to challenge her district in the first place. Despite her ultimate inability to reclaim her job, the case did anger lesbian and gay teachers who read gay media such as *The Advocate*. Some would organize.

John Gish, a Paramus, New Jersey, high school English teacher, triumphantly organized the Gay Teachers Caucus of the NEA in time for the annual Representative Assembly in June 1972. Gish had been active in the Gay Activists Alliance, a particularly successful grassroots political organization that attracted members, helped them develop political organizing skills, and staged public events designed to generate public awareness of discrimination against gay men and lesbians. Gish had served both as the vice president for public relations and then as president of the New Jersey Gay Activists Alliance. He decided that the next important front in the movement should be to gain rights for lesbian and gay teachers, so organizing the Gay Teachers Caucus of the NEA made sense to him. He told *The Advocate,* "Most gay teachers are known to be gay, or are assumed to be gay, by their students and Boards of Education. Just as long as nothing is said, the system tolerates them. I'm fed up with lying to them. I'm tired of using women to accompany me to proms so that a 'proper' image is preserved. I'm tired of listening to anti-gay jokes in the faculty room and being forced to laugh along with the straights."[26]

Later that summer, on hearing of Gish's work with the Gay Teachers Caucus of the NEA, his school board ordered him to undergo a psychiatric examination. Gish resisted. Then he enlisted the help of the ACLU and succeeded in winning an injunction against the board's order. The local newspaper reported that the school board members, and not Gish, should have their heads examined.[27] Nonetheless, the board removed Gish from his teaching duties, assigning him instead to administrative work in an office far from his school. The board also banned him from having any contact with students or graduates, a difficult feat for the popular instructor. Gish responded by waging a hunger strike to protest this prohibition. Meanwhile, that November, Gish addressed the annual delegation of the New Jersey Education Association to describe his plight. The Delegate Assembly then collectively decided to work for state antidiscrimination legislation that included sexual orientation.[28]

In 1976, the Superior Court of New Jersey decided that Gish's "actions in support of 'gay' rights displayed evidence of deviation from normal mental health which might affect his ability to teach, discipline, and associate with students."[29] Therefore they upheld the school district order that Gish submit to a psychiatric examination. Gish then appealed to the Supreme Court. A year later, the Supreme Court decided not to hear his appeal, thus letting the state decision stand.[30] In 1978, the superintendent of the Paramus schools released a list of eighteen instances of Gish's alleged "conduct unbecoming" a teacher including: serving as president of the New Jersey Gay Activists Alliance, talking to the media about the plight of gay teachers, helping to organize the Gay Teachers Caucus of the NEA, advocating that homosexuality was just fine, and suffering from deviant mental health.[31] The *San Francisco Examiner* then reported in June 1979 that Gish had decided to end seven years of legal battles, having exhausted his appeals, by submitting to examination by a school board-appointed psychiatrist.[32] Gish continued to seek his classroom job. In a hopeful development in 1981, the New Jersey State Board of Education decided that teachers could not be fired for advocating controversial causes outside the classroom. However, because police had confiscated drugs from Gish's apartment during a raid—which Gish maintained belonged to his roommate—the Paramus schools fired him anyway.[33] In the end, Gish could not resume his teaching position even though his case furthered the cause of lesbian and gay teachers. And his activism within the NEA produced long-standing changes in the organization, contributing to the eventual passage of a resolution adding sexual orientation to categories of school employees who must be protected from job discrimination.[34]

Shortly after *The Advocate* first reported John Gish's successful establishment of the Gay Teachers Caucus of the NEA in 1972, reporters covered another story about a gay teacher education student and his quest for a teaching certificate. Joseph Acanfora, a senior at Pennsylvania State University, had been active in the Homophiles of Penn State (HOPS). He explained that he should be awarded a teaching certificate because "There's absolutely nothing against me. I had a very high grade point average and got a B in student teaching." Apparently he had done exemplary work in his student teaching assignment, but supervisors assigned him a B after the principal learned of his involvement in HOPS. The principal refused to allow him to finish the student teaching term. Acanfora got a court injunction allowing him to complete the assignment. Meanwhile, the university teacher education council expressed uncertainty about whether it would approve Acanfora's candidacy for a certificate even with the matter of his student teaching resolved. It summoned him for questioning. He came with attorneys and answered a lengthy series of questions about his sexual orientation. He admitted sexual attraction to men, but clarified that he had never engaged in any homosexual acts. Eventually, the council approved his application for the certificate. Acanfora explained his reason for resisting the overwhelming obstacles in his path: "The point of being in the movement is, if you are homosexual, say it—and get your rights anyway."[35]

The Advocate then reported that Acanfora had been granted his teaching certificate primarily because, as the State Secretary of Education explained, he had not engaged in homosexual activities.[36] By then Acanfora had begun teaching in Maryland. However, on September 24, 1972, the *New York Times* featured a story on his battle to receive his teaching certificate. Two days later, Acanfora received a letter ordering him to report to a central office building where he would begin an immediate administrative assignment pending an investigation into the *Times* story. Both the NEA and ACLU expressed interest in his case as he considered his next steps.[37] A number of students and teachers at Acanfora's school lobbied the administration to reinstate him to the classroom. Three-quarters of the faculty and nearly every single student he taught signed a petition supporting him, but the administration stood its ground.

The nearby Gay Activists Alliance of Washington, DC, even labored on Acanfora's behalf. Earlier that spring, the DC Gay Activists Alliance had successfully petitioned the District of Columbia Board of Education for a policy banning discrimination against district employees on account of sexual orientation.[38] The board had adopted this policy over the superintendent's objections, becoming the first school district in the country to offer such protection to school employees. During heated board discussion of the matter, the vice-chairwoman apparently screamed, "I agree with the superintendent that this resolution is unnecessary and absurd, and I am at a loss as to what this committee is doing concerning itself with orientation, sexual orientation. If I thought that this would pass I would take my children out of the schools in order that they might not be contaminated by homosexuals and deviates." Board chairman, Marion Berry, Jr. (who subsequently became mayor) responded, "There was a time when black people and women were fired from a job, or not hired, and the reason given was never because of their color or sex, although we know that these were the reasons. We cannot condone de facto discrimination. We need to open our schools in order to discuss life in 1972. This resolution only confirms those rights granted to everyone, and for which I have fought in the past, which are guaranteed under the Constitution and under the Bill of Rights."[39] In this courageous stance, Berry effectively framed discrimination based on sexual orientation as a civil rights issue. As an effective civil rights leader himself, his words carried significant weight.

Following this remarkable turn of events catalyzed largely by Gay Activists Alliance efforts and impressive board leadership, DC Gay Activists Alliance members sought to influence the disposition of Acanfora's case. At an open forum for school board candidates in Acanfora's Maryland district, DC Gay Activists Alliance members grilled candidates on how they would assure equal rights for homosexuals. The Gay Activists Alliance president specifically asked aspiring board members if they were homophobic enough to rename Walt Whitman High School (Bethesda) because of Whitman's well-known homosexual relationships. One board candidate confronted Gay Activists Alliance members by declaring the urgent need for schools to keep homosexuality from spreading. This raucous forum received extensive television and newspaper coverage in the Washington, DC, area.[40]

Acanfora chose to file a lawsuit against the Montgomery County schools, with the legal support of the NEA.[41] After lower court defeats, he appealed. Meanwhile, his case continued generating significant media

attention. The Educational Broadcasting Corporation syndicated nationwide a television documentary featuring his battle for the right to teach.
In the film, Acanfora's parents staunchly supported him, discussing their
love for their son, whom they described as kind, sensitive, and talented.[42]
During the spring of 1974, the Fourth Circuit Court of Appeals ruled
that schools could not bar teachers on account of homosexuality. They
also indicated that gay educators should be allowed to discuss their orientation openly, that they should not be forced to hide it. However, they
specifically denied Acanfora's right to resume his teaching position because he had failed to list his membership in the campus homophile organization on his teaching application, a failure that they regarded as de-
ceitful. Although Acanfora appealed to the Supreme Court, it declined to
hear the case, thus letting the decision of the Fourth Circuit Court
stand.[43] Acanfora, like Burton and Gish, had achieved expanded rights
for lesbian and gay teachers; but in the end, like them, he could not regain
his teaching position.

   In 1972, during the same fall semester that school officials removed
Gish and Acanfora from their classrooms and forced them into make-
work administrative positions, James Gaylord, a high school teacher in
Tacoma, Washington, lost his job because of his supposedly immoral sexual orientation. Though Gaylord consistently had earned high evaluations during his twelve years of teaching, his teaching abilities would not
merit a reprieve from dismissal. School officials terminated him when
they learned of his homosexuality from a student, even though they knew
of no sexual misconduct on his part. They dismissed him because of a
homosexual *identity,* which Gaylord did not deny, rather than his *behavior.* Gaylord explained, "They came up with the idea that since I hadn't
denied any illegal conduct, I can be presumed to have engaged in it. . . . I
was discharged for status. I was never even asked if I engaged in improper
conduct, and no one suggested that I had." Prior to this event, Gaylord, a
Phi Beta Kappa graduate of the University of Washington, had kept information about his sexual orientation away from school officials.[44]

   The Tacoma school board dismissed him on grounds of his alleged immorality. Gaylord appealed. The Supreme Court of Washington upheld
the board's decision, claiming that Gaylord's admission of overt, rather
than latent, homosexuality sufficed for drawing the conclusion that he
also had engaged in homosexual activities, even though no one ever submitted evidence. Then, community knowledge of his homosexuality damaged his reputation and ability to teach, the court claimed.[45] Apparently
the school district explained in court that some of Gaylord's colleagues
objected to his reinstatement. However, the Tacoma Federation of Teachers strongly supported him, bearing the expense of his legal defense, and

even employing him following the case. The Assistant Superintendent of Personnel for the Tacoma schools testified that "I think there is a way of life that I have looked for in employing teachers through the years, and fundamentally I don't think that homosexuality is a way of life that I can tolerate in my position."[46] When Gaylord appealed the state ruling to the Supreme Court, it refused to hear the case—just as it had with Gish and Acanfora's cases. Both Justices Brennan and Marshall wanted to hear the case, but other justices outvoted them. Consequently, in 1977, the decision of the Supreme Court of Washington stood.[47] Not only did Gaylord then go to work for the Tacoma Federation of Teachers, but over the months that followed, he also would speak out in support of newly forming groups of lesbian and gay teachers in California who by then were preparing to fight against an upcoming state initiative to systematically dismiss lesbian and gay teachers and those who supported them.[48]

Finally, two other teachers experienced job terminations that garnered national attention. Both teachers transitioned to the other sex. New Jersey band director, Paula Grossman, formerly Paul Grossman, underwent sex-change surgery in 1971 and lost her job immediately afterwards. District officials claimed that students would suffer adverse psychological effects by working with a teacher whose sex had changed. The New Jersey Superior Court supported this contention, explaining that "the plain fact is that no school district will employ her because of her transsexual status and the feared effect that may have on pupils she might be called on to teach." Furthermore, the Court maintained that her transsexuality "incapacitated" her because of the social stigma that accompanied it. Grossman, who remained married throughout her transition, sought to distance herself from charges of lesbianism, and maintained that she and her wife were good friends and that the case had nothing to do with homosexuality.[49]

Similarly, school officials dismissed Steve Dain, formerly Doris Richards, a physical education teacher, following his surgery. Echoing the sentiments expressed in Grossman's case, officials in the Emmeryville, California, school district claimed that Dain's continued presence in school would cause psychological harm to students. Eventually, the California Supreme Court let stand a lower court ruling that the district owed Dain back pay.[50] In both the Grossman and Dain cases, school administrators claimed that, by definition, these teachers violated their gender roles by becoming the other sex—and, as such, they could damage the psychological well-being of their students and certainly provide supposedly poor gender-role modeling.

Burton, Gish, Acanfora, Gaylord, and Grossman had been relieved of their classroom responsibilities within a year of each other, Burton and

Grossman in 1971 and Gish, Acanfora, and Gaylord in 1972. Their legal battles stretched over years. Acanfora, Gish, and Gaylord's cases culminated in Supreme Court decisions not to consider their cases. By the time final news of Gaylord's appeal reached the headlines, Burton, Gish, Acanfora, and Gaylord had come to deeply appreciate the importance of organized activism for their employment rights. On the other hand, Grossman and Dain's transsexuality fell outside the mainstream of lesbian and gay activism of the time. Furthermore, Grossman denied any connection with homosexual identity, much less with the movement. As such, Grossman and Dain fought their legal battles largely with their own resources.

Meanwhile, Anita Bryant had begun agitating against the rights of lesbian and gay teachers in Florida. Around the country, conservative critics bemoaned the prospect of homosexuals corrupting children and male teachers wearing skirts to school. Lesbian and gay teachers would need to work with each other as well as in concert with the larger and increasingly powerful gay liberation movement if they ever hoped to claim their sexual orientation openly while serving in the schools.

As these early and widely publicized individual cases unfolded concerning the employment rights of openly lesbian and gay teachers, activism began on another front. A few teachers began to lobby their professional associations to add "sexual orientation" to the classes of persons protected from job discrimination. These early teacher activists decided to risk activism even though they knew they could—and often did—lose their jobs. John Gish had been instrumental in organizing the Gay Teachers Caucus of the NEA in 1972, an action that had contributed to his school district's decision to dismiss him from teaching duties.

Predating Gish's efforts with the NEA and only a few months after news of the Stonewall riot first appeared in *The Advocate,* however, Morgan Pinney and students at San Francisco State University successfully encouraged the California Federation of Teachers to pass an ambitious resolution supporting the rights of homosexual teachers. During the CFT's annual convention in 1969, the 250 delegates in attendance decreed that it would work for "the abolition of all laws or other governmental policy which involves non-victim sexual practice," and, further, that it would strive to implement an expanded sex education program that included discussion of "various American life-styles." Pinney wrote and presented the resolution, which stated as its rationale that millions of homosexuals are oppressed in the United States, that "homosexuals are harassed and intimidated by the police," that "the government's antihomosexual policies set the tone of homosexual oppression as national policy," and finally, that the worst problem of all was the self-hatred induced in many homosexuals. Initial snickers soon gave way to quiet respect as Pinney recounted the horrors faced by homosexuals who, as he maintained, were murdered by police and others. He described the deep pain experienced by men and women who feared the consequences of revealing their sexual orientation. He argued for offering sex education that included discussion of nonmonogamous and nonheterosexual orientations. In particular, he maintained that homosexual youth need to see positive models in the schools. When Pinney finished his eloquent remarks, the delegates greeted him with a standing ovation and a clear victory for the resolution.[51]

This groundbreaking vote by the California Federation of Teachers stood in contrast with the relative difficulty that other lesbian and gay educators would face in their newfound activism. One group of lesbian and gay teachers picketed the New York Board of Education in early 1971 to protest the discrimination they faced in their jobs. The chancellor deflected them by telling them that the State Board of Examiners created the policies against gay and lesbian teachers, not him. The group then instigated a sit-in at the State Board of Examiners office. Police arrested five of the protesters. The policies remained the same.[52] A few months later in Iowa City, a teacher lost his job after he brought two members of the Gay Liberation Front to speak to his eighth-grade sex education class. The popular teacher received vigorous support from the community, however. As a result, the board of education met with members of the Gay Liberation Front and then decided to reinstate the teacher.[53]

With greater regularity, these scattered incidents would intersect with national developments in the larger gay liberation movement. Late in 1973, the board of trustees of the American Psychiatric Association voted unanimously to remove homosexuality from its list of psychiatric disorders. *The Advocate* reported the event as the moment during which twenty million homosexuals experienced instant cure. This action, resulting in part from intense lobbying by gay advocacy groups, also included language calling for the removal of sodomy laws.[54]

Despite the support of this influential professional association, legislators in Missouri introduced a bill in early 1974 to classify homosexuality as a disease—and, further, to require homosexuals whose jobs brought them in regular contact with persons under twenty-one years of age to register with the state Division of Health. One legislator explained that he had introduced the bill "because we felt there was a need, and our constituents thought there was a need for protection of young persons from unwanted exposure to persons who openly flaunt this way of life." The state homosexual registry would have been available to all organizations responsible for hiring persons to work with youth, particularly schools. Persons appearing on the list would have had no legal recourse. They could be removed only if they provided a certificate, signed by two doctors, declaring them free of homosexuality. Though the measure did not pass, it indicates something of the peculiar attention lesbian and gay teachers received in the larger gay liberation movement.[55] It became increasingly obvious to gay activists that political conservatives would not necessarily focus their efforts on the broad, and at times diffuse, gay liberation movement, but rather on the narrow subset within the movement that aroused the strongest public fears: homosexual school workers. In time, such political figures would capitalize on these fears to raise funds and generate votes.

During the summer of 1974, the NEA Representative Assembly decided once again to take up the issue of including sexual orientation among the classes of persons it would support in fighting employment discrimination. John Gish and the group he had formed, the Gay Teachers Caucus, had introduced such a resolution two years earlier, which delegates had not approved. This time, the 9,700 delegates would discuss the resolution for over thirty minutes. When the president could not determine the outcome of the voice vote, she asked delegates to stand. In the end, the resolution carried with about two-thirds of delegates supporting the inclusion of sexual orientation in the NEA's nondiscrimination statement. In effect, this change committed the vast legal resources of the 1.4-million member organization to backing employees who faced job discrimination on account of their sexual orientation.[56]

Immediately following this headline-grabbing policy development, *The Advocate* broke the story in the fall of 1974 that ABC planned to run an episode of the then-popular television drama, *Marcus Welby, M.D.*, that would infuriate gay activists. The episode, "The Outrage," featured a junior high school science teacher who rapes one of his male students. As a result, the boy's intestinal wall becomes inflamed and needs treatment. He refuses to tell what happened out of shame. After the boy's relatives assure him that he is still "a man," he reveals the truth. Gay activists worried that if the show were aired as planned, it would unfairly reinforce the popular, though scientifically unsupported notion that homosexuality and child molestation were linked.[57]

Gay activists then protested the script, but ABC refused to alter the show. In response, Bruce Voeller, director of the National Gay Task Force, rallied the support of the American Psychiatric Association, the NEA—which had voted to include sexual orientation in its antidiscrimination statement only months earlier, and the American Federation of Teachers (AFT). Voeller explained, "All the ABC protests that homosexuality is not the issue in this episode are vain. It does in fact reflect poorly on Gays as a whole, and everyone who sees it will take that message away: Homosexuals are vicious, preying child molesters."[58]

In response, the Gay Tactical Force, which *The Advocate* described as a "semi-underground radical protest group," compiled a list of the companies likely to advertise during *Marcus Welby*. They urged gay activists around the country to write those companies and urge them to withdraw their sponsorship of that episode.[59] To the surprise of ABC and gay activists alike, the lobbying effort yielded impressive results. Seven major sponsors withdrew their support. Four network affiliates refused to air the episode. A number of top medical leaders and Albert Shanker, president of the AFT, contributed their expertise by writing letters of support. And, overall, the event provoked enormous national media coverage. *The Advocate* reported that this "demonstrated the growing muscle and intergroup cooperation of the organized Gay Liberation Movement across the nation." Voeller weighed in: "I think it has to be viewed as really the first great concerted national effort by gay groups around the country."[60] This was the first time that sponsors had ever withdrawn their support of a television show in response to political pressure. Also for the first time, stations had refused to air national network programs. In cities like Iowa City, Tulsa, and Fort Worth where activists could not persuade stations to cancel the show, raucous demonstrations occurred instead. *The Advocate* delighted in concluding:

> From the hinterlands as well as the great cities, and for the first time in history, a national movement seems to have emerged from gay liberation's battle with ABC-TV over its Oct. 8 episode of "Marcus Welby M.D."
> Claiming that the giant network had suffered great financial losses and a severe blow to its prestige, Gays were declaring a victory of David vs. Goliath proportions and announcing that gay liberation had itself become a giant in the land. . . . In this instance, at least, Gays had battered and bruised the ancient "child molestation" bogeyman that has haunted nearly every project of the fledgling movement.[61]

Inspired by such successful national activism, lesbian and gay teachers soon began organizing local associations devoted to securing their own employment rights, providing social support, and educating communities about issues they faced. The first such local group may have been the Gay Teachers Association of New York City, formed during the fall of 1974 as the *Marcus Welby* debacle unfolded. Marc Rubin, one of the founders of the group, recounted that an old friend and fellow Gay Activists Alliance activist called him over the summer asking for help in convincing the local AFT representative to support the rights of lesbian and gay educators. Altogether, five teachers met with Sandy Feldman, the representative to the local AFT unit for New York City, the United Federation of Teachers (UFT).[62] The group explained that "we wanted the UFT to acknowledge and support its thousands of gay teachers. We wanted a Gay Rights resolution, and we wanted the UFT to speak for us at the City Council." Feldman agreed to speak to the executive council, but the group heard nothing back from her. Then they arranged to speak with Albert Shanker, president of both the national AFT and also the local UFT. Shanker indicated that he did not object to the formation of a gay teachers caucus, but he did not want the UFT to take a public position on the rights of gay teachers, believing the matter to be too divisive. He did not necessarily believe that a gay bill would help, but he agreed to lobby members of the executive council quietly. He also reportedly told the group that its estimate of 6,000 homosexual teachers working in New York City was low because he believed that teaching attracted a larger proportion of lesbians and gay men than other professions. In retrospect, members of the group contended that no tangible results came from this meeting, just as none had from the meeting with Sandy Feldman.[63] Years later, Shanker also reportedly denied that he ever indicated that larger numbers of gay men and lesbians sought to enter teaching than other lines of work.[64]

Undeterred, the small group of teachers placed an ad in the *Village Voice* announcing a meeting of gay and lesbian teachers in New York City. Over fifty people came, far exceeding the expectations of organizers. Meryl Friedman, a school administrator and member of the Board of Directors of the National Gay Task Force, and Marc Rubin, a teacher with Gay Activists Alliance ties, became co-spokespersons for the newly formed Gay Teachers Association. Rubin recounts that many of the teachers who came to these early meetings wanted a social experience to counteract the loneliness and fear they encountered in their work. Only a handful wanted to engage in activism. To address these differences, some meetings were educational, others social, and the rest geared toward political actions. Remarkably, too, Rubin explained that "we have completely avoided political factionalism, we have been free of power struggles, and, most blessed of all, we have not been plagued by the sort of women/men discord that has struck so many other sexually integrated gay organizations."[65] Indeed, members of the organization demonstrated remarkable skill in negotiating gender relations. Other lesbian and gay teacher organizations, especially some on the West Coast, would segregate largely into separate lesbian and gay groups. With a commitment to pulling together, though, the New York group labored to address the needs of all its members.

Not surprisingly, secrecy remained an important issue for many of the persons interested in the Gay Teachers Association. To address this concern, newspaper ads included the reassuring language, "closet rights respected," so fearful individuals might feel comfortable attending. Rubin described many early participants:

> Gay teachers are, on the whole, an incredibly paranoid group of people. Smeared for years by the pre-Stonewall image of gays, and feeling intensely vulnerable to the vicious myth of child molestation, now masquerading under the more sophisticated label of "undesirable role model" or "threat to the family," most of the gay teachers that we have met are simply afraid that they will lose their jobs if *anyone* finds out their secret. We have had people come to our meetings who have been teaching together in the same school for years and did not recognize each other's homosexuality. We still have people who are afraid to give us their real names, and we still meet people who are afraid to be on our mailing list. Three-quarters of the teachers who call us, ask for information, and say they will come to our meetings, never appear.[66]

In addition to conducting increasingly well-attended meetings despite this difficulty, the Gay Teachers Association engaged in political efforts to end discrimination against lesbian and gay teachers. Friedman and Rubin worked to develop a strong and direct working relationship with Frank Arricale, Executive Director of the New York City Board of Education. Arricale attended a meeting of the Gay Teachers Association to answer questions posed by attendees. When Friedman asked Arricale directly if being a lesbian was a bar to employment in the New York schools, he wrote her a letter on January 24, 1975, explaining that "you can be assured that homosexuality is not a bar to entrance into teaching in New York City nor to the continuation of teaching in the City. . . . Homosexual teachers have exactly the same rights and protection as any other teacher in the system. Not only are we not involved in any process of ferreting out homosexual teachers, frankly, we are not particularly interested in whether or not teachers are homosexual or not."[67]

Fresh from this fruitful effort, the Gay Teachers Association pressed on another front. They had attempted several times to buy ads in the union newspaper, *The New York Teacher,* announcing Gay Teachers Association meetings. However, the newspaper would not accept these ads—for a variety of reasons that Gay Teachers Association members found unsatisfying.[68] In frustration, the group decided to "zap" union headquarters. With television reporters in tow, they stormed the building. They found, however, that the elevator to the offices somehow had stopped working. When they made their way up the stairs, they discovered headquarters offices

locked with officials inside.[69] Although Gay Teachers Association protesters could not meet with union officials that day, the tremendous
media attention they garnered helped the cause. Soon representatives of
the Gay Teachers Association were invited to speak to the 100-member
Executive Board of the union, during which their twenty minutes of allot-
ted time expanded to an hour and a half of frank discussion. Board members decided to bring the matter of Gay Teachers Association advertisements in the union newspaper back to every school system for discussion.
They also agreed to discuss a resolution supporting the right of all members, including homosexuals. The board later passed the resolution.[70]

In reflecting on the history of the Gay Teachers Association, Rubin described how a persistent obstacle that the association encountered was
the tremendous reluctance of lesbian and gay teachers to identify themselves openly. "Not one single NYC teacher who has come out at school
has lost a job," he said. To celebrate the powerful act of openly identifying as a lesbian or gay teacher, the Gay Teachers Association began to
participate in the annual Stonewall marches. He explained:

> For the past two years, there has been a huge lavender and red banner in
> the Christopher Street Liberation Day march. It will be in this year's march,
> and it will go down to Washington, DC on May 21. It centers around a
> giant-size red apple with two green leaves and a yellow lambda superim-
> posed on it. The words 'Gay Teachers Association—New York City' pro-
> claim not only that there are gay teachers, but that there are gay teachers
> who stand proud and united with their gay sisters and brothers. That, in it-
> self, is our most powerful political statement.[71]

The Gay Teachers Association grew larger and stronger over the years.
In January 1978, the association published its first *Gay Teachers Association Newsletter*, a well-written publication that chronicled association activities. Early issues described how the Gay Teachers Association increasingly pitched in with national efforts to support LGBT educators. Stories
also indicated that Gay Teachers Association members eagerly reached
out to fledgling LGBT teacher groups in other cities, to help them organize, to exchange newsletters, to share information, and occasionally
even to visit.

On the West Coast, the Bay Area Gay Teachers Caucus, later called the
Gay Teachers and Schoolworkers Coalition, soon would begin sharing its
experiences with its New York Gay Teachers Alliance colleagues. Ron
Lanza, one of the organizers of the Gay Teachers and Schoolworkers Co-
alition, explained how he first became interested in starting such a group.
He and his lover had been riding their bicycles through downtown San
Francisco when

We came across this ragtag collection of people on a flatbed truck in zany costumes and clanging bells and horns, maybe a couple of hundred in total. It was like the Christopher Street West celebration. A part of me was so drawn to that, it seemed so wonderful and so new and so revolutionary, and at the same time, as a teacher, I knew I should get back on my bicycle, because I wouldn't want my picture to be taken. I remember that day very clearly, like a seed was planted.[72]

Lanza then began attending meetings of the Bay Area Gay Liberation (BAGL), which members affectionately called "Bagel." BAGL inspired many activists to form affinity groups. The Gay Teachers and School Workers Coalition then became one of those associated groups—working specifically for the rights of LGBT teachers, school workers, and students throughout the Bay Area. With the leadership of Lanza, Hank Wilson, and Tom Ammiano, the group officially organized during the spring of 1975. As its first order of business, members decided to tackle the problem of increasing violence against LGBT persons in area school districts. When the school year ended, the ambitious members of the Gay Teachers and Schoolworkers Coalition decided to organize a mass demonstration on June 17, 1975. They posted fliers explaining, "Gay teachers and other schoolworkers live in constant fear of losing their jobs. When gays face discrimination in employment all workers are less secure in their jobs. An attack on gay schoolworkers is an attack on all gay people. The Board *does* respond to pressure. Your attendance *will* make a difference."[73]

This flyer calling for large numbers of protesters had been inspired by recent San Francisco school board actions that coalition members considered as acting in bad faith. At an earlier meeting, the board was to have considered adding sexual orientation to its nondiscrimination statement. Del Martin and Phyllis Lyon, organizers and leaders of the Daughters of Bilitis, had petitioned the board to add sexual orientation, but the board tabled action until a later date. Reportedly, as soon as Martin and Lyon left the room, the board voted down the proposal to add the language to the nondiscrimination policy.[74] A week later, Tom Ammiano led an angry crowd of over 300 lesbians and gay men who marched into the chamber while singing "When the Gays Go Marching In." In response to this pressure, the board agreed to revisit the issue of adding sexual orientation to the nondiscrimination policy at its meeting slated for June 17.[75]

Gay Teachers and Schoolworkers Coalition members not only plastered fliers around the city in anticipation of this meeting, but they also strategized carefully how they could best advocate for the revised board policy. Someone on the school board would need to place a resolution on the table to include sexual orientation in the nondiscrimination policy. Understanding this, coalition activists lobbied behind the scenes for the entire week prior to the board meeting to persuade one official to take this politically risky action. A few hours before the meeting began, coalition activists had no idea if the issue would be put on the table—but then one member discreetly called and said he would introduce the resolution. An hour before the meeting, hundreds of resolution supporters rallied outside and then, once again, filed into the meeting room singing, "When the Gays Go Marching In." This action reportedly had a salutary effect on Board members who then extended themselves courteously to the large crowd.[76] Eventually, the crowd hushed, the meeting began, and then board member, Tom Reed, former principal of St. Ignatius High School, placed the resolution on the table. He explained that when he had served as principal, some of his students had started what they called the "Queer Hunters Club." He continued, "The purpose of this club was to prey upon gays, attack them and beat them up. The whole thing turned my stomach that students should think they had some right to attack their brothers simply because they had a different sexual orientation than their own." Then one night after a school dance, they found a teacher whom they considered gay waiting for a streetcar outside. They "attacked this person, robbed him, threw him on the streetcar tracks, and he was run over by the streetcar and killed." Ever since, Reed had felt the weight of his action or inaction as principal in contributing to this event. Reed's story powerfully affected those in attendance as well as other board members. They then unanimously approved the measure. Immediately after the vote, the crowd burst into applause that lasted for over two minutes.[77] As an additional benefit, the board also agreed to include information about upcoming coalition meetings in its future district newsletters.[78]

Among the many other actions of the Gay Teachers and Schoolworkers Coalition that would follow in the years ahead, one important tradition was marching as a group in annual gay pride parades. This action represented a public display of teachers openly claiming their gay and lesbian identities. At a time when teachers around the country could be fired on account of their sexual orientation, participation in public marches required courage. In turn, teachers who saw parade participants sometimes later described such events as deeply moving. Consequently, these annual events played a significant role in growing activism among teachers. One member of the coalition wrote a brief piece for the newsletter describing the experience:

> There I was marching down Market Street carrying a giant red-apple, support gay teachers banner and hundreds of people clapped and shouted their support! It would be impossible to explain the feeling that filled my insides as I walked that one mile but I know that it was entirely new.

It has been some twelve years I have been teaching and some thirteen years I have been gay but until very recently those two things never came up together. Years of listening to straight teachers talk about their trips to Tahoe with their husbands, years of donating to wedding presents in the social fund, years of hearing about their husbands' new jobs and years of deciding if I could stand to go to one more faculty function.[79]

By marching, however, this teacher found exhilarating the public support she received for who she was, for the job she did, for her willingness to take a risk, and for working together with other LGBT teachers. This affirmation offered lesbian and gay teachers and the groups they organized a heightened sense of purpose.

Exactly one year after the momentous meeting where the San Francisco Board of Education added sexual orientation to its nondiscrimination policy, a group of eight gay and lesbian teachers in Los Angeles gathered to discuss their conditions and status within the schools. They considered the recent Los Angeles City Council resolution that included sexual orientation in its nondiscrimination policy. They noted the impressive successes scored by the Bay Area's Gay Teachers and Schoolworkers Coalition in winning employment protection for lesbian and gay school workers. And they debated the implications of the NEA's 1974 non-discrimination policy that included sexual orientation. In the end, they decided to form the Gay Teachers of Los Angeles. They agreed to work closely with local organized gay academics as well as with the Bay Area's Gay Teachers and Schoolworkers Coalition and New York's Gay Teachers Alliance. In that first meeting, the group ceremoniously passed a bowl and collected $8.25 to cover expenses—and then agreed to meet again soon.[80]

By the next meeting, one of the new group's members had approached the president of the United Teachers of Los Angeles, the local teachers union, to discuss his support for the rights of lesbian and gay teachers. Another had written a school board member about support as well and received a favorable reply. Then, fearing that a strictly political agenda might alienate many potential members, the group decided to split future business between social and political activities. The author of the newsletter dutifully noted that the group's membership appeared to be growing rapidly and that thirty-five had indicated interest by the time of publication.[81]

By the September meeting of that year, the group decided on a new strategy. Because they all agreed that the support of teacher unions was essential to their cause, they would try to get Gay Teachers of Los Angeles members elected to union representative bodies. Then in reviewing political actions since the previous meeting, the group learned that one of their members, Hank Springer, had spoken before the board of directors of the local teachers union, the United Teachers of Los Angeles (UTLA), to discuss the need for support of lesbian and gay teachers. Though some board members initially resisted his logic, Springer reminded them that New York, Chicago, and San Francisco teachers unions already had passed resolutions offering such support. He also reiterated that the NEA and AFT both had gone on record with support of lesbian and gay teachers as well. Local union board members then softened a bit and Springer agreed to help draft a resolution that included sexual orientation in its nondiscrimination policy. The union's House of Representatives would vote on the resolution later.[82]

Soon the Gay Teachers of Los Angeles would see fruits of its political organizing efforts. By February 1977, the newsletter proudly announced that "Infiltration of GTLA into United Teachers of Los Angles has begun. Our GTLA President has been elected into the UTLA House of Representatives. Out of 250 UTLA House members, four whole people are in Gay Teachers of Los Angeles. Yes, four today. Tomorrow the whole House."[83] A month later, a resolution supporting the rights of lesbian and gay teachers was introduced to the Executive Board of the local teachers union, which then approved it unanimously. The resolution stated: "Just as parents and teachers want children to grow up and make their own choices about careers and philosophies, UTLA recognizes the rights of teachers to choose from a variety of lifestyles. Part of that choice may be a pattern of sexual activity which is thought by some to be unconventional. UTLA supports the rights of teachers to fair treatment regardless of sexual orientation or life style. UTLA believes in a policy of 'live and let live,' a policy which is the essence of a free people."[84] In April, the resolution passed with 95 percent of the members of the House approving.[85]

By the late spring of 1977, the newsletter of the young Gay Teachers of Los Angeles boasted a circulation of ninety-two, a number that continued growing during the turbulent years ahead. Members marched in the annual Los Angeles Gay Pride Parade, sporting an attractive banner, a canine member, and numerous supporters who joined them along the route.[86]

Beyond covering these encouraging developments, the newsletter also began mentioning Anita Bryant and her campaign 3,000 miles away to overturn the new Miami nondiscrimination ordinance that included sexual orientation. The newsletter noted: "On March 8, Anita Bryant said on nationwide television that homosexual teachers were teaching children how to be homosexuals and therefore should be fired."[87] LGBT teachers in Los Angeles, and indeed around the country, would follow

Bryant's campaign over the coming months both with alarm as well as a sense of the inevitability and justness of their own efforts, a belief that momentum was on their side.

In the meantime, LGBT educators formed associations in other urban areas around the country. Eric Rofes organized the Boston Area Gay and Lesbian Schoolworkers in May 1977.[88] A Philadelphia organization started during the summer of 1977. These groups were joined quickly by other organizations in Denver, Oregon, Texas, Maryland, and Melbourne, Australia. Camaraderie and cooperation among these groups fortified them as they eventually confronted the reality of Bryant's increasingly powerful campaign against LGBT school workers.

Late in 1976, Ruth Shack, a Miami school board administrator as well as civil rights and women's movement activist, won a seat on the Dade County Metro Commission. Soon after, she agreed to introduce an amendment to the local civil rights ordinance that included the language "affectional or sexual preference." This would have protected lesbian, gay, and bisexual persons against discrimination in employment, housing, and public accommodations. The Metro Commission unanimously agreed to move the amendment forward and scheduled a public meeting. A second reading would follow after which the revised ordinance would become law.[89]

At this point, Robert Brake, a conservative Catholic, learned about the amendment. He feared that it would require schools, like the parochial school his children attended, to hire openly homosexual teachers. He understood that one of the only ways to overturn the vote of the Metro Commission was to gather 10,000 names on a petition, which would then bring the matter to a public vote.[90]

Anita Bryant, another Miami resident, also learned about the amendment. Bryant, the beauty queen whose singing career had netted her several gold records, numerous television appearances, a role as Florida orange juice spokesperson, and a prominent broadcasting position with the Orange Bowl, was also a devout southern Baptist. She recounted how she first heard the news:

> Word came to our pastor that there was a proposed ordinance in Miami which I thought, if passed, would give special privileges to homosexuals. . . . He noted the effect this ordinance would have on private and religious schools. I suddenly started to realize what he was saying. The thought of known homosexuals teaching my children especially in a religious school bothered me. . . . All of a sudden I began to see that God doesn't tolerate a lot of things that people say they are willing to tolerate "in love." I couldn't say no to God when His Word is so plain.[91]

Bryant called Ruth Shack, who, coincidentally, was married to Dick Shack, Bryant's booking agent. Bryant warned Ruth Shack that she was condemning herself to damnation by proposing the expanded language for the nondiscrimination ordinance. Then Bryant attended the public meeting on the amendment to the ordinance, along with Brake and hundreds of other religious conservatives bussed from around the area. Bryant had prepared a brief speech with the assistance of a team of religious leaders united in their fear of the amendment. After Bryant delivered her speech, to powerful effect, Brake came over to her, introduced himself, and asked her to lead the petition drive. A few weeks later, Bryant and her followers delivered 64,304 signatures, several times more than needed to force a public referendum.[92]

In January 1977, Bryant appeared on Jim Bakker's nationally broadcast Christian television show, *The PTL Club*. Later, Bakker dubbed her appearance "the bombshell that exploded over America." A month later, she booked an appearance on Pat Robertson's *700 Club,* another popular conservative Christian program. Each of these appearances apparently resulted in the heaviest positive viewer mail experienced by these programs. Consequently, national contributions poured into her "Save Our Children" campaign.[93]

As the campaign wore on, Bryant gathered even greater support when she raised the specter of a "national homosexuality bill." She described the threat: "The hurt in my heart and the agony in my soul were of such intensity that when I heard . . . the news of a national homosexual bill similar to the one in Dade County, all I could do was cry. This bill, HR2998, would have had the effect of making it mandatory nationwide to hire known practicing homosexuals in public schools and in other areas."[94] Although the Miami ordinance concerned housing, public accommodations, and protection from job discrimination on account of sexual or affectional orientation, Bryant clearly focused on what she regarded as the chief problem: lesbian and gay teachers in schools and their supposed recruitment among children. She explained, "First, public approval of admitted homosexual teachers could encourage more homosexuality by inducing pupils into looking upon it as an acceptable life-style. And second, a particularly deviant-minded teacher could sexually molest children."[95] These points described the central mission of her crusade.

Early in Bryant's "Save Our Children" campaign, lesbian and gay leaders did not take her seriously. The Metro Commission had been completely supportive of the amendment adding their rights. Cities around the country had taken up similar measures and passed them. Even up until a month before the vote, gay rights supporters expressed mild confidence that their rights would be preserved because, as the *Miami Herald* reported, a poll showed 42 percent in favor of the gay rights amendment, 33 percent opposed, and the rest undecided.[96] Besides, as one writer for the *Lesbian Tide* explained:

> At first it seemed comical. The same day the Dade County (Florida) Commissioners passed a pro-gay rights ordinance, singer Anita Bryant led a protest before the Commission pledging she would overturn their "evil" decision to prohibit discrimination against gays. . . . An obsolete singing career, followed by years of pushing orange juice on national television, coupled with her role as back up vocal to Billy Graham, Bryant's image was not one to strike fear into the heart. Rivaling the Lennon Sisters for blandness, Anita Bryant seemed laughable when she started talking about "men wearing dresses" teaching in public schools, and "the devastation of the moral fiber of the youth of America." Her ignorance of homosexuality was so complete, her prejudice so simplistic, she seemed a ludicrous parody of 1950s style American "womanhood"; a sort of "Ozzie & Harriet" gone mad.[97]

Gay activists realized, though, that staggering sums of money poured into Bryant's "Save Our Children" campaign from Christian conservatives all over the country. With this largess, Bryant's forces ran television commercials in late spring that opened with wholesome clips of the Orange Bowl Parade with its marchers, twirlers, and beauty queens—and then abruptly switched to footage of a San Francisco Gay Pride parade. The announcer intoned: "In San Francisco, when they take to the streets, it's a parade of homosexuals. Men hugging other men. Cavorting with little boys. Wearing dresses and makeup. The same people who turned San Francisco into a hotbed of homosexuality . . . want to do the same thing to Dade." A newspaper ad read: "This recruitment of our children is absolutely necessary for the survival and growth of homosexuality—for since homosexuals cannot reproduce, they must recruit, must freshen their ranks. . . . And who qualifies as a likely recruit: a 35-year-old father or mother of two . . . or a teenage boy or girl who is surging with sexual awareness?"[98]

These commercials and ads took a devastating toll on voter support. With weeks remaining, even though ordinance supporters led opponents by nearly 2 to 1, few supporters seemed likely to turn out to vote. Bryant's supporters, however, could not be stopped.

During the evening of the vote, Bryant's supporters celebrated a resounding 2-to-1 victory—the opposite of polling results from a few weeks earlier. Meanwhile, gay liberation activists mourned and struggled to find hope in the sweeping upset. Reportedly a number of lesbians and gay men in the Miami area were fired or suspended the next day. Many others around the country feared what might happen to them because they had risked coming out to resist Bryant's efforts.[99] Two weeks after Bryant's victory, Robert Hillsborough, a thirty-three-year-old man who lived in San Francisco, enjoyed the evening with his longtime partner. On his way home, a gang of youths stabbed Hillsborough fifteen times in the chest and face, yelling "Faggots! Faggots!"[100]

Bryant, however, faced her own backlash. Nationwide supporters of lesbian and gay liberation successfully campaigned against the products she endorsed, the television shows on which she appeared, and other events for which she provided entertainment. She became a highly controversial figure to her previous sponsors. NBC eventually replaced her as host of the Orange Bowl parade.[101] In the days and weeks following the Miami defeat for the gay liberation movement, lesbian and gay communities staged marches around the country. Annual gay pride parades boasted record numbers. New lesbian and gay liberation organizations emerged and membership in others exploded.[102] What worried most, though, was that Bryant would take her campaign on the road and launch similar efforts in other states, perhaps even the nation.

Bryant had found a great vulnerable spot in the gay liberation movement: lesbian and gay adults who work with youth—particularly teachers. As long as the public generally believed that homosexuals molested and recruited children, regardless of the evidence to the contrary, then campaigns like "Save Our Children" could become common fare. A Gallup poll conducted within a month of the June 7 Miami referendum underscored the point. It indicated that even though the majority of the 2,000 persons surveyed believed that homosexuals should have equal rights in job opportunities, 65 percent objected to their serving as elementary school teachers.[103]

Lesbian and gay liberation activists would muster their strength in the wake of the Miami ordinance vote. Despite the immense risks involved, a growing number of lesbian and gay teachers also would organize during the next few years to agitate for an end to school employment discrimination. Bryant had raised the stakes not only in Florida, but also across the nation. California would become the next front in the larger battle. By this time, everyone clearly understood that the increasingly organized Christian Right regarded LGBT teachers as the most politically charged facet of the larger gay liberation movement. LGBT teachers effectively had become the wedge issue that divided public support for gay civil rights. Until lesbian and gay activists confronted the child molestation bugaboo directly, conservative political groups would continue to exploit this vulnerability in order to roll back gay rights.

CHAPTER 7

How Sweet It Is!

A nita Bryant and her supporters gathered in a hotel ballroom to watch the returns from the Miami-Dade ordinance vote. Her guests included California Senator John Briggs, a supporter who had flown in for the festivities. Briggs took pleasure in the emerging landslide vote. "We won! We won!" he told a reporter from KQED, a San Francisco television station. Briggs did not realize it at the time, but that reporter was Randy Shilts, a gay man and former reporter for *The Advocate* who subsequently authored several landmark volumes on pivotal events in gay history. Briggs told Shilts that night that the Miami-Dade victory would aid him in his gubernatorial bid to unseat Governor Jerry Brown. Briggs observed that proportionately as many voters had turned out for a mere referendum as had for the last California governor's race. He described the demographics of California and Miami-Dade as similar, each with significant populations of religious fundamentalists and homosexuals. He indicated that if he were to campaign against homosexuality, he would go from a long shot to a contender for the governorship. He would begin by introducing a bill in the legislature to prohibit homosexuals from teaching. The legislature, he surmised, would refuse to consider it—in which case he would bring the matter to a public referendum like the one he celebrated that night with Bryant.[1] One week later, Bryant flew to California to support Briggs as he launched his new initiative.[2]

When Briggs returned to California, he quickly introduced a resolution commending Bryant on her Miami campaign, but the Senate Rules Committee refused to allow floor debate on the measure. Then, on June 14, 1977, with police escort, Briggs approached the steps of the San Francisco City Hall where he announced his measure to remove openly homosexual teachers from California schools. Briggs did not choose his hometown of Fullerton, or the state capitol, or even the most populous city in the state. Instead, he introduced his measure in the heart of San Francisco, which he considered "in a captured nation status and wanting to be liberated" from a teeming population of homosexuals. As hoped, journalists, camera crews, and hundreds of vocal gay activists awaited his arrival. He started speaking, but angry shouts of "Stop the New Hitler Now" easily overpowered his words. Barely above the din, Briggs declared that "normal" people should be heard, too. Perhaps as a small concession to gay activists, he explained that his bill would not deny homosexuals the right to housing, jobs, or their sexual lifestyle. Instead, it simply would keep "children from being exposed to homosexual teachers." His voice hardly audible, he quickly finished his remarks and moved toward his waiting car. Immediately he tripped and fell—after which protesters taunted him even more aggressively. Police escorts quickly helped him back into his car and he sped away.[3]

Over the next two months, gay activists and Briggs's supporters alike kept a relatively low profile on the antigay teacher measure as they waited for a Supreme Court decision in the case of James Gaylord, the Tacoma, Washington, teacher dismissed for supposed "immorality." If the Supreme Court decided in Gaylord's favor, then the Briggs Initiative likely would be deemed unconstitutional. On the other hand, if the Supreme Court ruled against Gaylord, the decision probably would inflame public opinion further against the rights of lesbian and gay teachers. Meanwhile, Jean O'Leary, co-director of the National Gay Task Force, concluded, "One thing I know for sure is that in the next two years the focus of debate over gay rights is going to be on teachers and students. . . . It's a hot, rising issue." Not only had Bryant scored a lopsided victory in Miami, but other cities like Wichita and Eugene similarly considered dropping new antidiscrimination ordinances protecting lesbians and gay men. Rhetoric against the supposed threats of homosexual schoolteachers topped the headlines in each case. Briggs, however, demonstrated a particular flair for conjuring sensational images to drive home his points. He taunted, "Believe it or not, right now in California a teacher can stand up in the classroom, say he is homosexual and introduce his wife, Harry, and not a single thing can be done about it. . . . The bottom line in the initiative, if it passes, is that if you lead a homosexual lifestyle—preaching it, practicing it or showing up in drag at gay bars—and your students find out about it, a school board may conduct hearings to consider your dismissal. At present it can't." As Briggs would explain repeatedly over the course of the campaign, his measure would not penalize lesbian and gay teachers who *hid* their sexual orientation. He sought instead to penalize teachers who *publicly* pronounced their sexual orientation—in gay pride parades, at rallies, to the media, through LGBT teacher organizations, and by word of mouth.[4] He wanted all visible and activist LGBT educators to return to the closet.

By this time, the rapidly emerging issue of gay rights attracted the attention of diverse professional and civil rights organizations. Among them, the American Bar Association decided to consider gay rights during its annual meeting in August 1977. Delegates introduced the following resolution: "Resolved, that the American Bar Association urges Congress, the states, and municipal governments to enact legislation prohibiting discrimination against homosexuals in housing, employment, and public accommodations." A distinguished panel of speakers lined up to speak for the resolution, including the U.S. attorney general, the president of the American Psychiatric Association, and Michael Greene, a gay former elementary school teacher from New York. Greene explained, "The whole question of whether or not homosexuals should be allowed in the classroom is academic. We *are* in the classroom, in virtually every school in the country, teaching effectively at every level in both public and private schools." He argued that the central issue instead concerned whether or not homosexuals could claim their identities openly while retaining their teaching positions. However, forcing lesbian and gay teachers to remain secretive about their sexual orientation essentially damaged them psychologically. Dismissing teachers because of their religious, political, or social views, Greene argued, remained a highly problematic practice. He reminded listeners that only a few decades ago, "female teachers in the New York City public school system were absolutely prohibited from marrying." Though this seemed ludicrous to listeners in 1977 in light of the significant presence of married women teachers, Greene argued that so too would the practice of dismissing homosexual teachers appear unconscionable to future generations. Although Greene reported that members of the American Bar Association seemed sympathetic, they tabled the resolution for action later in the year.[5] Meanwhile, the Supreme Court decided not to consider the Gaylord case, which meant that the battle in California over the Briggs Initiative would receive neither boost nor hindrance from the nation's highest court. Activists on both sides of the issue then began mobilizing.

On August 3, 1977, Briggs staged a press conference during which he announced that the "California Save Our Children" campaign would seek 312,000 petition signatures. This would remove the decision from legislators and instead place it directly in the hands of voters in a popular referendum—like the Miami Metro referendum. The California attorney general then needed to frame the legal language for the referendum by mid-September, after which Briggs would have 150 days to gather the signatures. The *Lesbian Tide* reported that because the California attorney general planned to run against Briggs in the June 1978

Republican gubernatorial primary, he probably felt no urgency about moving Briggs's proposal through the process. The *Tide* also contended that Briggs's measure might fail on legal grounds because it was "hopelessly unconstitutional."[6]

In California's largest cities, gay liberation advocates started preparing for a major fight. Although Briggs's measure might be dismissed for technical or legal reasons, early activists wanted to take no chance. The Reverend Troy Perry, a prominent gay spokesperson who also had established the gay-oriented Universal Fellowship of Community Churches, launched a hunger strike to raise money for the effort. Determined to raise $100,000, Perry drank only water until his goal was reached—sixteen days later.[7] The Gay Teachers and School Workers Coalition immediately called on all teachers to build support networks with teachers around the state.[8] The group organized a media team specifically to work with journalists and reporters because "in the past others, both straight and gay have presumed to speak for us; we will speak for ourselves." Although the Gay Teachers and School Workers Coalition enjoyed membership both of lesbians and gay men, several women organized the Lesbian Caucus to assure that the public heard their views. This strategy also made sense to the lesbian school workers who lived as separatists. The Gay Teachers and School Workers Coalition formed an education committee to challenge "the lies and myths surrounding gay lifestyles and most especially the outrageous stereotypes of those gays who work with children in whatever the capacity." The speakers' bureau sent members to a wide variety of civic groups requesting their services. And finally, the Gay Teachers and School Workers Coalition pressured the influential AFT to go on record in full support of lesbian and gay teachers at this particularly challenging moment.[9]

The long-standing efforts of the Gay Teachers and School Workers Coalition and allied groups around the country such as the New York Gay Teachers Association began paying off. In October 1977, the AFT released an official position statement on the Briggs Initiative—one that left no doubt about its stake in the battle. Don Liles, Executive Vice President of the AFT wrote:

> Every individual and organization in California concerned with quality education at all levels should take an unequivocal position opposing the Briggs initiative, the provisions of which would launch a campaign in our schools reminiscent of the red witch-hunts of the late unlamented 1950's.
>
> Because of the initiative, California is about to become a massive test of human rights in a renewed struggle going on in America, as a result of resurgence of the radical right. The issues singled out are: equality for women, abortion, school desegregation, public employees bargaining

rights, academic freedom, freedom of the press, gay rights, and federally financed child-care assistance.

The radical right has found that one of the most successful tools is the conversion of civil concerns into moral issues, cloaked in the symbol of the "American family." The easiest issue for mustering broad-based support for the rest of the radical right's campaign is the issue of gay rights.

Senator Briggs has chosen to attack gay women and men, and has singled out a minority within a minority: gay educators. He has shrewdly found a "sitting duck" issue, but his initiative is merely the first in a series of major "moral crusades" supported by the radical right.

The Briggs initiative is dangerous for the following reasons:

1. Any educator anywhere, anytime, would be vulnerable to charges, if he or she participated in (or countenanced) any mention of homosexuality that did not judge it as sin, crime, and/or sickness. Any educator could be accused of "advocating, soliciting, imposing, encouraging or promoting of private or public homosexual acts directed at, or likely to come to the attention of school children and/or other employees." One signed complaint by anyone—colleague, student, parent, etc.—would trigger a hearing by the school board.

2. The initiative endangers academic freedom because it would establish in the Education Code that a significant area of human behavior must be prejudged and that educators must serve as uncritical indoctrinators of a single view of a behavioral choice central to the healthy development of every human being.

3. The initiative would officially deprive a minority of civil and human rights and would encourage a majority to tyrannize a minority, thus endangering the rights of *all* minorities in California.

The initiative would officially establish a climate in California schools and colleges dominated by intimidation and oppression in which all educators and students would become informers on one another.

The consequent witch-hunts would be a tragic spectacle in which "guilt by association" would destroy teaching careers, whether or not the accused is exonerated.[10]

Liles thus made it clear that the AFT viewed the Briggs Initiative not just as a campaign targeted at lesbian and gay educators, but rather as a broad attack on the rights of all teachers. Because of the sweeping language of the initiative, *any* teacher who publicly supported the rights of homosexuals could be scrutinized and dismissed. Perhaps of even greater concern to the teachers union leader, if Briggs's measure passed, its terms would override union contracts. Teachers union members—and indeed, union members across professions—quickly suspected that Briggs intended to weaken unions with the measure. His previous anti-union stances seemed to confirm this possibility.[11]

Finally, Liles indicated that Briggs mainly focused on lesbian and gay teachers because, as "sitting ducks," they faced a nearly irresolvable dilemma: to fight the Briggs Initiative, lesbian and gay educators needed to identify themselves publicly; however, should the initiative pass, educators who had identified themselves publicly could and probably would be dismissed. The threat of job loss already loomed so large that only a relatively small proportion of lesbian and gay educators in California joined LGBT teacher organizations, marched in pride parades, or identified themselves among colleagues, students, and parents. If the initiative passed, that fear would increase substantially.

Gay activists also experienced some initial reticence about fully supporting the rights of LGBT teachers. Some gay activists did not want to "liberate" education without LGBT teachers openly fighting for themselves. An important part of being in the movement was, as the dismissed Maryland teacher, Joe Acanfora, had observed, "If you are homosexual, say it—and get your rights anyway." However, educators notoriously resisted "saying it" because most believed they would *not* get their rights anyway. School districts around the country consistently demonstrated why. For example, the Iowa Civil Liberties Union released a survey indicating that 83 percent of Iowa superintendents surveyed indicated that they would not hire a gay teacher.[12] Also, gay activists understood quite clearly that no matter how much credible scientific evidence they offered to suggest that homosexuals molested children proportionately far less often than heterosexual men, the linkage remained strong in public thought. Anita Bryant had capitalized successfully on this potent association in Miami—and she attempted to strengthen it further. To defend lesbian and gay teachers successfully, opponents of the Briggs Initiative would need to confront the gay child molestation bugaboo squarely. They also would need to convince voters that lesbian and gay teachers did not otherwise harm the gender and sexual development of their students.

Finally, LGBT activists could reach no agreement about the most effective strategy to employ. Most believed they would lose, but that campaigning hard might soften the ground for the future. Some argued that voters might respond best if they viewed the Briggs measure as a civil rights issue. Surely persons of color, women, and other marginalized groups would recognize common elements in the fight for basic rights. Others believed that the real issue in voters' minds concerned homosexuality—and not the specific employment rights of LGBT teachers. To these activists, the best way to gain public support lay in helping voters understand homosexuality better and opening a larger discussion about sexuality in our society. Essentially, they maintained that skirting the real issue made no sense. The best path led right to the core of voters' fears and concerns. Then a few leaders contended that LGBT leaders possessed little clout with voters, so they suggested raising money and hiring allies to conduct the bulk of the campaign. Most activists overwhelmingly rejected this hands-off strategy as playing into the oppression of LGBT persons and accepting their second-class status.[13]

While activists planned, help in fighting Briggs's measure immediately arrived from unanticipated supporters. The well-respected national education reporter, John Merrow, wrote a featured article for the September 1977 issue of *Parents' Magazine*. In his provocatively titled piece, "Gay Sex in the Schools," Merrow cited evidence supplied by recent studies of child sexual abuse. He concluded that "my way of answering the question, what do homosexual teachers do to children, is: nothing in particular by virtue of their homosexuality, neither by inclining children toward homosexuality, nor by sexual seduction or molestation. Despite what many parents may fear, homosexuals are almost never child abusers or child molesters. Those crimes are nearly always committed by 'straight' males."[14] A popular columnist wrote in the *Saturday Review,* "As more communities discover that gay teachers are no more prone to abuse their students than straight teachers, and that when they do, the abuse is much more likely to be rooted in hostility or stupidity than in homosexuality, the question of gays in the classroom may look as quaint as the prohibitions of the Twenties against women teachers who smoked or kept late hours. The question then was not homo or hetero, but whether the person who entered the classroom could have any sexual feelings at all."[15]

Other national figures weighed in to express their indifference or even their contempt for LGBT educators, however. "I know that there are homosexuals who teach, and the children don't suffer," said then-President Jimmy Carter. Signaling his intention to stay out of the issue, he continued, "But this is a subject I don't particularly want to involve myself in."[16] The extremely conservative Max Rafferty, who had served for years as California Superintendent of Public Instruction, also joined the fray. During the early 1970s, Rafferty had relished his statewide duties authorizing the dismissal of teachers deemed homosexual. Despite the fact that courts struck down California's sodomy law in May 1975, Rafferty argued in a 1977 issue of *Phi Delta Kappan,* the widely circulated magazine for professional educators, that

> Sodomy is against the law everywhere I've ever been or heard of, and its illegality alone should make the matter moot. . . . The ancient Jews who wrote the Torah used an interesting term to identify the act of sodomy:

"confusion." That's what it is, you know. Confusion of the sex roles. Confusion of the biological purpose behind the sex act. Confusion of masculinity with femininity. Confusion thrice confounded. . . .

For eight clangorous and combative years, I chaired the statewide credentials commission of the most populous state in the nation. Our job in large part was to decide each month whether certain teachers were morally fit to be allowed to teach in California schools. And from the beginning, I do assure you, we took for granted the self-evident proposition that a homosexual in a school job was as preposterously out of the question as a heroin mainliner working in the local drugstore. . . .

I am asked: "Would homosexual teachers influence children?" My answer: "Of course they would. All teachers influence children. Good teachers have a good influence on children. Bad teachers have a bad influence on children. And homosexual teachers have a homosexual influence on children. So what's new?". . . Teachers colleges should weed out the sexually abnormal before they qualify for the credential.

School principals and superintendents should refuse to rehire probationary teachers who turn out to be abnormal despite the efforts of preliminary screening. And no one who suffers from this kind of abnormality should be recommended for tenure.

Don't tell me it can't be done. I've been a school administrator for 30 years and I know darned well it can. I repeat: No one has the "right" to be a schoolteacher. It's a privilege, dearly bought and stringently conferred.[17]

Rafferty's closing thought lacked subtlety: "Can't we really find something more important educationally to spend our time and energy on? If not, how about a rousing *Kappan* on 'techniques of defecation?'"[18] Although Rafferty professed the unimportance of the issue, he had devoted a significant and visible portion of his career as California Superintendent of Public Instruction pursuing allegedly homosexual teachers, even while a wide variety of other challenging education issues begged for attention.[19]

Also, clearly Rafferty found disturbing what he considered the "confusion of masculinity with femininity." With this statement he indicated that he shared the long-standing view from the 1940s and 1950s that homosexuals supposedly could be identified by cross-gender behaviors and characteristics. To Rafferty, gender and sexual orientation marched in parallel. "Straight" persons appeared and acted in accordance with their gender, which in turn aligned with their biological sex. Homosexuals, however, blurred and crossed the lines. In addition, Rafferty maintained that one of the fundamental problems with homosexuals concerned their "confusion of sex roles." By this reasoning, lesbians and gay men necessarily would wish to step out of their traditional gender-linked realms and into another. Gay men might wish to teach young children and lesbians might foreseeably pursue administrative work, putting them in positions of authority over men. To Rafferty, these various vexations shared a common root: homosexuality.

Gay activists understood quickly enough that they had a significant fight on their hands. Even though Briggs, Bryant, Rafferty, and other opponents of the rights of LGBT educators frequently offered arguments that could not be substantiated, they tapped a powerful sentiment among many voters. Such leaders basically played on voters' fear of homosexuality, about which most knew quite little. When reporters asked Briggs point-blank if he knew of any circumstances in California schools when homosexual teachers had cross-dressed, solicited among their students, or promoted homosexuality in classrooms, he reportedly held up what he called a "recruitment booklet," a pamphlet for students that answered their questions about being gay. He never offered any other evidence. When Ellen Broidy and Jan Zobel, two members of the Gay Teachers and School Workers Coalition, appeared on a San Jose television news show with Briggs, Broidy thought things went well at first. The interviewer asked reasonable questions that both Broidy and Zobel handled skillfully. Then Briggs requested permission to "answer." Broidy recounted that Briggs flew into a tirade, using phrases like "sick" and "militant lifestyle." She concluded, "There was little pretense of rational thought on his part during this concluding portion of the show. The demagogue of fear came across loud and clear."[20] At this early stage, gay activists argued, "We can't look at this thing rationally. . . . California is a big state and we have our share of hysterics." The only way to respond, they contended, was to prepare for "our biggest battle yet."[21]

That battle took shape quickly. Briggs needed to produce 312,000 signatures by January 1978 to place his initiative in a public referendum. Gay activists feared that if popular vote decided the matter, Briggs would win overwhelmingly. Instead, they hoped technicalities or a ruling on the measure's unconstitutionality would spare them.[22] Preparing for the worst, gay activists organized a statewide conference in Sacramento in September. At this conference, participants unanimously agreed that they should invest fully in campaigning against the Briggs Initiative. Subsequently, they organized a larger conference in mid-December on the campus of the University of Southern California. During this event, activists from around the state coordinated their strategies. They arranged speak outs that featured such notables as the eminent researcher, Evelyn Hooker, and the feminist, Gloria Steinem.

Participants in the state activists' caucus articulated their core principles for the campaign against Briggs's handiwork. These key activists agreed that strong links existed between oppressions directed at "third world" persons (persons of color), women, lesbians and gay men, and other groups. To work against the oppression of LGBT persons, activists pledged to fight racism, sexism, and other oppressions. The Gay Teachers and School Workers Coalition sent five of its members to the meeting. One teacher reported that "the plenary session was an amazing experience. . . . Over 40 resolutions were presented and passed, mostly by large majorities. The resolutions dealt with many issues, including the rights of Gay people, Third World people, women and other oppressed groups. It was encouraging to hear that most people at the conference agreed that there is a connection between all these oppressions and that it's important not to treat the oppression of Gay people as a single isolated issue; we need to support other struggles." Attendees agreed on a representative structure with racial, sex, and geographical balance.[23] This development both recognized and countered a prevailing tendency in many LGBT organizations in which whites dominated numerically, led proceedings, and demonstrated little commitment to or understanding of issue important to persons of color. Attendees agreed that resisting one oppression meant understanding and resisting kindred oppressions.

The *Lesbian Tide* further reported that the Briggs Initiative posed such a serious threat that, despite long-standing differences, lesbians and gay men were beginning to work together. Their reporter quoted one lesbian activist who said, "I'm a separatist" who agrees with the necessity of working with gay men "on limited projects of mutual benefit. . . . After all, if we're all put in concentration camps, there can't be Lesbian Nation." The reporter concluded that "the women's caucus agreed that the majority of men at the [state activists'] conference were making an effort to be friendly and non-sexist." Gay and lesbian conference attendees eagerly passed resolutions assuring support of the Equal Rights Amendment, full custody rights for lesbian mothers, lesbian and gay representatives in media and other public events where possible—or only lesbians if only one representative were permitted, and co-sexual conveners at meetings.[24]

Meanwhile, Briggs's campaign encountered early problems. One Briggs worker allegedly encouraged signatories to forge their names. Briggs accused the campaign worker of being a plant by gay activists. Briggs then missed his January deadline for producing 312,000 signatures. Finally, however, on May 1, 1978, Briggs filed over 500,000 signatures—which placed the referendum on the November 1978 ballot.[25] The official wording of the referendum, released by the California attorney general, read:

One of the most fundamental interests of the State is the establishment and the preservation of the family unit. Consistent with this interest is the State's duty to protect impressionable youth from influences which are antithetical to this vital interest. This duty is particularly compelling when the state undertakes to educate the youth and by law, requires them to be exposed to the state's chosen educational environment throughout their formative years.

A schoolteacher, teacher's aide, school administrator or counselor has a professional duty directed exclusively towards the moral as well as intellectual, social and civic development of young and impressionable students.

As a result of continued close and prolonged contact with schoolchildren, a teacher, teacher's aide, school administrator or counselor becomes a role model whose words, behavior and actions are likely to be emulated by students coming under his or her care, instruction, supervision, administration, guidance and protection.

For these reasons the state finds a compelling interest in refusing to employ and in terminating the employment of a schoolteacher, a teacher's aide, a school administrator or a counselor, subject to reasonable restrictions and qualifications who engages in public homosexual activity and/or public homosexual conduct directed at, or likely to come to the attention of, schoolchildren or other school employees.

This proscription is essential since such activity and conduct undermines that state's interest in preserving and perpetuating the conjugal family unit.[26]

By this time, Briggs knew he would not receive the Republican nomination for California governor. However, he still harbored lofty political aspirations for the future—and he reportedly hoped that his initiative would earn the support he needed. To file the half a million petition signatures, he chose to return to the steps of the San Francisco City Hall because, as he explained, "it is the moral garbage dump of homosexuality in this country." The last time he had spoken there, he had tripped and fallen in front of hundreds of protestors. This time, only around forty demonstrators greeted him—and they kept their distance.[27] From this point forward, Briggs's measure would bear the official title of "Proposition 6," which would appear on the November 7 ballot for all Californians.

Despite legal challenges and petition irregularities, when Briggs filed the half-million petition signatures, many gay activists, though preparing themselves for this eventuality, voiced disbelief and pessimism. The editors of *The Advocate* gave in to their sense of foreboding in an unusual lead editorial in the June 1978 issue:

> Five hundred thousand Californians signed petitions to take away teachers' rights to privacy and freedom of speech. The chief proponent of this outrage, State Senator John Briggs, filed the signatures May 1 in San Francisco and began the campaign by calling gay people "garbage."
>
> In the 10½ years *The Advocate* has been published, we pride ourselves in never knowingly telling you untruths, no matter how unpleasant the

facts have been. This is one of those times when the truth we have to report is very unpleasant. The bottom line is that it is most unlikely that the Briggs initiative can be defeated in this November's election. We shall have waged a good campaign if the vote ratio is less than the 2 to 1 majority against us that occurred in St. Paul and Miami. We may lose even in San Francisco. We can expect a multimillion-dollar media campaign of lies and hate directed at us. Some gay people probably will commit suicide under this onslaught of hate. Few gay Californians will not experience a lot of pain and anger between now and November. . . . There is not one example in history where a majority has voted for rights of a minority. Despite many people's false beliefs in right triumphing in democratic ways, history clearly shows that success for minority groups has been the result of patient, careful and sophisticated economic and political power applied skillfully and persuasively to rulers and legislatures, not to the votes of the masses. . . . Thanks to many of you, The Concerned Voters of California (CVC) financed an excellent voter survey in California. It told us many things. Among them, the most important is that, except for Boy and Girl Scout leaders, there is no profession Californians wish less open to gay people than teaching. Although they are willing to have us quietly in their midst in many ways, they don't want us near their children. Yes, I know we make superior teachers and that the only people for whom we might be role models are gay children. The public doesn't believe this truth. The issue is too emotional and there isn't time to change their minds. In an election campaign, our truth will have to compete with bigoted lies. Our enemies can and will outspend us, about 10 to 1. Voters who are at all confused will undoubtedly follow their emotional reaction. In short, John Briggs has struck at the weakest point in our line of defense.[28]

Despite the editor's sense of the futility of the anti-Briggs effort, gay activists and increasing numbers of writers for national media voiced support for defeating Proposition 6. *McCall's* ran an article titled, "Should Homosexuals be Allowed to Teach?" To prepare the story, reporters surveyed 1,300 school officials around the country and interviewed a number of others. Reporters gave the views of Meryl Friedman, co-spokesperson for the New York Gay Teachers Association, considerable weight in the piece, as they did for those of Drs. Jack Weinberg, president, and John Spiegel, former president of the American Psychiatric Association, both of whom supported the rights of lesbian and gay teachers. The authors indicated that clearly a "double standard" existed in teaching in one form or another over the past century. In describing the views of Max Rafferty, the authors wrote that he "went into paroxysms of indignation at merely being asked whether homosexuals should be allowed to teach." They reaffirmed the recent studies indicating that heterosexual men molested children proportionately far more often than gay men and lesbians. "The available record does not support parents' and school administrators' concern that homosexual teachers may seek to convert children by proselytizing, seduction or molestation. . . . The records indicate that child molestation is more often committed by heterosexuals." The piece concluded, "If only the issue could be freed of the exaggerated claims and irresponsible fear mongering, no rational obstacle should stand in the way of letting homosexuals remain and become teachers, subject to those controls and standards of behavior that the profession applies to all teachers."[29] In its monthly newsletter, the New York Gay Teachers Association reviewed the piece and deemed it "more reasonable than flashy."[30]

Around this time, *Psychology Today* ran a story describing the experiences of a gay teacher. Using the pseudonym, Michael Trent, the author wrote that he could not come out at work, which, he argued, exacted a tremendous psychological toll. If he were to reveal his sexual orientation, he probably would not be fired outright, but administrators, colleagues, and parents would do what they could to run him out. He might be removed from children by being forced into a central office desk job. If he refused to leave voluntarily, the stakes would rise. Every aspect of his work would be scrutinized closely—despite years of exceptional performance reviews. Parents would remove their children. He would be threatened physically and his property vandalized. "Finally, the children would lose respect for me, and I would lose all effectiveness."[31]

The *Ladies Home Journal* published the results of a poll of 800 junior and senior high school students around the country. According to the poll, Anita Bryant figured prominently in the thinking of adolescents—earning the honor of the famous female who makes teenagers "angriest" and making the list of persons who has "done the most damage to the world," a list led by Hitler.[32]

By early fall, editors of the *Los Angeles Times* registered their stance on Proposition 6. Although they considered the measure to be "so repugnant to basic American freedoms that we'd prefer to ignore it altogether," they decided to go on record early and strongly in opposition to it. In short, they described it as "an invasion of privacy, and a potential disruption of the education process. It's vicious and mean-spirited, too." If the issue were child molestation, they argued that sufficient laws already existed to remedy problems that might arise. On the contrary, to Proposition 6 supporters, the issue seemed to boil down to opposing homosexuality. Further, editors declared the initiative "so vaguely worded that it would subject teachers to sweeping allegations on baseless charges; it would dignify rumor and innuendo." Any child who disliked his or her teacher would have a powerful weapon for harassing them. For these and other reasons, the editors concluded that "the teachers deserve support now, and the protection of votes against Proposition 6 in November."[33]

As the battle over Proposition 6 played out in state and national media, gay activists worked intensely at the grassroots level. The recently established Lesbian Schoolworkers organized a demonstration supporting a San Francisco Board of Education resolution opposing Proposition 6.[34] Briggs had successfully staged a number of media events over the early months of the campaign, including speaking on television talk shows and participating in radio interviews. Members of the Gay Teachers and School Workers Coalition decided to protest outside radio and television stations each time Briggs made an appearance. Occasionally, such demonstrations netted activists the opportunity to choose a representative to debate Briggs on the air. "Anytime we can find out about a scheduled Briggs appearance we plan to be on hand to demand equal time, preferably with Briggs."[35]

Anita Bryant joined Briggs in working for Proposition 6. During the months after her successful "Save Our Children" campaign, Bryant formed a new group, Anita Bryant Ministries. Through this organization, she sought funds from a national audience of conservative Christians to support advertising and other efforts to assure passage of Briggs's handiwork. In one mailing to millions across the country, Bryant claimed:

> When the homosexuals burn the Holy Bible in public . . . how can I stand by silently? Dear Friend: I don't hate the homosexuals! But as a mother, I must protect my children from their evil influence. And I am sure you have heard about my fight here in Dade County, Florida—and nationwide—for the rights of my children and yours. But I had no idea my speaking out would lead to such frightening consequences: . . . ugly persecution at the hands of militant homosexual groups. . . . the attempted blacklisting of my career. . . . misguided individuals hounding me and my family—even when we go to church. All this, because I stood up for my children—as a mother—as an American—as a Christian. Then, when the militant homosexuals lost the public vote in Dade County, their friends in New England burned the Holy Bible! . . . That's why I am writing you today—because I cannot remain silent while radical, militant homosexuals are raising millions of dollars and waging a campaign for special privileges under the disguise of "civil rights". . . and they claim they are a legitimate minority group. Do you realize what they want? They want to recruit our school children under the protection of the laws of our land! . . . And remember, militant homosexuals want their sexual behavior and preference to be considered respectable and accepted by society. They want to recruit your children and teach them the virtues of becoming a homosexual. One militant homosexual group actually published a newsletter giving techniques to entice and recruit young men to commit unnatural sex acts. . . . I don't hate

the homosexuals. I love them enough to tell them the truth . . . But I insist they leave my children and your children alone. We must not give them the legal right to destroy the moral fiber of our families and our nation. . . . Shall I be silent? . . . If you want me to speak out, will you consider sending a special love gift to support the work of Anita Bryant Ministries? . . . I must depend on your $10 tax-deductible gift of love—or perhaps even $15 or $25 or $100, if these issues really shake you as they do me. . . . Will you help me stop the militant homosexuals?[36]

Along with this letter, Bryant enclosed her photo taken with her husband and four children. The millions of dollars raised through this and other solicitations paid for television and other advertisements similar to those employed by the "Save Our Children" campaign. Some of the funds supported centers around the state designed to "cure" homosexuals.[37] One gay activist in Des Moines, Iowa, used a decidedly low-budget means of countering Bryant's message, however. He smashed a cream pie in her face during a televised and subsequently much-publicized event— which ignited activists on both sides.[38]

Briggs and Bryant conveyed urgency to their contributors by conjuring images of wealthy gays raising millions of dollars to fund a major media blitz. Contrary to this portrayal, however, gay activists struggled to raise funds to mount a credible campaign. When one organization hosted a large fund-raising reception, reporters and photographers showed up to cover the event—which sent closeted guests fleeing. Wealthy allies who sponsored other receptions found that guests resisted attending because they dreaded being seen. Many supporters reportedly refused to wear buttons or place bumper stickers on their cars out of fear that if the measure passed, they might face retroactive punishment. Because the law decreed that political contributions of $50 or more must be reported to the secretary of state, gay activists typically collected checks of $49. Although gay activists had hoped to raise at least one million dollars to stage a credible media effort, they only collected around half this amount altogether.[39] And because many volunteers refused to disclose their identities fully, one activist observed, "We have the largest first-name volunteer list in the history of politics."[40]

Despite these formidable obstacles, momentum began shifting slightly against Proposition 6. During the 1978 annual summer meeting of its Representative Assembly, the NEA approved a resolution affirming its opposition to Proposition 6. The resolution also committed the NEA's legal and legislative resources to defeating this and similar measures.[41] Then in September, Wilson Riles, the California Superintendent of Public Instruction, announced that Proposition 6 served no useful purpose. "We have enough laws on the books to protect the youngsters," he argued.[42] A number of prominent state politicians across the political spectrum registered their opposition to Proposition 6 as well, including former governor Ronald Reagan, San Francisco Mayor Willie Brown, and Governor Jerry Brown.[43] Entertainers including Cher, Jane Fonda, John Travolta, Norman Lear, and other celebrities attended fundraisers to defeat the Briggs Initiative—even though many notable LGBT entertainers stepped away from the spotlight out of fear of career ruin.[44] In mid-October, the archbishop of San Francisco went on record against Proposition 6.[45] The Los Angeles Board of Education also officially and unanimously opposed the measure.[46]

As the statewide battle over Proposition 6 entered the final weeks, activities on both sides reached a climax. Gay activists handed out leaflets, bought advertising space in newspapers, and purchased radio and television spots. The "No on 6" organization produced and placed two commercials on prime-time television. One spot featured a kindly older woman teacher who explained to viewers that although she had always believed in privacy rights, she could lose her job for saying that. Another showed a hearty young male teacher and father of three children who made a similar pitch.[47] Beyond the media, activists countered Briggs wherever and whenever he appeared, pointedly refuting his arguments. Poll results showed unmistakable momentum building for the anti-Briggs effort. The *Los Angeles Times* reported rapidly declining support for the initiative. In August the margin was for Proposition 6—41 percent, against—49 percent, and undecided—10 percent; in September, for Proposition 6—38 percent, against—52 percent, undecided—10 percent; and in October for Proposition 6—29 percent, against—62 percent, and undecided—9 percent.[48] Although activists hoped Proposition 6 might go down in defeat given these promising polling results, they also understood that the vote would hinge on who showed up. Miami polling had looked promising, too, but, at the last minute, thousands of committed ordinance opponents packed the polls.

Some of the most sensational events of the campaign included debates between John Briggs and proposition opponents, staged as the referendum approached. One televised debate broadcast in September featured Briggs and Claudia Norby, a lesbian activist assisted by Sandy Lowe, a gay man. Although Norby assumed the role as Briggs's primary debate opponent, cameramen rarely showed her face. Instead, they filmed Lowe—so the debate appeared to be primarily between two men with a woman's voice thrown in. One lesbian, writing for the *Sonoma SCLGA*, complained that this had become a typical pattern in the campaign to defeat the Briggs Initiative. Lesbians' substantial contributions were being marginalized at every turn, she argued. Even though other lesbians

sought to debate Briggs after this event, Briggs only chose gay male opponents, particularly Harvey Milk, the first openly gay man elected to the
San Francisco Board of Supervisors, and Larry Berner, a little-known
teacher from Healdsburg.[49] Milk and Briggs frequently tangled in high-
profile debates around the state. Briggs reeled off well-practiced lines
from cards that he carried. With great regularity, he charged that homosexuals accounted for a third of teachers in San Francisco and a fifth in
Los Angeles. "Most of them are in the closet, and frankly, that's where I
think they should remain." Hoping to inspire fear, Briggs alleged that
"homosexuals want your children. . . . They don't have any children of
their own. If they don't recruit children or very young people, they'd all
die away. They don't have any means of replenishing. That's why they
want to be teachers and be equal status and have those people serve as
role models and encourage people to join them." Milk, on the other hand,
responded to these serious and dogmatic accusations with incisive wit.
"How do you teach homosexuality—like French?" or "If it were true
that children mimicked their teachers, you'd sure have a helluva lot more
nuns running around."[50]

Briggs also debated Larry Berner several times. Berner, a shy, tall,
bearded, and well-liked second grade teacher, initially wanted no central
role in the "No on 6" effort. He had written an article in the *Sonoma
SCLGA* describing his experiences as a "spy" in the Briggs petition effort. When his article attracted broad attention, the parents of several
children in his class requested transfers. However, Berner enjoyed strong
support from colleagues and his school administration. Briggs learned of
Berner's activities and decided to make an example of him. Berner rose
to the challenge, though, deciding to fight Proposition 6 actively.[51] In
late October, Briggs came to Berner's hometown to debate him in a spectacle that attracted over half of the town's residents—as well as substantial media interest from around the state. The *Los Angeles Times* described the event as "strange" and "weird" because of colorful protests
outside as well as the heated rhetoric exchanged inside. During the
ninety-minute debate, Briggs charged that "we don't allow prostitutes to
teach. . . . You can't get married in the state of California if you're a
homosexual couple . . . If they're not good enough to get married, how
are we to support the notion that they're to serve as role models (for
schoolchildren) when they can't bear children themselves?" Briggs made
clear the importance he attached to heterosexual modeling for students.
After Briggs described the sexual activities of gay men, Berner countered, "Your mind is in the gutter. . . . The children at my school are not
obsessed with my sexuality, as you seem to be, senator." The *Los Angeles
Times* indicated that around two-thirds of those in attendance appeared

to be staunch Berner supporters who applauded his statements vigorously. In the end, Briggs denied that Proposition 6 would require schools
to get rid of all homosexual teachers. Instead, once again he maintained
that he only intended to purge the ones who came out or otherwise vo-
cally supported gay rights. Berner challenged Briggs convincingly, match-
ing him point for point, something Briggs had not anticipated. Berner
then became an instant celebrity among gay activists around the state.[52]

In the final days before the vote, national media ran powerful editori-
als encouraging Californians to strike down Proposition 6. The *New Republic* explained that Anita Bryant's "Bible-thumping bombast works
well on conservative voters with Dark Age attitudes about job discrimination and equal rights. The California vote will be the first statewide
poll on the issue, and its passage would be one of the most damaging and
ugly uses of referendum politics in recent memory."[53] The *Boston Globe*
quoted Briggs as declaring, "One-third of San Francisco's teachers are
homosexuals. I assume most of them are seducing young boys in toilets."
The *Globe's* report compared Briggs's effort to a tent-revival and described Briggs as a pariah among California's politicians.[54]

Briggs had hoped to air hard-hitting television ads during the final
weeks, but his campaign ran short of funds. He already had transferred
much of his funding for the Proposition 6 campaign from his unsuccess-
ful bid for the Republican nomination for governor. Then, during the fall,
contributions fell off. He fired his professional staff and instead placed
his son-in-law in charge of the effort. Reportedly he racked up $657,000
in debt, for which he mortgaged his house.[55]

On November 7, when voters filed into their polling places, they received the official voters' pamphlet explaining Proposition 6. At first, the
pamphlet warned voters that "the fiscal impact of the proposition would
depend on the total number of hearings initiated." Because the total number of cases to be brought potentially could be enormous, state fiscal
agents indicated, "we thus conclude that the proposition could result in
substantial costs to the state, school districts, and school employees due
to an increase in dismissal hearings, plus additional court costs to the
state and county governments." The pamphlet then offered brief statements both for and against the measure.[56]

As votes came in throughout the day, gay activists began celebrating.
By evening, reporters announced that Proposition 6 had gone down in a
resounding defeat—by a margin of 58 percent to 42 percent. Less than
two hours after the polls closed, Briggs conceded. Meanwhile, Los Angeles Mayor Tom Bradley triumphantly addressed a crowd of 3,000 lesbian and gay activists, telling them, "How sweet it is! You have put on
the greatest campaign ever seen in California, uniting all religions, all

parties, all minorities. You have carried the message to all. May this be a lesson that Briggs will never forget. The spirit of justice lives in California because of you." Briggs, however, vowed that he would reintroduce the same measure in two years with a better and stronger organization. This would be difficult, though, given that even his conservative home district rejected it.[57]

Over the weeks following the dramatic vote, activists and editorialists took stock of what had transpired. In assessing the aftermath, however, mainstream media did not call the overwhelming defeat of the bill a victory for lesbian and gay teachers—or even for LGBT rights. Instead, the *San Francisco Chronicle, Los Angeles Times,* and the Associated Press indicated that the defeat was more about resisting governmental interference in personal rights than about homosexuality.[58] A local station, KHJ, aired a similar view with an editorial explaining, "We at KHJ-TV believe that the reason such a majority of voters went against the measure was not necessarily great sympathy for homosexuals in our schools so much as it was a real antipathy for any laws which open the way to serous erosion of the hard won civil rights statutes. Clearly, many felt that this potential loss was greater than any present danger from the sexual preferences of school personnel."[59] An editorialist for *The Nation* argued that although both "Yes" and "No" forces in the Proposition 6 effort operated with the pretense that the issue mainly concerned LGBT teachers, instead he argued that the central and larger issue was about changing views toward homosexuality in this country. He summarized, "Gay Rights won a victory in the protection of homosexual schoolteachers. The movement won even more by further establishing homosexuality in American culture as a viable sexual alternative."[60]

In the final analysis, many voters did reject Proposition 6 because it threatened basic free speech rights. It would have provided a point of entry through which further restrictions on basic rights might pass. Although many Californians did not particularly like the thought of LGBT persons working in schools, they also recognized that this measure would have taken away rights from a targeted group of persons. They would not want LGBT persons to gain special rights, but they also did not especially want them to lose them, either. African American voters, the group that most strongly opposed the initiative, expressed grave concerns about a measure that targeted one group for oppression. Latino voters, however, largely supported Proposition 6. Some analysts concluded that this may have been due in part to the influence of rural Catholic churches that staunchly opposed homosexuality. Union members opposed Proposition 6 because it challenged the right of unions to negotiate contracts. For a number of voters, though, the Briggs initiative centrally concerned not basic rights, but homosexuality. The highly public debates inspired by the measure stimulated many to rethink what they thought they knew about persons who desire others of the same sex. And ironically, even though Briggs purportedly introduced the measure to protect students from exposure to homosexuality, the vigorous and very public discussions provoked by the referendum dramatically increased students' knowledge about LGBT persons.[61]

In a retrospective piece, the *San Francisco Examiner* reported that second grade teacher, Larry Berner, seemed much happier than he was when Proposition 6 loomed. When he dined in restaurants, he felt freer to hold hands with his male companions. "I don't need to worry any more about what people think of my being gay," he explained. "It's been a joyous experience, being out of the closet. I always expected that something horrible would happen to me if people knew, but the most amazing thing is that absolutely nothing has happened. I'm surviving beautifully." When one of his school board members, a minister, called him a "moral carcinogenic among the tender treasures of the heavenly Father," Berner responded, "That just cracked me up. It was so outrageous that anybody would say that about me."[62] Berner also decided that during the course of the Proposition 6 campaign, Briggs had defamed him by implying and stating outright that Berner could not be trusted with children. Berner eventually won a $10,000 judgment in a defamation lawsuit against Briggs. Berner explained, "I'm happy with the judgment that Briggs has admitted he damaged me. Maybe this will be a warning to other opportunists and politicians."[63]

Media reflection on the Briggs vote ended abruptly, however. On November 27, only twenty days after the referendum, San Francisco Supervisor Dan White assassinated Harvey Milk along with Mayor George Moscone. White, an anti-gay conservative, quickly confessed to the murders in which he saved a set of hollow-headed, exploding bullets for Milk, who had debated Briggs on a number of occasions. After the news broke, thousands of gay activists and their supporters filled the streets from Castro Street to City Hall, holding lit candles and moving slowly to the sound of a drum.[64] A jury handed White a light sentence: five years in prison and parole. It had accepted the defense argument that White's penchant for Twinkies and other junk food had contributed to his depression and the eventual murders.[65]

These proved to be painful months for Briggs as well. Reports emerged that he might face investigation by the IRS.[66] Then during November 1981, Briggs announced that he would not seek reelection. Echoing an earlier Nixon speech, Briggs said, "You won't have me to kick around any more." Explaining that he was burned out, he told reporters that he planned to invest in real estate and do consulting work.[67]

Newly energized activists had rallied around the cause of lesbian and gay teachers because figures such as John Briggs and Anita Bryant identified them as potent fund-raising targets—ones who fought back only at their professional peril. Even though activists rallied to support LGBT teachers, and by extension all LGBT persons, some also resisted championing a class of persons who came out only reluctantly. Before Proposition 6, LGBT school workers rarely stepped forward to identify themselves and resist employment discrimination because they believed they would lose their jobs with little recourse. However, this battle inspired many LGBT school workers to work openly for their own rights as well as those of all oppressed persons. Together with LGBT activists, larger national teacher associations, and other allied organizations, the No on 6 activists had waged a formidable campaign. After the vote, though, some activists wanted to distance the larger gay movement from the issue that continued to make it the most vulnerable: the unfounded, yet continued public perception that LGBT persons either molested children or influenced them to become "deviant." LGBT school workers still worked at the center of this zone of vulnerability. In the years ahead, they would need to find new bases of support to resist the oppression of LGBT persons in schools.

CHAPTER 8

By the Students

With his Harvard undergraduate degree fresh in hand, Eric Rofes prepared for his first day of teaching in a small, independent, New England elementary school during the fall of 1976. After his class settled, one girl asked if he was married. "No, I'm not married," he responded. Rofes, in fact, identified as gay and worked actively in Boston's fledgling gay liberation movement. He also wrote for the *Gay Community News* using a pseudonym. As a teacher, though, he wanted to respond to students' questions honestly. This would become increasingly difficult as his sixth grade class intermittently quizzed him about his personal life—and as Rofes encountered a variety of gay jokes and put-downs around the school. About a month into the year, a reading group broke into laughter. "Mr. Rofes, do you know what the word 'gay' means?" He asked the students to use the word in context. One student read, "The gay colors of the peasants' clothing made the festival a joyous sight." The group burst into hysterics again. He replied, "Yes, Ann, in that sentence, 'gay' means bright, vivid, pretty blues and yellows and reds." The blank look on students' faces registered their amazement that Rofes did not seem to know the meaning they found so funny. One patiently explained to him that "gay" had another meaning, too. He responded, "Oh. You mean 'gay' like 'homosexual.' Men who are attracted to men and women who are attracted to women. I don't think that's what the author meant in this case." Sensing rapt attention from the class, he continued, "I don't think that gay people are anything for you to laugh at. You might not know any gay people yourselves, but that's no reason to be afraid or prejudiced. It's something that may be confusing or scary to you now, but when you're older, I expect you'll understand a lot better." With this, the students returned to their work.[1]

Then in January 1977, shortly after Anita Bryant delivered enough petition signatures to prompt a public referendum on the inclusion of sexual orientation in the Miami Metro antidiscrimination ordinance, Rofes asked students to write essays about "One Important Person" who inspired a tremendous amount of either good or bad in the world. When two students chose to write their papers on Bryant, each with an opposing view, Rofes quickly found himself in the middle of a spirited student discussion. It seemed that he could not avoid the topic.[2]

For the remainder of that school year and the next, a variety of situations confronted Rofes that tested his resolve to work for gay liberation and report for gay media while simultaneously teaching. When his friends encouraged him to join them in the Boston gay pride parade before he believed he could come out at work, Rofes resolved this thorny dilemma by marching with a paper bag over his head and carrying a large sign saying, "Dick and Jane have come out. Their teachers can't. Gay rights now!"[3] LGBT teachers around the country would repeat this powerful gesture in their own local gay pride parades during the coming years.

Rofes quickly demonstrated his gifts as a teacher. School officials and parents praised the astonishing increases in his students' achievement. However, he believed that to continue teaching, he needed to be open with the school community about his sexual orientation. Toward the end of his second year of teaching, he came out to his headmistress and explained that he no longer wanted to conceal his sexual orientation while teaching. The headmistress, who remained unmarried throughout her life, called a meeting of the school's trustees to decide how to handle this news. After prolonged discussion, the trustees offered Rofes a contract for his position provided that he remain closeted and continue using pseudonyms when writing for the gay press. Rofes, thoroughly energized by his gay activism and reporting, believed he no longer could hide his sexual orientation. Consequently, he chose to leave the school. Eventually, he found a position in a different independent school that welcomed him warmly.

Other teachers, like Rofes, chose to teach and live openly as gay men or lesbians. Tom Ammiano taught special education in San Francisco. Along with Ron Lanza and Hank Wilson, he formed the Gay Teachers and School Workers Coalition in 1975. Although Ammiano's leadership in this capacity greatly influenced the San Francisco school board to include sexual orientation in the district's nondiscrimination statement, he eventually would win even grander political successes. In 1990, he ran for and won a seat on the school board of the San Francisco Unified School District, the first openly gay person to serve in this capacity. He became chair of the board only two years later. Then, in 1994, he won a seat on the San Francisco Board of Supervisors, eventually serving two terms as president. Ammiano, who also performed stand-up comedy, raised ire among some opponents not only because of his sexual orientation, but also because of the views he expressed from the stage. Nonetheless, he proved to be a resilient and popular political figure who helped enact such changes as enhancing AIDS education and ensuring the presence of at least one designated "gay- and lesbian-sympathetic staff person" in each middle and high school in the city.[4]

Rofes and Ammiano joined a small but growing number of LGBT teachers around the country who decided to reveal their desire for persons of the same sex—and keep their jobs. Some LGBT teachers in California disclosed their sexual identities to help defeat the Briggs Initiative. Others came out as an inevitable part of their gay political activism, rooted in claiming a lesbian or gay identity openly. Some decided that as their LGBT friends in other professions came out, they, too, should make this statement that mattered so much to the movement. And in a few urban areas, clusters of LGBT teachers joined organizations of LGBT school workers, groups that provided invaluable support by easing the isolation and silence most such educators experienced.

Although Rofes, Ammiano, and a few other teachers around the country chose to come out during the late 1970s, the vast majority of LGBT teachers decided against revealing their sexual orientation. The hazards remained too great, many reasoned. Some school workers who chose to come out or otherwise faced unwanted exposure did in fact lose their jobs. Mildred Doyle, who for thirty years served as superintendent of the Knox County, Tennessee, schools, lost her reelection bid in 1976 when someone anonymously circulated a letter questioning the nature of her relationship with Mildred Patterson, her longtime companion.[5] During the fall of 1977, the superintendent of the Dallas schools warned that school officials would dismiss any known lesbian or gay teacher regardless of whether or not the person engaged in "improper conduct." Intense public criticism later forced him to retract this statement, especially given that he lacked the legal means to execute the directive. However, his comment justifiably concerned school workers in the district.[6] Late in 1978, Marc Rubin, co-spokesperson for the Gay Teachers Association of New York, told *Newsweek* reporters that an anonymous gay teacher recently called to report his dismissal—and that he had swallowed thirty Thorazines. The reporters also quoted a Cleveland teacher who indicated that although school officials would not fire him for being gay, he believed they would make his life miserable if he came out.[7] And a counselor at a Bronx high school lost her job after she revealed to students her lesbian identity. With the support of the Gay Teachers Association (New York), the local teachers union (UFT), and the New York Civil Liberties Union, she won her case and a teaching position. The difficulty she faced in regaining her job, though, undoubtedly discouraged other teachers.[8] These stories represent only a small portion of the far-reaching toll exacted on LGBT school workers during these tumultuous years.

Eric Rofes's story stands out for several reasons. First, like Tom Ammiano, he decided to come out while teaching. Second, early in his career, he helped establish the Boston Area Gay and Lesbian Schoolworkers, which joined its peer associations in New York, Los Angeles, and the Bay Area. He regularly exchanged newsletters with these and a growing number of new chapters. Third, after school officials warned him to exercise discretion about his sexual orientation to keep his job, he managed to find another position in a school where he could identify openly as a gay man; thus he chose to continue teaching rather than pursue another profession. For most LGBT teachers, leaving a teaching position on account of sexual orientation usually meant they would not receive favorable recommendations when applying for new teaching positions. Rofes left his first job on his own terms and thus could find another position that better met his requirements. Admittedly, few such jobs existed at the time. Fourth, at Rofes's new school, he and his students coauthored the book, *The Kid's Book of Divorce*. Rofes split the royalties equally with each of the twenty student contributors with a share left for the school.[9] In later years, Rofes would launch similar projects: *The Kid's Book about Parents*, and *The Kid's Book about Death and Dying*. His accomplishments as a teacher stand out as remarkable by any standard.

Fifth, in 1985 Rofes continued his activism on behalf of LGBT teachers by writing *Socrates, Plato, and Guys Like Me: Confessions of a Gay Schoolteacher*, an autobiography describing his first two years of teaching. This firsthand account documented Rofes's daily experiences with homophobia in his first school. In it, he also detailed his struggle to balance his expanding gay identity with the requirement that he remain closeted. This book inspired many students, teachers, and other readers to write him explaining the elements of his story that they recognized in their own lives. It remains one of exceedingly few detailed firsthand accounts describing the experiences of LGBT teachers ever—much less during one of the most important transitional periods for LGBT school workers. Another decade would pass before many others would publish their stories.[10]

During the years that Rofes taught, LGBT school workers faced challenges on a number of different fronts. As Briggs gathered signatures for Proposition 6 in California, a strikingly similar measure appeared in Oklahoma. State Senator Mary Helms introduced a bill permitting the dismissal of teachers who engaged in "public homosexual conduct," which meant, among other things, teachers who revealed that they desired persons of the same sex or who expressed the opinion that homosexuals deserved any civil rights.[11] The Oklahoma House overwhelmingly passed Helms's bill, 88–2, but the Senate went further, approving it unanimously.[12] Before any teacher could be dismissed with this new law, however, the National Gay Task Force immediately challenged its constitutionality, arguing that it violated First Amendment guarantees of free speech.[13] It appealed the matter to the U.S. Court of Appeals, which in 1984 sided with the National Gay Task Force in its contention that the law violated the First Amendment. A year later when the state appealed the case to the Supreme Court, Lawrence Tribe, who represented the National Gay Task Force, argued that the law had a chilling effect on teachers' speech. The Supreme Court deadlocked on the matter. Consequently, the decision of the lower court stood. The National Gay Task Force essentially won the case, which rendered the Oklahoma law moot.[14]

This would not be the end of legislative measures designed to limit gains won by the gay liberation movement. Three years after the Oklahoma legislature passed Senator Helms's bill barring teachers who engaged in "homosexual conduct," Representative Hanson from Idaho introduced a bill in Congress that would have produced an even greater chilling effect on LGBT school workers around the country. The Family Protection Act of 1981, with a broad collection of provisions championed by conservative Christian groups, would have terminated any municipal or state antidiscrimination laws that protected LGBT persons from housing or employment discrimination. One section stipulated that "no Federal funds may be made available under any provision of Federal law to any public or private individual, group, foundation, commission, corporation, association, or other entity which presents homosexuality, male or female, as an acceptable alternative."[15] Debate on the Family Protection Act dominated much of the 1980 presidential election. Presidential candidate Ronald Reagan endorsed the bill on the campaign trail, but, when elected, he opposed it, claiming simply that it discriminated against a class of people. The bill then failed to make it through the Democrat-controlled Congress.[16]

Despite such setbacks, political conservatives kept "homosexuality" at the front of their agenda. During the late 1970s and early 1980s, writers from increasingly well-funded conservative think tanks and right-wing Christian organizations published and distributed a variety of anti-homosexual materials. In 1978, William Bennett—who later became Reagan's Secretary of Education wrote an article, "The Homosexual Teacher," that appeared in *The American Educator*. Essentially, Bennett argued that LGBT school workers should remain closeted and, furthermore, that communities should determine what values are conveyed in schools. He concluded, "I believe that homosexuals who are overt and self-declared about their homosexuality, who have an interest in arguing for homosexuality as a lifestyle, and who make efforts to change student values about homosexuality in ways fundamentally inconsistent with values that the school and community affirm, should not be teaching in the public schools."[17] Leaders of the Gay Teachers Association (New York) drafted a response to Bennett's article, rebutting each contention. However, once Bennett became Reagan's Secretary of Education, he exerted tremendous influence over national education policy.

Then, in 1982, George Alan Rekers, a conservative Christian psychologist, published two influential books on children's sexual identity development—and its "correction."[18] The books, *Shaping Your Child's Sexual Identity* and *Growing Up Straight: What Families Should Know about Homosexuality,* cautioned parents to watch for signs that their children might become "homosexuals."[19] In both books, Rekers established his credentials at the start: He earned his Ph.D. in psychology from the University of California at Los Angeles. Then, as a visiting scholar, he conducted research on "sexual-identity development" at Harvard's Center for the Behavioral Sciences. He received over a half-million dollars of grant support from the National Institute of Mental Health to study "sexual-identity disorders" in youth, and further, the amelioration of these "disorders." The books, he promised, would reveal the expertise he had developed and would assist parents in assuring their children's heterosexuality.

Rekers began *Shaping Your Child's Sexual Identity* by charging, "A fierce battle is being waged today over male and female roles in family life." The problem, he explained, was that "unisex notions," supported by radical feminists and homosexuals, had gained credence across society, which supposedly confused children.

> The unisex notions are not based upon the findings of child-development research. . . . Instead, the feminist and unisex ideas are rooted in the relativism of humanistic thinking. These ideas are based on the worldview which rejects the philosophical idea of antithesis. The idea of natural sex-role boundaries embedded in creation is anathema to the relativistic humanists. Traditionally, the concept of antithesis would clarify that choosing a male sexual mate is a feminine sex-role behavior, properly the role of the female. However, the relativistic humanists do not hold up heterosexuality as a desired norm.[20]

Using language and logic reminiscent of works from earlier decades, Rekers argued that when children grew up with gender identities that did not align with those traditionally associated with their biological sex, they risked becoming homosexuals. He argued, "In most cases, men involved in homosexuality have reported specific feminine behavior patterns indicative of a difficulty in adjusting to the male role in early childhood." Conversely, he contended that although many girls go through tomboy phases, "there is a pattern of masculine identification and masculine role adoption by girls in childhood which can be distinguished from tomboyism and which places the girl at high risk for homosexual temptation in the teen-age years and adulthood."[21] Thus, if parents noticed when their children strayed into nontraditional gender development, then effective interventions could be arranged. In boys, Rekers told parents to watch for "dressing in feminine clothing," "using feminine body gestures and gait," "talking with a high femininelike voice and/or talking predominantly about feminine topics instead of masculine ones," or "taking a female role in play constantly." The fairly predictable watch-list for girls included "repeatedly refusing to wear girls' clothing, jewelry, or cosmetics," "using masculine gestures and gait," or "projecting her voice to a masculinelike tone and/or predominantly talking about male activities."[22]

Rekers urged parents to provide appropriate sex-role modeling for their children. He clearly distinguished between feminine and masculine parental roles in a neatly polarized table. He expected women to be mothers, wear "modest clothing of upper torso," abstain "from sexual relations with females," and be "submissive to husband's leadership at home." Meanwhile, men should impregnate "female by sexual intercourse," abstain "from sexual relations with males," and provide "moral and spiritual leadership in the home."[23] Essentially, if men and women honored their traditional gender roles, or "sex-roles" as he called them, then children would avoid sexual confusion, thus thwarting homosexual development. For Rekers, gender and sexual orientation walked in lockstep. His work ignored the existence of vast numbers of lesbian, gay, and bisexual persons whose gender behaviors and characteristics aligned with those traditionally associated with their biological sex. And it overlooked the transgender individuals who sexually desired persons of the other biological sex.

Finally, Rekers explained that "in some cases, it is necessary to introduce treatment procedures for the child in school." Boys needed to be coached patiently in learning proper athletic behaviors. And school workers needed to model correct sex-roles.[24] Homosexual teachers presented a grave threat to children, he warned, because he believed they could not model correct sex roles. Parents should be especially wary of the gay liberation movement since, as he described it, homosexual activists promoted "changes in sex-role stereotyping."[25]

Rekers's books are somewhat reminiscent of Peter and Barbara Wydens's earlier book, entitled, *Growing Up Straight* (1969), in that each of these authors sought to assure parents that they could steer their children away from homosexuality, as well as toward proper gender behaviors and characteristics. The Wydens relied heavily on then-current research, especially that published by Dr. Bieber's team in 1962, which blamed faulty parenting for homosexual development. Rekers drew substantially on his own research, but he reached some of the same conclusions as Bieber's team. A significant difference between the Wydens's book and Rekers's is that the latter are suffused with biblical passages, which may not be surprising given that the Moody Bible Institute published Rekers's *Growing Up Straight*. Indeed, much of the antigay political and social movement of the late 1970s and early 1980s arose from conservative Christian organizations, several of which supported the Family Protection Act of 1981.

Rekers eventually figured prominently in establishing "gender identity disorder" (GID) as a pathology recognized by the American Psychiatric Association. Psychiatrists diagnosed individuals with GID if they demonstrated gender-variance or sought sex reassignment surgery or hormones. Gay activists later protested that although the APA had removed homosexuality from its *Diagnostic and Statistical Manual of Mental Disorders* in 1973, its inclusion of GID amounted to a backdoor way to "pathologize transgender people and 'gender-variant' youth—i.e., those children who exhibit behavior that may be viewed as 'pre-homosexual' or 'pre-transsexual.'"[26] Rekers's research on preventing or suppressing GID led to his eventual leadership in the Christian organization, Exodus, started in 1977, which, to this day, endeavors to convert LGBT persons into gender-conforming heterosexuals. Much of Rekers's published work through the years stressed his view that adults must clearly demonstrate normal gender behaviors and characteristics for children to emulate. Otherwise, he maintained, children would develop sexual problems.[27]

As significant adults in the lives of children, teachers commonly have been expected to demonstrate traditional gender characteristics and behaviors—as Rekers implored. Teachers have discovered that failure to do so can be as fraught with difficulty as revealing sexual desire for persons of the same sex. Transgressing the bounds of "gender-appropriateness" cost one West Virginia teacher her job in 1983. School officials told Linda Conway, a kindergarten teacher, that she did not act "feminine enough." Her school district dismissed her because, as officials maintained, she developed a "reputation in the community" for being a lesbian even though she staunchly asserted her heterosexuality. Conway explained that officials fired her because "I wasn't prone to wearing dresses. I'm not feminine to begin with. I'm heavy-set, and I wouldn't look good in some of the things those petite women wear." She argued that, given her working conditions, she needed to wear comfortable clothing. "I taught in cafeterias, and I had to lean over tables to teach, so I wore pants. They were colder rooms, too, so I wore a lot of blazers and sweaters. Even though I had long hair, I still looked too 'manly' to them. It's funny because since then I read that if a woman wants to be taken more seriously in the business world, she should dress more manly." Apparently Conway's clothing provoked rumors. Then when she invited another teacher to live with her who recently had left her husband and when Conway chose to cut her hair short, as she explains it, "People were saying 'she left her husband to marry that other woman.'"[28]

In response to these rumors, the superintendent attempted to transfer Conway, but his bid failed on procedural grounds. When parents circulated a petition to pressure school officials to fire her, the superintendent hastily imposed a dress code requiring her to "wear a dress at least twice a week, no boots or manly clothes." Meanwhile, the superintendent consulted with the state attorney general to determine if he could dismiss Conway outright. The attorney general indicated that she could be fired because of her "reputation in the community." With this legal opinion in hand, the superintendent promptly pressured Conway to resign. Conway later changed her mind. She wanted her resignation nullified and her job back. A jury trial returned a decision in favor of the school board. However, with the legal assistance of the West Virginia Education Association, Conway appealed the matter to the West Virginia Supreme Court. Conway's attorneys argued that the jury had been improperly instructed. Finally, in December 1986, the State Supreme Court dismissed the appeal, ruling that the school district could fire Conway because the community perceived her as a lesbian.[29] Conway's case offers another example of the link between gender nonconformity and same-sex desire. Persons who display gender qualities that do not align with their biological sex often feel the sting of oppression purportedly aimed at persons who desire others of the same sex.

Despite some modest gains made during the fight against the Briggs Initiative and in other municipalities that passed sexual orientation antidiscrimination ordinances, school workers clearly still faced substantial threats to their livelihood during these early years of the organized gay movement. As a number of conservative religious and political groups rallied together to battle a host of recent social changes such as women's rights and abortion that they deemed "antifamily," they took aim at

LGBT persons. Consequently, the 1980s witnessed backlash against LGBT advances.

The most significant challenge to the nascent movement, though, became public on July 3, 1981, when the *New York Times* ran a small article on page 20 with the header, "Rare Cancer Seen in 41 Homosexuals." The story indicated that eight men died of a rare cancer and thirty-three others exhibited its symptoms. All identified as sexually active gay men. Most lived in or had recently visited New York, though some also resided in California.[30] Over the next few years, the number of gay men infected by what came to be known as the AIDS virus exploded and thousands died slowly and painfully. News media usually dodged the story of AIDS, however, until the disease reached heterosexual populations. Until that time, the federal government dispensed little funding for studying or fighting what has become one of the most devastating epidemics in human history.[31]

The LGBT movement shifted in response to this unfathomable killer. Some gay men, who only had begun to enjoy newfound freedoms and an emerging, rich gay culture, denied the magnitude of the problem and insisted that their sexual activity remain unfettered. Others saw their companions, friends, and members of the gay community die in shocking numbers. Playwright-turned-activist Larry Kramer fumed about gay men's denial as well as the lack of governmental and societal concern about the epidemic. Out of that anger, he founded the AIDS Coalition to Unleash Power (ACT-UP) to agitate for research and social support. He also established the Gay Men's Health Crisis (GMHC) to raise funds to care for infected people. In a provocative article published in the *New York Native* in 1983, he warned, "Our continued existence as gay men upon the face of this earth is at stake. Unless we fight for our lives, we shall die. In all the history of homosexuality we have never before been so close to death and extinction. Many of us are dying or already dead."[32] Many gay men and lesbians answered Kramer's charge by getting angry and involved. ACT-UP activists organized extravagant protests that attracted widespread media attention—such as blocking traffic around Wall Street and unfurling banners at Shea Stadium proclaiming "Men Wear Condoms," and "AIDS Kills Women." These actions prompted similar actions among other activists around the country. Urvashi Vaid, Executive Director of the National Gay and Lesbian Task Force, said, "There had not been a direct street response to the myriad problems of AIDS until ACT-UP came along."[33]

Schools soon confronted AIDS directly. In December 1984, doctors diagnosed thirteen-year-old Ryan White with AIDS. The Kokomo, Indiana, student had contracted the virus through a routine transfusion to treat his hemophilia. Then in June 1985, the superintendent announced that White could not return to school because of fears that other students and school staff might contract the virus through skin contact, sneezing, accidental cuts, or other means. Although by this time researchers had established that AIDS spread through exchange of bodily fluids, mainly blood and semen, many in the school community feared White would spread the virus easily. White's family filed a suit against the school district, after which officials allowed his return. However, a group of parents then sued to keep White from stepping onto school grounds. White studied at home for a brief time, but then his family moved to a more welcoming school district in which he enrolled. After his first day in his new school, White explained that "everybody was real nice and friendly."[34]

White's experiences garnered national attention, inspiring both sympathy and panic about the possibility that schools might become conduits in the spread of AIDS. Over the next few years, the NEA tackled several AIDS-related issues during its annual Representative Assembly. In 1986, the extreme right-wing political figure, Lyndon LaRouche, introduced an initiative in California to require all AIDS victims to be quarantined, regardless of whether or not medical professionals believed the measure necessary. Furthermore, the initiative would have forced all school employees to be tested for the virus. Any employee who tested positive or who associated with AIDS patients would have been barred from schools. After brief discussion, the NEA Representative Assembly quickly voted to oppose the LaRouche initiative on AIDS.[35]

In 1987, the Representative Assembly took up the matter of mandatory AIDS testing of students. One teacher from Minnesota argued passionately for mandatory student testing: "I am very much concerned about the individual rights of every person, student or adult. . . . But when the rights of others infringe so much upon my right, I am even more concerned. The problem of AIDS is a great problem. I am concerned during the school year when students will come up to my desk and face me and cough all over me, practically spitting on you."[36] A teacher from California countered, "I have heard concerns about protecting students with AIDS, and I believe those concerns are real. However, we as advocates of individual rights know that forced testing, even when it's done for the student's own good, is not the answer. We need to concern ourselves with the protection of students with AIDS by fighting for AIDS research funding, by providing accurate education about AIDS, and by showing compassion and concern for the welfare of students with AIDS." A teacher from Oregon added, "We do not have the right to submit students to any mandatory or involuntary testing that we are not willing to submit to ourselves." The Representative Assembly then voted to oppose mandatory AIDS testing of students.[37]

During the 1988 Representative Assembly, the NEA addressed general LGBT issues in addition to AIDS. One particular resolution, concerning the needs of LGBT youth, inspired a vigorous floor debate—and signaled a larger shift in LGBT activism in schools away from the rights of school workers and toward students. Resolution C-11 would have the effect of throwing the collective weight of the NEA behind the idea that LGBT youth should be entitled to sensitive counseling to help them accept and adjust to their sexual orientation—rather than ignoring their needs or referring them to counselors or medical professionals who would attempt to make them heterosexual. Earlier in the day before debate on this issue commenced, through a remote video connection, an obviously weakened Ryan White had delivered a moving speech to the Representative Assembly about the need to address AIDS and LGBT issues thoughtfully. When debate on the resolution began, the NEA Secretary-Treasurer spoke as an individual:

> Fourteen years ago [1974], the very first time I spoke on the floor of this Representative Assembly. . . . It was for inclusion of sexual orientation in our list of nondiscriminatory personnel policies. Two years earlier I had spent the spring of 1972 working with a student who had survived an extended coma as a result of an attempted suicide due to her depression over social oppression she was experiencing because of her own sexual orientation. Had she had access to a supportive counseling system years prior to her coming to college, she may have had the option to build a strong self-concept based on a sense of self-esteem and dignity, no matter her sexual preference. As I watched her in a state of convulsion for over 70 hours sitting by her bedside, I vowed I would never again be silent on this issue. Fourteen years have not changed my commitment to this belief that one's sexual orientation should not be an excuse for limiting rights afforded to any other citizen; nor does it give any excuse for blind discrimination, particularly during this time of ignorance surrounding the issue of AIDS.[38]

A representative of the Oklahoma delegation spoke against the resolution, explaining that "we have already in Oklahoma confronted many of the prejudices and have worked through the Supreme Court system to see bad laws struck down," he said, speaking of the state law barring homosexual teachers. However, "We are going to see this used against the membership so they can't be as successful as they'd like to be and need to be."

A delegate from Ohio countered, "I know of a young man who tried to hang himself after a school administrator told him he would die in the streets as a result of addiction to drugs, prostitution, and AIDS if he continued to believe that he was gay. . . . The student I know who tried to hang himself, through outpatient counseling is now a productive member of our society and fairly well adjusted. But we need this resolution to help all of us work with these students." Gladys Graves, president of the North Carolina Education Association, added her support: "C-11 is about children, it is about giving all children a sense of self-esteem, it is about children who are being denied equal access to education, who are at a greater risk for suicide, who face isolation, rejection, and verbal and physical abuse, who comprise a disproportionately large percentage of homeless youth, who often resort to dropping out and running away. The human potential of a segment of our student population is being wasted through inappropriate counseling. These students need our support, our counsel, and our love. Let's not fail them today." After several more exchanges, the matter came to a voice vote. President Mary Hatwood Futrell declared that the resolution passed—but disgruntled calls for a division, or standing vote, quickly rose above the commotion. After a lengthy process of counting the votes of the several thousand delegates in attendance, Futrell finally announced that the resolution passed.[39]

The positive vote on this resolution soon lent significant support to an innovative counseling program for LGBT youth in Los Angeles. Virginia Uribe, a science teacher with nearly thirty years of experience, established "Project 10" to provide support services to students questioning their sexual orientation or being subjected to hate or bigotry. She confessed that initially she resisted using the words "lesbian" and "gay" in the name of the group, fearing that already hesitant students might be driven way. She settled on "10" because of the Kinsey reports showing that around 10 percent of all people engaged in sexual activity with persons of the same sex.

In 1984, she started the project when taunting students drove an effeminate male student away from school—which made her angry and then compelled her to act. At first, she facilitated discussion groups for students who wanted to talk about sexual orientation. Then, in the fall of 1987, she brought the program to high schools throughout the district with the support of the Los Angeles school board and her principal. She spoke before school assemblies. She compiled and distributed information pamphlets and other materials for students to read—discreetly if necessary. She eventually trained contact people in each high school to spread the reach of the program. And, by 1991, Project 10 extended to school districts around the country.

Along the way, Uribe encountered bracing resistance from the Reverend Lou Sheldon, leader of the Traditional Values Coalition, a conservative Christian organization. Sheldon argued that Uribe, an "avowed lesbian," essentially used the project to recruit students to homosexuality. He prompted a state assembly member to introduce a bill "which would prohibit schools operated by school districts or county superintendents of schools from implementing or continuing a program that by design or effect encourages homosexuality as a viable life alternative." The bill failed, but Sheldon and his supporters continued to trouble Uribe over the years—which she believes made her stronger. She maintained that "withholding these vital counseling services to teenagers because of sexual orientation is nothing more than criminal prejudice, and this community should deal with it as such. . . . As responsible adults, we should let our elected officials know that this legislative gay-bashing, particularly when it is aimed at children, is not going to be tolerated."[40]

In contrast, a wide variety of local and national media offered favorable reporting on the novel program and its founder. During interviews, Uribe frequently mentioned that the NEA had recently passed a resolution (C-11) supporting counseling for students struggling with sexual/ gender orientation. The NEA then developed a handbook for advising and teaching LGBT youth—with Uribe serving as consultant.[41]

A year and a half after Uribe brought Project 10 to the entire Los Angeles school system, the U.S. Department of Health and Human Services released a landmark study on youth suicide. The *Report of the Secretary's Task Force on Youth Suicide,* prepared during the Reagan administration, reached publication in January 1989, around the time that George Bush became president. The printed report, however, remained boxed for seven months.[42] Then, Louis Sullivan, Bush's new Secretary of Health and Human Services, voiced his strong objections to the conclusions reached in one particular chapter of the thick, four-volume report. The existence of that single chapter soon generated considerable controversy and national media attention. Entitled "Gay Male and Lesbian Youth Suicide," it began with force:

> A majority of suicide attempts by homosexuals occur during their youth, and gay youth are 2 to 3 times more likely to attempt suicide than other young people. They may comprise up to 30 percent of completed youth suicides annually. . . . The root of the problem of gay youth suicide is a society that discriminates against and stigmatizes homosexuals while failing to recognize that a substantial number of its youth has a gay or lesbian orientation. Legislation should guarantee homosexuals equal rights in our society. . . . Schools need to include information about homosexuality in their curriculum and protect gay youth from abuse by peers to ensure they receive an equal education. Helping professionals need to accept and support a homosexual orientation in youth. Social services need to be developed that are sensitive to and reflective of the needs of gay and lesbian youth.[43]

Paul Gibson, a social worker, therapist, and consultant in San Francisco, compiled the chapter. In doing so, he relied heavily on the scholarship of Gary Remafedi, a medical researcher at the University of Minnesota, who documented a disproportionately high attempted and actual suicide rate among gay male youth.[44] Gibson also drew from a variety of sources produced by LGBT persons with extensive experience working with LGBT youth. These materials included those produced by the National Gay and Lesbian Task Force, statistics gathered from youth centers, and Eric Rofes's1983 book, *I Thought People Like That Killed Themselves: Lesbians, Gay Men and Suicide.* Gibson's report discussed suicide statistics among LGBT youth, how such youth came out, the unique experiences of transsexual youth, AIDS, and risk factors in LGBT youth suicide.

Upon release of the larger, four-volume report on youth suicide, Representative William Dannemeyer, a conservative Republican from California, wrote to Dr. James Mason, Assistant Secretary of HHP, explaining that "after all the public has had to endure from unwise stewards within the Department of Health and Human Services, I suppose the *Report of the Secretary's Task Force on Youth Suicide . . .* should come as no surprise." He then listed quotes from the chapter on gay and lesbian youth suicide. Finally, he threatened, "I am calling upon your leadership to publicly denounce at least the portion of the *Report* dealing with homosexuality and ask that you take a serious look at the entire analysis on suicide. Individuals plagued by homosexuality and seeking help should receive professional help to overcome their problem. . . . You will need to decide whether you will side with traditional family values or the National Gay and Lesbian Task Force."[45] When Dannemeyer did not hear back from Mason—who had participated in drafting the report—he wrote President Bush a few weeks later:

I suggested to Dr. Mason that he will need to decide whether he will side with traditional family values or the National Gay and Lesbian Task Force. He has obviously chosen the latter. As of Monday . . . the National Gay and Lesbian Task Force, the Human Rights Campaign Fund (a homosexual PAC), the Municipal Election Committee of Los Angeles (another homosexual PAC), Parents and Friends of Lesbians and Gays, and surprisingly, the National Parents and Teachers Association and the National Association of State Boards of Education are sponsoring a Senate staff briefing promoting homosexuality among America's youth—using the HHS Report as a federal cloak of legitimacy.

The briefing is a lobbying effort intended to maintain support for school districts which give aid and comfort to militant homosexuality through pro-homosexual instruction and counseling in public schools.

Frankly, Mr. President, this effort puts to rest any notions of innocence regarding homosexual recruitment among youth. The recommendations of the Report and public school programs such as Project 10 in the Los Angeles Unified School District simply add legitimacy to the heretofore crime of child molestation.

Now is your opportunity to affirm traditional family values by denouncing the portion of the *Report* dealing with homosexuality and helping those plagued by homosexuality to seek professional help to overcome their problem. On the other hand, you could say nothing thereby condoning the substance of the *Report*. . . .

If you choose to affirm traditional family values my next suggestion would be to dismiss from public service all persons still employed who concocted this homosexual pledge of allegiance and then issue my draft Executive Order that would seal the lid on these misjudgments for good.[46]

Urvashi Vaid, Executive Director of the National Gay and Lesbian Task Force, immediately wrote President Bush explaining that Dannemeyer failed to address the substance of the report in his earlier letter. She outlined the significant findings of the report and then requested, "What is needed now, Mr. President, is not prejudice and moral posturing, but moral leadership. Accordingly, and in keeping with your admirable pledge to foster a 'kinder and gentler nation,' we ask you to reject Mr. Dannemeyer's request that you 'denounce' the sections of the report focusing on lesbian and gay youth suicide issues. Furthermore, we ask that the Department of Health and Human Services actively work to ensure that the report's recommendations are fully and quickly implemented." She concluded by asking to meet with Bush's domestic policy staff to discuss issues raised in the report.[47]

A month after Vaid sent her letter to President Bush, Louis Sullivan, his new Secretary of Health and Human Services, wrote directly to Representative William Dannemeyer, explaining that persons in the previous Reagan administration wrote the *Report*. "Moreover, I want to reemphasize that the views expressed in the paper entitled 'Gay Male and Lesbian Youth Suicide' do not in any way represent my personal beliefs or the policy of this Department. Indeed, I am strongly committed to advancing traditional family values. . . . In my opinion, the views expressed in the paper run contrary to that aim." However, he did admit that the Department of Health and Human Services must at least review the findings on youth suicide before making final recommendations.[48] Again, Urvashi Vaid countered by writing Sullivan on behalf of the Task Force:

We are concerned about your statement regarding "traditional family values." We believe strong family values have traditionally meant the nurturing, affirmation, protection and understanding of young people, not their alienation and stigmatization. We believe, as we hope you do, that suicide and violence are not family values. . . . Congressman Dannemeyer in no way represents responsible health policy in this country. The Congressman has a clear, discriminatory, anti-gay political agenda. His homophobic accusations are based in intolerance and hatred, not fact. Your letter to Dannemeyer politically validates his positions and distracts public attention from the fundamental problem: teen suicide.[49]

Again, she closed her letter by requesting a meeting to discuss the implications of the *Report*. However, Sullivan staffers subsequently told her they could not find the letter. When Vaid sent another copy, staffers told her that Secretary Sullivan's busy schedule would not permit a meeting. Months later, during the spring of 1990, Sullivan relented and voiced agreement to meet with gay and lesbian leaders. However, a year later, he continued evading such a meeting.[50]

By the summer of 1991, the findings in the *Report* concerning gay and lesbian youth suicide garnered national media attention. The *Washington Post* covered the story not only as concerning the findings on youth suicide, but also as a high-level governmental "cold-shoulder" to LGBT issues.[51] *The Advocate* went even further in calling the issue a governmental cover-up and charging that the Department of Health and Human Services printed only 2,000 copies of the original report, then widely released a much diluted version of the report on gay and lesbian youth suicide.[52]

Unwilling to wait for federal support, a few LGBT adolescents around the country began taking matters into their own hands. They formed LGBT and queer youth groups in their local communities so they could support each other, hang out, enjoy themselves, and work together to reduce the isolation and harassment they faced. In 1991, Chance Claar, a sixteen-year-old lesbian living in Atlanta, wrote a feature for *The Advocate* explaining why she started one such group:

> Generally ignored by the adult community, queer youth have had to provide for ourselves, with resources limited due to the constraints of our age group. This has primarily meant creating our own youth groups and support networks. Because the adult community is almost exclusively centered around the bars, which you must be 21 to enter, lesbian and gay youth have no social connections to the community at large. The message we have been given is that in order to become accepted as legitimate queers, we must be over 21. Until we reach that age, the adult community is unwilling, maybe even afraid, to accept any responsibility for us.[53]

She argued that LGBT adults sometimes resisted working with youth because they feared being tarred with the pedophilia label—or they believed, "let them fend for themselves, as we did." In the meantime, she maintained that queer youth would help themselves even as they very much wanted the active involvement of queer adults.[54]

In 1993, LGBT students in Massachusetts asserted themselves by working for a state law outlawing discrimination against them in schools. For several years a bill to this effect had languished in the state legislature. However, hundreds of students from all over the state began writing legislators, urging them to move the bill forward and vote for it. They recorded poignant stories about their own experiences of harassment and discrimination. They arranged to meet with legislators and even organized a widely reported demonstration outside the statehouse. Eventually, the bill made it to the floor where a majority approved it. Since then, Massachusetts students who believe they have been the object of homophobic bias have been entitled to file lawsuits. This represents the first time a state granted such protections to students.[55]

Immediately afterwards, Massachusetts students and teachers organized regional workshops about LGBT youth in schools. A $450,000 grant from the Massachusetts Department of Education's Safe Schools Program for Gay and Lesbian Students funded these workshops in which students and teachers described the discrimination they had witnessed or felt. They discussed effective strategies for confronting this treatment. And workshop leaders also provided technical assistance to attendees in setting up gay/straight alliances at their schools.[56] By the spring of 1995, hundreds of LGBT and high school student allies from around the state converged on the statehouse in Boston for the nation's first Gay/Straight Youth Pride March. The students brought a list of actions they wanted, including gay/straight alliances in every Massachusetts high school, more out LGBT school workers, "visible penalties for anti-gay harassers in school," and LGBT people and issues included in the curriculum.[57]

This remarkable feat on the part of LGBT youth in Massachusetts was not easily duplicated in other parts of the country, however. In Salt Lake City, Kelli Petersen organized a gay/straight alliance at her East High School. She decided to do this after coming out during her sophomore year, immediately losing all her friends, and then seeing the same thing happen to other students. When she tried to arrange after-school meetings for the new club, the principal denied her request. Eventually the school board voted 4–3 to ban all after-school clubs rather than allow the gay/straight alliance to meet. School board members justified their actions by explaining that the Federal Equal Access Act of 1984 gave them two options: allow all student clubs to meet including the gay/straight alliance, or allow none of them. Ironically, this act had been sponsored by Utah's Senator Orrin Hatch specifically so religious clubs could meet in school. In response to the school board's decision, Peterson told a reporter, "The school board decision will only exacerbate the hate and violence that's been going on against us for years. . . . But this is not over by a long shot. This is a declaration of war." News of Peterson's club then spread quickly around the state, apparently inspiring a ninety-minute, closed-door meeting between state senators and state education officials during which senators accused school leaders of advocating homosexuality through faculty advisors. A few senators indicated that they might seek to ban all school clubs in the state. Some threatened that they would risk $100 million in federal aid to Utah schools to keep gay/straight alliances out. State Senator Craig Taylor explained, "Young people reach their teen-age years, and their sexuality starts developing . . . and I believe they can be led down that road to homosexuality." Peterson calmly retorted, "Nobody led me to become a lesbian. My parents are heterosexual. I was taught to be heterosexual. I was taught to get married and to have children." Meanwhile, in the spirit of solidarity with Peterson's efforts, Clayton Vetter, a debate teacher, publicly announced his gay identity, making him the first teacher in the state to do so. Given that the statehouse was considering an "illegal conduct" bill at the time, Vetter risked his job by making this statement.[58] Later that spring, Utah lawmakers crafted and then passed a bill requiring school districts to forbid student clubs that "promote bigotry, encourage criminal conduct, or discuss issues of sexuality."[59] Peterson then graduated and began speaking across the country about the need for LGBT youth rights. "Out of the Past," the nationally broadcast PBS documentary on LGBT history, featured her story prominently. Then in 1997, one of the other pioneering members of the East High gay/straight alliance, Jacob Orozco, hanged himself, making overwhelmingly clear the magnitude of the problem LGBT youth and their allies faced. Despite the school board's stunning continued resistance in the wake of this tragedy, the school's principal reportedly moved forward and implemented a no-harassment policy with "sexual orientation" listed along with race and ethnicity.[60]

Late in 1996, LGBT students and their allies received a shocking piece of good news when Jamie Nabozny, a young man from Wisconsin, won a nearly $1 million judgment against administrators in his schools, who he argued did nothing to stop years of antigay verbal and physical abuse. Nabozny recounted how his middle school principal told him that he should expect to be abused if he insisted on claiming an openly gay identity. The attacks Nabozny faced included one where students urinated on him and kicked him. Another attack sent him to the hospital for surgery. Upon winning the judgment, Nabozny said, "I'm very glad the truth came out. Now I can go on with my life. . . . I feel like I have justice, and that this means justice for all other kids out there who aren't sure if they should stay in school or stay alive."[61] Although this unprecedented judgment did much to hearten LGBT students and allies, it would not prevent further abuses. During the fall of 1998, Adam Colton, a seventeen-year-old gay student in Novato, California, formed a gay/straight alliance at his high school. Twice after that, gangs of teenagers beat him savagely.[62] That fall also brought the brutal murder of University of Wyoming student, Matthew Shepard, which riveted national attention on the issue of violence against LGBT persons, particularly students.

LGBT students and allies responded by organizing even more aggressively. By the spring of 2001, one report indicated that students had formed gay/straight alliances at more than 800 schools in forty-seven states. This idea, which originated in Massachusetts, had spread with breathtaking speed as LGBT students around the country understood the profound need for mutual support in resisting violence, preventing suicide, and educating their communities about the realities they faced. In many cases, LGBT school workers sponsored these gay/straight alliances. They did so out of a commitment to ending discrimination against all LGBT persons in the school community.[63]

Kevin Jennings, a teacher in an independent school in Concord, Massachusetts, sponsored the first recorded gay/straight alliance in 1989.[64] Jennings had begun teaching history a few years earlier at a private school in Rhode Island, but when the principal pulled him aside and told him he must remove the jewelry from his left ear or not bother showing up the next day, he knew his work there would be unsupported and difficult. Two years later, Jennings moved to the Concord school where students and staff seemed unfazed by his gay identity. He revealed his sexual orientation if anyone asked, but did not raise the topic otherwise. Then, during the fall of 1988, his second year in Concord, Jennings delivered a speech during chapel in which he told the school community how he experienced growing up gay in a system that did not tolerate it. He explained that he abused drugs and attempted suicide, but that only by accepting and appreciating his sexual orientation could he thrive. Much to his surprise, the student body warmly and enthusiastically embraced him and his message.[65]

Jennings sponsored the school's innovative gay/straight alliance the next academic year. Also, he published a piece in the trade journal, *Independent School,* discussing his experiences as an openly gay teacher. This piece generated substantial interest among readers and quickly propelled Jennings into a fast-paced schedule of speaking engagements around the country. The extended contact with LGBT and ally teachers that these opportunities provided inspired Jennings to find ways to offer teachers social support, too. With the full cooperation of the Independent School Association of Massachusetts, Jennings started an LGBT and ally group for teachers in 1990. The first conference of such teachers convened in 1991 and attracted 100 people, far beyond expectations. The annual event grew rapidly and, within a few years, the Gay, Lesbian, and Straight Teachers Network included teachers from both private and public schools around the country.

Some local associations of LGBT educators chose to join with the Gay, Lesbian, and Straight Teachers Network as did the Bay Area Network of Gay and Lesbian Educators (BANGLE) in 1995. The president of the Bay Area group explained to members that becoming a chapter of the Gay, Lesbian, and Straight Teachers Network would mean that the focus of the organization would shift:

> Currently, BANGLE could be described as teacher resource and support group. BANGLE allows anyone to join but in practice has mostly members who are lesbian, gay, and bi teachers. We try to support queer youth and to eliminate homophobia from schools, but this has come second to maintaining BANGLE as a viable teacher group. GLSTN actively recruits straight members who are committed to eliminating homophobia in schools. While the majority of its members are educators, it actively seeks broadbased community support. Anyone interested in eliminating homophobia from schools is encouraged to become a member. BANGLE [if it joined with GLSTN] would still provide support to lesbian, gay, and bi teachers, but primarily because doing so creates a safer school environment for all queer school community members. There would probably be a relative increase in support for teachers who want to come out at school, although closeted teachers would also be welcome in the organization. Straight teachers who make the school safe for sexual minority students would become a significant focus.
>
> It is the difference in focus, I believe, that accounts for GLSTN's dramatic success in schools. Its members were largely responsible for Massachusett's landmark policies that provide real, meaningful support to lesbian and gay youth in schools statewide. GLSTN has also had much more success than BANGLE in putting together educational training conferences.[66]

This shift in focus captures well a significant trend among LGBT teacher associations over the 1980s. Organizations of LGBT teachers fighting for their rights had enjoyed limited success. However, by broadening the focus to include students—and straight teachers—the organization could cultivate vastly greater public support. Reflecting this larger development, the Gay, Lesbian, and Straight *Teachers* Network eventually changed its name to the Gay, Lesbian, and Straight *Education*

Network (GLSEN). Today, GLSEN is a truly national organization committed to fighting homophobia in schools. Membership in GLSEN has grown significantly over its brief existence along with private and corporate donations. LGBT educators account for a noticeable segment of GLSEN's membership, but its roster also includes a notable number of students and educators who identify as allies. Although GLSEN devotes some resources to ending employment discrimination in schools, clearly the greatest portion of funding, staff time, and conference attention is dedicated to assisting *all* LGBT persons and allies in schools.

Without question, LGBT school workers still face tremendous risks in their work. Although activism over the past three decades has helped thousands of such educators to become visible, keep their positions, and sometimes even to thrive, vastly more believe that conditions still remain too unsafe for such a move.[67] Recently a teacher in California came out and subsequently became Teacher of the Year at his school; another teacher in the same state announced that she is a lesbian and promptly lost her job. Some teachers come out and must sue their districts to retain their positions; others find welcome support.[68] In February 2002, the NEA's Task Force on Sexual Orientation concluded that "employment discrimination against g/l/b/t education employees is commonplace." Nonetheless, this problem, "while often acknowledged—has not received the same level of systematic and comprehensive scrutiny as the problems confronting g/l/b/t students, and the Task Force is not aware of any statistical studies documenting the incidence of such discrimination." Even without such systematically collected data, "the evidence suggests that such discrimination is severe and widespread." Furthermore, many LGBT school workers continue to feel they are caught in the long-standing double bind: they are vulnerable to dismissal if they reveal their sexual orientation, but, unless they reveal their sexual orientation, they are unlikely to secure full employment rights. The authors of the NEA Report closed:

> This discrimination against g/l/b/t education employees is damaging not only to the affected employees themselves, but to g/l/b/t students as well. In a discriminatory environment, g/l/b/t education employees may be reluctant to intervene on behalf of victimized g/l/b/t students or otherwise be supportive of such students in order to avoid disclosure of their own sexual orientation/gender identification, and both g/l/b/t and non-g/l/b/t education employees may be reluctant to do so out of concern that they might be perceived as promoting homosexuality. Moreover, when students observe employment discrimination on the basis of sexual orientation/gender discrimination, it reinforces attitudes in a way that places g/l/b/t students in a form of double jeopardy: "Abusive youth justify their harassment by pointing to

societal and governmental support for discrimination, and abused youth get the message that even adults in positions of authority can be attacked because of who they are."[69]

As the twenty-first century opens, school workers who identify as LGBT continue facing immense social resistance and lack of job security. Despite important legal and political victories won by courageous LGBT school workers, the larger LGBT movement, and an expanding array of allies, remarkably few such school workers believe they are free of workplace discrimination on account of their gender identity or sexual orientation. And regardless of abundant and carefully executed research to the contrary, a large portion of the population still believes that LGBT teachers either wish to molest youth or that they will damage the "normal" sexual and gender development of their charges.

When the previous century began, the male teachers of the New York City schools fought for higher wages than women and substantial recruiting initiatives to employ more male teachers. They argued that a greater male presence in schools would ensure that children developed proper gender qualities, in part because males long had been expected to patrol and enforce gender boundaries. They rationalized their campaign largely by invoking the needs of students.

Over the remainder of the century, a wide variety of others have similarly couched their rhetoric in terms of students' welfare. Those who wished to purge schools of persons desiring others of the same sex or manifesting nonconforming gender qualities have explained their efforts as protecting students. The recurrent logic holds that such persons either will sexually molest students or, through their influence, inspire students to become homosexual and/or gender-nonconforming. Just as the male teachers in New York offered no proof that a larger presence of male teachers would make boys more manly and females more womanly, critics have offered no compelling evidence that LGBT school workers change students' sexual and/or gender identities any more than gender-conforming heterosexuals. And as Kelli Petersen, the student activist from Utah, might argue, generations of seemingly heterosexual and gender-conforming teachers have not kept LGBT youth from identifying as such.

The New York male teachers of the last century took their campaign to the public, hosting discussions, writing letters to the *New York Times,* and generating significant news coverage for their concerns. Since that time, school workers who have desired others of the same sex and/or crossed conventional gender bounds mostly have resisted pleading their cases publicly because stepping forward could entail job loss. School workers as a group tend to be economically vulnerable, so they do not take threats to their employment lightly, careers for which they have earned college degrees and licenses.

The LGBT school workers who have spoken up, resisted discrimination, and built politically effective organizations have done enormously important work on behalf of their colleagues. Even though Peggy Burton, John Gish, Joseph Acanfora, James Gaylord, and others who fought similar cases could not retain their teaching positions, their legal battles have resulted in much improved conditions for many others. The hostile climate for LGBT persons in schools has been mitigated somewhat over the years by the activists who organized LGBT school worker associations, marched in pride parades—thus inspiring the wrath of those who believed such school workers should remain in the closet, have told their stories to others, and have organized gay/straight student alliances. And the larger LGBT movement, which at times has provided strong support for the rights of LGBT school workers, has inspired the rise of activism by and for LGBT school workers even as it retains some ambivalence about supporting persons who work so near its zone of greatest political vulnerability.

The welfare of students has been invoked in each of these battles, from that of the male teachers of New York through more recent ones in which political and religious conservatives maintain that it is for the sake of the students that they wish to keep LGBT persons out of schools. Over the 1990s, LGBT school workers, too, have argued that their rights need to be recognized for the benefit of students, so they might serve as positive role models for LGBT youth.

Remarkably, though, during the 1990s and early twenty-first century, students have taken matters into their own hands. Not content to have adults speak on their behalf or make vital decisions for them without understanding the realities of their lives, students around the country have organized and rapidly won expanded rights for LGBT persons and their allies in schools. Such student activists have enlisted the support of straight students, teachers, and community members, thus broadening their base and effectiveness. These students have leveraged the security of the requirement that they attend school against the job insecurity experienced by their LGBT teachers and other school workers. And they have shifted the contours of these debates from "for the students" to "by the students."

Epilogue

At the start of the twenty-first century, the experiences of school workers who desire others of the same sex and/or possess nonconforming gender identities differ remarkably from those 100 years earlier. Today, growing numbers of teachers claim LGBT identities openly while retaining their jobs, although the overwhelming majority still fear employment reprisals. In 1900, few would have thought it possible that any among the legions of unmarried women teachers might have desired other women emotionally and/or sexually. Lesbian identity largely did not exist in popular thought. Besides, the public benefited mightily from the service of these inexpensive, willing, and qualified workers. Some urban communities sought greater numbers of male teachers—yet they also disparaged such men for their close association with what had become known as "women's work." Essentially, teaching was thought to emasculate men. Also, a few schools dismissed male teachers who had been caught engaging in sexual activities with other males, but such dismissal hinged on individual instances of supposedly deviant behavior rather than homosexual identity.

Despite these differences, some present conditions greatly resemble those of a century earlier. Currently, women account for the overwhelming majority of teachers. A recent NEA report indicates that in 2001, women held 79 percent of all teaching positions and men only 21 percent.[1] This is comparable to the ratio that existed nearly 100 years ago. Although men entered teaching in greater numbers during mid-century, the work largely has returned to its highly female-associated status.

In parallel fashion, the school superintendency has remained male-associated throughout the twentieth century. In 1910, men held 91 percent of all superintendencies.[2] A recent study indicates that in 2000, men accounted for a notably similar proportion: 87 percent.[3] Furthermore, in 2001, an astonishing 95 percent of these men were married—in contrast with the current rate among men in the general population of 58 percent.[4] Although women have begun attaining school administrative positions in

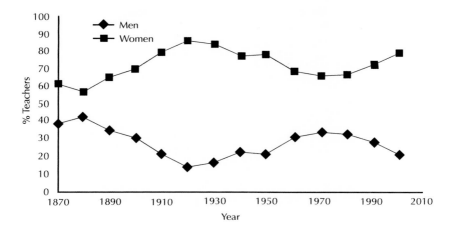

Figure E.1. Sex of Teachers, 1870–2001. Data for 1870–1950 can be found in *The Statistical History of the United States from Colonial Times to the Present* (Stamford, CT: Fairfield Publishers, Inc., 1965), 208. Data for 1961–2001 is in NEA, *The Status of the American Public School Teacher, 2000–2001* (Washington, DC: NEA, 2003), 90. Also available online at http://www.nea.org/edstats/images/status.pdf.

growing numbers, their presence in the positions of greatest responsibility and remuneration is still quite limited, especially in light of women's dominating presence in teaching, the field from which superintendents are eventually drawn.

School work has been and remains highly sex-stratified. To generalize, women teach and men administer. Although many factors contribute to this persistent condition, one powerful, yet underexplored cause is the ongoing fear of school workers who transgress the bounds of conventional sexuality and/or gender. As I have shown throughout this volume, this deep-seated concern about the sexuality and/or gender of school workers has profoundly affected policymaking, personnel practices, curriculum, school-related activities, and, of course, it also has significantly affected informal social aspects of schooling.

Today, for example, school administrators, particularly high school principals and superintendents, are called on to police the boundaries of acceptable sexuality and gender. They make decisions about whether or not gay/straight alliances may meet in their high schools. They decide which teaching candidates to hire. They reprimand any personnel deemed inappropriate on account of gender presentation/identity or sexual orientation, real or perceived. They choose whether or not dress codes will be implemented, including those that are gender-associated.

They oversee gender-associated school activities and officially approved courtship rituals such as dances. In these and so many other ways, they are charged with setting and maintaining sexuality and gender bounds for schools. Not coincidentally, the vast majority of high school principals and school superintendents are married men, many of whom also have coached high school male athletics. As such, they symbolically epitomize heterosexual masculinity.

Conversely, few men teach in elementary school classrooms. Men accounted for only 9 percent of such positions in 2000.[5] Because of the historically strong association of elementary teaching with women, men essentially cross the line of gender-propriety by working in this area. And, as I have indicated throughout, such gender transgression in the case of men is presumed to indicate gay or bisexual status. In turn, many still contend that LGBT persons prey on children or otherwise confound their sexual/gender development. Because of the formal and informal punishments that LGBT persons often endure in schools, the small proportion of men in this work hardly comes as a surprise.

Just as they were 100 years ago, school workers today are hired in part to model and preserve normative sexuality and gender. When parents, community members, and school workers plead for more men in schools so that youth will be exposed to "strong male role models," really this often means that they want heterosexual men who will regulate the sexuality and gender of students and school personnel. Men who pursue traditionally female-associated jobs, display gender-nonconformity, remain unmarried, or openly identify as gay, bisexual or transgender, typically are not hired in the first place, or, if hired, endure heightened scrutiny. In much the same manner, women who seek male-associated educational positions such as high school principalships or superintendencies, coach certain sports, remain unmarried, or identify openly as lesbian, bisexual, or transgender, tend to face internal resistance, if not overt employment discrimination.

In these early years of the twenty-first century, however, an astonishing variety of events are unfolding that either reflect or promise improved conditions for LGBT school workers. On June 26, 2003, the Supreme Court struck down the "Texas Homosexual Conduct Law," which criminalized private sexual activities between persons of the same sex. Immediately, sodomy laws in thirteen states disappeared and whole classes of persons became law-abiding citizens. Matt Foreman, executive director of the National Gay and Lesbian Task Force, commented, "While this is a victory for individual liberties of all Americans, it is particularly welcome for gay people, who have been singled out for persecution and discrimination by these laws for decades." Sodomy laws such as the one in

Texas have been employed to justify discrimination against lesbian, gay, and bisexual persons. The authors of the "Friend of the Court" brief filed by the Human Rights Campaign; the National Gay and Lesbian Task Force; Parents, Families and Friends of Lesbians & Gays; and a number of other LGBT and allied organizations explain that "sodomy laws are most commonly used by states *not* to punish particular persons for having engaged in proscribed acts, but to impose legal disabilities on persons who can be identified as 'homosexual' without regard to any proof that they have engaged in the proscribed conduct. In other words, the primary function of sodomy laws today is to brand gay people as 'criminals,' a brand that itself works to inflict a variety of psychological and legal harms."[6] As a consequence of the Supreme Court's *Lawrence v. Texas* decision, lesbian, gay, and bisexual individuals may win expanded rights. However, even with the elimination of criminal status for LG and B persons, discrimination against such school workers may continue unabated. Laws against discrimination must also exist. As of February 2004, only fourteen states banned discrimination based on sexual orientation—and of these, only four also included gender identity in their laws.[7]

Beyond using the legal system to challenge discriminatory policies and practices, over the past three decades LGBT school workers also have banded together in a variety of organizations. GLSEN has become the primary organization in the country working specifically for improved conditions for all LGBT persons and their allies in schools. GLSEN members endeavor to educate school communities about LGBT persons, to raise awareness of the harassment that LGBT students continually face, as well as to track the discrimination endured by LGBT school workers. Often, LGBT school workers sponsor gay/straight alliances in their schools and find that this participation connects them with other such school workers as well as the larger organization. Over 900 gay/straight alliances existed within a decade of the first such recorded group in 1989—and the pace of growth shows no sign of slackening.[8]

GLSEN has been spectacularly effective in raising awareness of LGBT issues in schools and developing leadership skills among students wishing to start or maintain gay/straight alliances or otherwise work for their political rights. LGBT school workers who face job discrimination, however, must seek legal support from other organizations such as the NEA and AFT.

Although expanding numbers of LG and B teachers are coming out and keeping their jobs, matters remain relatively more difficult for transgender and transsexual school workers. Extraordinarily few school workers with cross-gender identities or those who have transitioned to the other sex have kept their jobs. For example, in the late 1990s, a Sacramento teacher lost his position when he revealed a planned sex-change operation.[9] More recently in Colorado, however, Randey Michelle Gordon similarly underwent male-to-female sex-change surgery, but she kept her job and maintained the support of administrators, colleagues, and the school community.[10] And when an Illinois principal chose to transition from a man to a woman, Deanna Reed's school board supported her continued employment, provided that she implement a plan for informing all members of the school community.[11] These cases may signal a critical shift in climate for transgender and transsexual school workers.

Conditions generally remain especially difficult for LGBT school administrators, however. LGBT school administrators who come out typically face problems with parents and school board members. Furthermore, most do not enjoy much legal support from school administrator organizations. And relatively few school administrators belong to the NEA and AFT, which have gone on record in support of LGBT school workers and also provide legal representation for members faced with employment discrimination on account of sexual orientation or gender presentation.[12] Finally, because many school administrators serve at the pleasure of their school boards, their employment security is reduced even further.

When the twentieth century opened, awareness of same-sex desire had begun seeping into public consciousness as the word "homosexual" found its way into common expression; as new British laws made high-profile spectacles of men such as Oscar Wilde who were charged with this crime; as research produced by sexologists reached the shelves of medical doctors and growing ranks of psychologists; and as elite boarding schools on both sides of the Atlantic struggled to maintain their images after reports circulated about rampant sexual activity among their charges. The notion of same-sex desire, commonly conflated with nonconforming gender, eventually encompassed not only men, but also women as the larger women's movement achieved expanded social, political, and economic power for half of the population. By mid-century, vast numbers of unmarried women teachers found that their communities no longer regarded them as valued members of the community—but rather, they had come to be regarded as suspected deviants, if not lesbians. This suspicion of deviance gave way to widespread panic after World War II as school officials aggressively sought to remove men and women from schools who remained unmarried, exhibited unconventional gender qualities, or otherwise provoked suspicion of homosexuality. This system depended on total intimidation, which compelled self-identified homosexuals to hide and everyone else to conform strictly to narrow notions of sexuality and gender. As post-Stonewall lesbians and gay men flouted the requirement that they remain hidden, as their visibility in urban areas increased around the country, and even as a few lesbian and gay teachers began challenging discrimination in court, religious and political conservatives organized to force such school workers back into hiding. Then, when Anita Bryant proved that campaigning against homosexual teachers could galvanize powerful political support and inspire vast fund-raising, conservative religious and political groups around the country raised with increasing regularity the specter of "homosexual" teachers who molested children or otherwise corrupted their proper sexual and/or gender development. They have continued to employ this as a wedge issue, dividing otherwise cohesive, socially moderate, and liberal constituencies. Even some LGBT persons experience ambivalence about supporting LGBT school workers—individuals who work close to where LGBT persons have been attacked with great ferocity—those who work with youth. Furthermore, because so many LGBT persons have experienced great harassment, discrimination, and other social trauma during their own school experiences, they may feel reticent about supporting workers associated with an institution that either has inflicted or allowed so much harm.

Over the 1990s and into the early twenty-first century, however, LGBT issues have moved into the mainstream as lesbian and gay characters appear with great regularity in television shows, major motion pictures, novels across genres, magazines, and local newspapers. LGBT school workers and students no longer exist in theory only. Instead, communities are coming to terms with the fact that LGBT school workers and students exist in every school.

Though high-profile stories continue to capture national attention, such as the opening of the new Harvey Milk High School building in New York City during the fall of 2003, increasingly, the story of LGBT school workers and students is unfolding at the local level—everywhere. Hundreds of high school principals every year must figure out how to support newly proposed gay/straight alliances. Millions of teachers must determine how best to help LGBT students who confront harassment and discrimination in schools on a regular basis. Millions of young people must come to terms with their own nonconforming sexuality/gender or that of their friends. Hundreds of teacher preparation programs must learn how to assist teacher candidates in understanding LGBT issues in schools. And hundreds of thousands of self-identified LGBT school workers must decide how best to honor their identities while engaging in their chosen profession—all too frequently in unsupportive school environments. It is in these local and very personal arenas that conservative religious and political groups currently are waging intense battles.

Without question, school work remains highly sex-stratified, gender-polarized, and hostile to those who desire persons of the same sex or manifest unconventional gender. These conditions conspire against educating students in a manner that best realizes their humanity, their potential. Schools that remain locked in fear of LGBT school workers inevitably will cripple the development of students, confining them to narrowly defined gender paths and tormenting them for same-sex desires. And by severely constraining the daily experiences of hundreds of thousands of LGBT school workers, the profession loses the services of a talented, dedicated pool that includes some of its best workers. Indeed, despite all that has been done to make us disappear, to diminish our contributions, and even to punish us, the ranks of school workers are filled with vast numbers of LGBT persons who are deeply committed to the welfare of students—and also who possess exquisite skill. Undoubtedly, we are highly fit to teach.

Notes

Introduction

1. Karen V. Hansen, "'No Kisses Is Like Yourses': An Erotic Friendship between Two African-American Women during the Mid-Nineteenth Century," *Gender and History* 7, 2 (1995): 153–182.
2. Kellie McGarrh, "Hanging' in Tough: The Life of Superintendent Mildred E. Doyle, 1904–1989," Dissertation completed at the University of Tennessee, Knoxville (August 1995), 121–122. McGarrh's dissertation was published posthumously as Clinton B. Allison, ed., *Kellie McGarrh's Hangin' in Tough: Mildred E. Doyle, School Superintendent* (New York: Peter Lang, 2000). See p. 84 for McGarrh's description of Doyle's reelection campaign experience.
3. "Gay Teachers Organizing," *The Advocate*, 5 July 1972, 17.
4. Jamie Malernee and Peter Bernard, "Teacher of the Year Comes Out (FL)," *South Florida Sun-Sentinel*, 1 March 2002.
5. John D'Emilio, *Sexual Politics, Sexual Communities: The Making of a Homosexual Minority in the United States, 1940–1970*, 2nd edition (Chicago: University of Chicago Press, 1998).
6. Irving Bieber, *Homosexuality: A Psychoanalytic Study of Male Homosexuals* (New York: Basic Books, 1962).
7. George Alan Rekers, *Shaping Your Child's Sexual Identity* (Grand Rapids, MI: Baker Book House, 1982); and George Alan Rekers, *Growing Up Straight: What Families Should Know About Homosexuality* (Chicago: Moody Press, 1982). Currently, Rekers teaches in the School of Medicine at the University of South Carolina.
8. The National Gay and Lesbian Task Force maintains an up-to-date map of states that ban discrimination based on sexual orientation and gender identity. In February 2004, the states that ban discrimination based on sexual orientation are: Wisconsin, Massachusetts, Connecticut, Hawaii, New Jersey, Vermont, New Hampshire, Nevada, Maryland, Minnesota, Rhode Island, New Mexico, California, and New York. The states that also ban discrimination based on gender identity are: Minnesota, Rhode Island, New Mexico, and California. See http://www.ngltf.org/downloads/civilrightsmap.pdf.
9. Catherine Gewertz, "Fired Beverly Hills Superintendent Claims Anti-Gay Bias," *Education Week*, 8 March 2000, 3.
10. Tom Kertscher, "Court Dismisses Gay Teacher's Case (WI)," *Milwaukee Journal-Sentinel*, 22 March 2001, N.p.

11. The ability of GLSEN leaders and members to minimize the effects of this tactic employed so commonly against LGBT school workers is a testament to their willingness to confront the bugaboo head-on and reveal its fallacy. There have been skirmishes, though. In May 2000, GLSEN sponsored a "Teach Out" at Tufts University for students to ask questions about sexuality in a safe setting. The leaders of one session (out of over fifty) apparently responded to some student questions with discussion of specific sexual behaviors. Two parents in attendance, who belonged to the conservative Parents Rights Coalition, recorded the event illegally and then threatened to distribute the tapes. Kevin Jennings, Executive Director of GLSEN, responded, "GLSEN believes that children do have a right to accurate, safer sex education, but this needs to be delivered in an age appropriate and sensitive manner." The two instructors employed by the state were fired or resigned. The parents group staged a rally to protest the session as well as state funding for LGBT student programs. Then thousands of students and other GLSEN supporters organized a much larger rally to preserve state funding for programs supporting gay and lesbian teens. See Heidi Perlman, "Graphic Workshop for Gay Teens Run by Education Officials," Associated Press, Boston, 16 May 2000; and Raphael Lewis, "Thousands Rally to Preserve Funding for Gay Student Program," *Boston Globe*, 21 May 2000, B2.

12. Karen M. Harbeck, "Personal Freedoms/Public Constraints: An Analysis of the Controversy over the Employment of Homosexuals as School Teachers," dissertation completed at Stanford University, 1987. Harbeck, who also holds a law degree, structured much of her analysis on case law regarding the employment of lesbian and gay school workers. Both Harbeck's dissertation and her book, *Gay and Lesbian Educators: Personal Freedoms, Public Constraints* (Malden, MA: Amethyst Press, 1997), remain seminal works in the field.

13. "Homosexuality in America," *Life* 56, 25 (1964): 66–81.

14. I have worked extensively in the research libraries of the following institutions: University of North Carolina at Chapel Hill, Iowa State University, University of Wisconsin, University of Iowa, University of California at Los Angeles, and the University of Illinois. I also have used a number of others to a much lesser degree.

15. I visited the following LGBT historical collections: June Mazer Collection (West Hollywood), One International (West Hollywood), Lesbian History Collection (Los Angeles), LGBT Historical Society of Northern California (San Francisco), Harvey Milk Collection and Pulp Novel Collection (San Francisco Public Library), and the Gerber Hart Library (Chicago).

Chapter 1

1. Grace Strachan, *Equal Pay for Equal Work* (New York: B. F. Buck & Co., 1910). See also Robert E. Doherty, "Tempest on the Hudson: The Struggle

for 'Equal Pay for Equal Work' in the New York City Public Schools, 1907–1911," *History of Education Quarterly* 19, 4(1979): 413–434.

2. "Appeal for Men Teachers," *New York Times,* 4 October 1911, col. 7, 12.

3. *Statistical History of the United States from Colonial Times to the Present* (Stamford, CT: Fairfield Publishers, 1965), 208.

4. Joanne Meyerowitz, *How Sex Changed: A History of Transsexuality in the United States* (Cambridge: Harvard University Press, 2002).

5. Anthony Rotundo, *American Manhood* (New York: Basic Books, 1993). Also see footnote 1, 300.

6. John D'Emilio and Estelle B. Freedman, *Intimate Matters: A History of Sexuality in America,* 2nd edition (Chicago: University of Chicago Press, 1997).

7. W. E. B. DuBois, *The Philadelphia Negro* (New York: Lippincott, 1899), which also is available online at http://www2.pfeiffer.edu/~lridener/DSS/DuBois/pnchvi.html. See Chapter VI, "Conjugal Condition."

8. Rotundo, *American Manhood,* 3–5. Also see R. W. Connell, *Masculinities* (Berkeley: University of California Press, 1995); Michael Kimmel, *Manhood in America: A Cultural History* (New York: The Free Press, 1996); J. A. Mangan and James Walvin, *Manliness and Morality: Middle-Class Masculinity in Britain and America, 1800-1940* (Manchester, U.K.: Manchester University Press, 1987); Harry Brod, *The Making of Masculinities: The New Men's Studies* (Boston: Allen & Unwin, 1987); and Máirtín Mac an Ghaill, *The Making of Men: Masculinities, Sexualities and Schooling* (Buckingham, U.K.: Open University Press, 1994).

9. Rotundo, *American Manhood,* 3–4.

10. Ibid., 5–6.

11. Nancy Cott, *The Bonds of Womanhood: "Woman's Sphere" in New England, 1780-1835* (New Haven: Yale University Press, 1977).

12. For a discussion of the laws that both reflected and helped solidify separate spheres ideology, see Wendy W. Williams, "The Equality Crisis: Some Reflections on Culture, Courts, and Feminism," *Women's Rights Law Reporter* 7, 3 (1982): 175–200.

13. D'Emilio and Freedman, *Intimate Matters,* 60–61.

14. Ibid., particularly Chapter 4, "Within the Family," 55–84. Also see Carl N. Degler, *Out of Our Past: The Forces that Shaped Modern America,* 3rd edition (New York, Harper Torchbooks, 1984), especially the chapter, "The Shaping of American Families," 451–490; and Carl N. Degler, *At Odds: Women and the Family in America from the Revolution to the Present* (New York: Oxford University Press, 1980).

15. Angus McLaren, *The Trials of Masculinity: Policing Sexual Boundaries, 1870-1930* (Chicago: University of Chicago Press, 1997).

16. Walt Whitman, "A Death in the School-House," *Democratic Review,* August 1841, 177–182, which also is available at http://cdl.library.cornell.edu/cgi-bin/moa/moa-cgi?notisid=AGD1642-0009-26.

17. Washington Irving, *The Legend of Sleepy Hollow* (1819), 1, available at http://www.schooltales.com/sleepyhollow/.

18. Hubert Marshall Skinner, a former schoolmaster, compiled stories and satires about schoolmasters in late 1800s. This may have been a way to preserve something of the disappearing schoolmaster tradition. See his two collections, *The Schoolmaster in Literature* (New York: American Book Company, 1892), and *The Schoolmaster in Comedy and Satire* (New York: American Book Company, 1894).

19. Joseph Alva Baer, "Men Teachers in the Public Schools of the United States," Abstract of Dissertation, Ohio State University (1932), 4–5.

20. Thomas Morain, "The Departure of Males from the Teaching Profession in Nineteenth-Century Iowa," *Civil War History* 26, 2 (1980): 161–170, particularly 165.

21. W. E. B. DuBois, "A Negro Schoolmaster in the New South," *Atlantic Monthly,* January 1899, 99–104, which also is available at http://www.schooltales.com/negroschoolmaster/.

22. Baer, "Men Teachers."

23. Kimmel, *Manhood.*

24. Edward Eggleston, *The Hoosier Schoolmaster* (New York: Orange Judd and Company, 1871), which also is available online at http://www.schooltales.com/hoosierschoolmaster/.

25. Horace Mann, "Report for 1843," *Annual Reports on Education,* 2 (Boston: Horace B. Fuller, 1868); Mary Hurlbut Cordier, *Schoolwomen of the Prairies and Plains: Personal Narratives from Iowa, Kansas, and Nebraska, 1860s-1920s* (Albuquerque: University of New Mexico Press, 1992); John Rury, "Who Became Teachers? The Social Characteristics of Teachers in American History," in *American Teachers: Histories of a Profession at Work,* ed. Donald Warren (New York: Macmillan, 1989), 9–48.

26. Catharine Beecher, *The True Remedy for the Wrongs of Women* (Boston: Phillips, Sampson, 1851); Kathryn Kish Sklar, "Catharine Beecher: Transforming the Teaching Profession," in *Women's America: Refocusing the Past,* 3rd ed., ed. Linda K. Kerber and Jane Sherron De Hart (New York: Oxford University Press, 1991), 171–178; and Catharine Beecher, "Petition to Congress," *Godey's Ladies Book* (1853), 176–177.

27. Henry Raab, "Women as Teachers in Ungraded Schools," *Annual Report of the Secretary of the Interior for the Year Ending June 30, 1891,* Vol. 5. (Washington, DC: Government Printing Office, 1894), 1058.

28. Horace Mann, ed., *Common School Journal* 8 (1846), 117; May Wright Sewall, "Woman's Work in Education," *Proceedings of the National Educational Association 1884* (Boston: J. E. Farwell & Co., 1885), 153.

29. Myra Strober and David Tyack, "Why Do Women Teach and Men Manage? A Report on Research on Schools," *Signs: Journal of Women in Culture and Society* 5, 3 (1980): 494–503.

30. One of my very favorite discussions of the early history of women teachers in the United States is the first chapter in Kathleen Weiler's important book, *Country Schoolwomen: Teaching in Rural California, 1850-1950* (Stanford, CA: Stanford University Press, 1998), 8–34.

31. "Women Teachers in American Public Schools," *School Life* 14, 3 (1928): 50–51.

32. Jackie Blount, *Destined to Rule the Schools: Women and the Superintendency, 1873–1995* (Albany: State University of New York Press, 1998); *Statistical History,* 208; James C. Albisetti, "The Feminization of Teaching in the Nineteenth Century: A Comparative Perspective," *History of Education* 22, 3 (1993): 253–263; Alfred A. Cleveland, "The Predominance of Female Teachers," *Pedagogical Seminary* 12, 3 (1905): 289–303; Paul H. Mattingly, "Academia and Professional School Careers, 1840–1900," *Teachers College Record* 83, 2 (1981): 219–233; George K. Pederson, *The Itinerant Schoolmaster: A Socio-Economic Analysis of Teacher Turnover* (Chicago: Midwest Administration Center, University of Chicago, 1973); Solomon Schindler, "Men and Women Teachers," *Journal of Education* 39, 23 (1894): 357; Michael Sedlak, and Steven Schlossman, "Social Origins and Composition of the Teaching Force," *Who Will Teach? Historical Perspectives on the Changing Appeal of Teaching as a Profession* (Santa Monica, CA: Rand Corporation, 1986), 26–38; Myra H. Strober and Audri Gordon Lanford, "The Feminization of Public School Teaching: Cross-Sectional Analysis, 1850–1880," *Signs: Journal of Women in Culture and Society* 11, 2 (1986): 212–235; and Strober and Tyack, "Why Do Women Teach and Men Manage?"

33. Kimmel, *Manhood,* 1–10.

34. C. W. Bardeen, "Why Teaching Repels Men," *Educational Review* (April 1908): 352–355. Also see Lotus Delta Coffman, *The Social Composition of the Teaching Population. Contributions to Education, No. 41* (New York: Teachers College, 1911), 82. Here, Coffman attributes the decreasing number of male teachers to "the changed character of the management of the public schools, the narrowing of the intellectual range or versatility required of teachers," and, of course, to the fact that women teachers could be employed for much lower wages than men.

35. Bardeen, "Why Teaching Repels Men," 351.

36. Earl Barnes, "The Feminizing of Culture," *Atlantic Monthly,* June 1912, 770–773.

37. Henry Armstrong, "Report," *Reports of the Mosely Educational Commission to the United States* (London: Co-operative Printing Society Limited, 1903; repr. New York: Arno Press & The New York Times, 1969), 13.

38. "Male Teachers Needed," *American School Board Journal,* December 1908, 8.

39. C. F. Adams, "The Development of the Superintendency," *Addresses and Journal of Proceedings of the NEA 1880* (Salem, OH: Allan K. Tatem, 1880), 65.

40. Bardeen, "Why Teaching," 358.

41. Thomas W. Churchill, "The Superintendent as the Layman Sees Him," *Addresses and Proceedings of the NEA, 1916* (Washington, DC: NEA, 1916), 940–945.

42. Blount, *Destined to Rule the Schools,* 46–60.
43. Susan B. Anthony and Ida Harper, eds., *History of Woman Suffrage,* 4 (1900; repr. Salem, NH: Ayer, 1985): 575–578; Helen Laura Sumner Woodbury, *Equal Suffrage* (New York: Collegiate Equal Suffrage League, 1909), 128–144; and Kathleen Underwood, "Schoolmarms on the Upper Missouri," *Great Plains Quarterly* 11, 4 (1991): 225–233.
44. Grace Strachan, "Two Masters Cannot be Served," *The Woman Voter* 5, 12 (1914): 12.

Chapter 2

1. Thomas Woody, *A History of Women's Education in the United States,* Vol. 2 (New York: The Science Press, 1929), 225–229.
2. Carroll Smith-Rosenberg, "The Female World of Love and Ritual: Relations between Women in Nineteenth-Century America," *Signs: Journal of Women in Culture and Society* 1, 1 (1975): 19–27; and Karen M. Harbeck, *Gay and Lesbian Educators: Personal Freedoms, Public Constraints* (Malden, MA: Amethyst Press and Productions, 1997), 165.
3. Martha Vicinus, "Distance and Desire: English Boarding School Friendships, 1870–1920," *Signs: Journal of Women in Culture and Society* 9, 4 (1984): 602.
4. Ibid.
5. Ibid., 603–604.
6. Ibid. For further discussion of romantic friendships among nineteenth-century women, see Susan Albertine, "Heart's Expression: The Middle-Class Language of Love in Late Nineteenth-Century Correspondence," *American Literary History* 4, 1 (1992): 141–164; and Lillian Faderman's work on the subject, *Surpassing the Love of Men: Romantic Friendship and Love Between Women From the Renaissance to the Present* (New York: William Morrow, 1981).
7. Vicinus, "Distance and Desire," 604–605.
8. Ibid., 605, 611.
9. Sara Burstall, *English High School for Girls* (London: Longmans, 1907), 160–161, quoted in Vicinus, "Distance and Desire," 617.
10. Havelock Ellis, *Sexual Inversion in Women* (1895), Appendix D.
11. E. G. Lancaster, *Pedagogical Seminary* (1897): 256–257. Also, Nancy Cott describes the early 1800s as a period during which girls and women commonly maintained intense friendships with other women. In "Sisterhood," in *The Bonds of Womanhood: 'Woman's Sphere' in New England, 1780–1835,"* (New Haven: Yale University Press, 1977), 160–196, she describes the nature of many of these close friendships in the context of female academies and seminaries.
12. Anne Firor Scott, "The Ever Widening Circle: The Diffusion of Feminist Values from the Troy Female Seminary, 1822–1872," *History of Education Quarterly* 19, 1 (1979): 3–25.

13. Vicinus, "Distance and Desire," 618–619.

14. Lillian Faderman, *Odd Girls and Twilight Lovers: A History of Lesbian Life in Twentieth-Century America* (New York: Penguin, 1991), 50–51.

15. Havelock Ellis, "*Sexual Inversion of Women*," in *Gay/Lesbian Almanac: A New Documentary,* ed. Jonathan Ned Katz (New York: Harper & Row, Publishers, 1983), 269–273.

16. Irving D. Stenhardt, *Ten Sex Talks to Girls* (Philadelphia: Lippincott, 1914), 57–62, quoted in Faderman, *Odd Girls,* 50.

17. A College Graduate, "'Your Daughter: What Are Her Friendships?" *Harper's Bazaar,* October 1913, 16.

18. R. W. Shufeldt, "Dr. Havelock Ellis on Sexual Inversion," *Pacific Medical Journal* XLV (1902): 199–207, quoted in Carroll Smith-Rosenberg, *Disorderly Conduct: Visions of Gender in Victorian America* (New York: Oxford University Press, 1985), 280.

19. Quoted in William G. Shade, "A Mental Passion: Female Sexuality in Victorian America," *International Journal of Women's Studies* 1, 1 (1978): 16.

20. Anna Mary Wells, *Miss Marks and Miss Woolley* (Boston: Houghton Mifflin Co., 1978), 107.

21. Patricia Palmieri, *In Adamless Eden: The Community of Women Faculty at Wellesley* (New Haven: Yale University Press, 1995), 137–142. Palmieri offers a sensitive discussion of the close relationships of these women faculty members, carefully avoiding the historical distortion that occurs when contemporary labels are applied to the experiences of earlier generations.

22. Helen Lefkowitz Horowitz, *Alma Mater: Design and Experience in the Women's Colleges from Their Nineteenth-Century Beginnings to the 1930s* (Boston: Beacon Press, 1984), 187–193, especially 190.

23. Nancy Sahli, "Smashing: Women's Relationships Before the Fall," *Crysalis* (Summer 1979): 17–27; and Sheila Jeffreys, *The Spinster and Her Enemies* (London: Spinifex Press, 1997), 105.

24. Carol Lloyd, "Was Lincoln Gay?" *Salon.com,* 3 May 1999. Also see Richard A. Kaye, "Outing Abe," *The Village Voice,* 25 June—1 July 2003, which is available online at http://www.villagevoice.com/issues/0326/ kaye.php.

25. Rotundo, *American Manhood,* 77; and E. A. Rotundo, "Romantic Friendship: Male Intimacy and Middle-Class Youth in the Northern United States, 1800-1900," *Journal of Social History* 23, 1 (1989): 1–25.

26. Edward Carpenter, *The Intermediate Sex: A Study of Some Transitional Types of Men and Women* (New York: Mitchell Kennerley, 1912), 78–81, 82. Noël Greig describes Carpenter's life and work in "Introduction," *Edward Carpenter: Selected Writings,* Vol. 1 (London: GMP Publishers, 1984), 9–77.

27. J. R. de S. Honey, *Tom Brown's Universe: The Development of the English Public School in the Nineteenth Century* (New York: Quadrangle, 1977), 178.

28. Ibid., 192–193.

29. Ibid., 183, 185; and Vern and Bonnie Bullough, "Homosexuality in Nineteenth Century English Public Schools," in *Homosexuality in International*

Perspective, eds. Joseph Harry and Man Sing Das (New Delhi: Vikas Publishing House, 1980), 123–131.

30. Honey, *Tom Brown's Universe,* 192–193.

31. Martha Vicinus argues, however, that Havelock Ellis's work was banned in England at the time, having been deemed pornographic. She contends that his influence was not felt strongly in England until early in the twentieth century.

32. Evelyn Waugh, quoted in Jonathan Gathorne-Hardy, *The Public School Phenomenon, 597-1977* (London: Hodder and Stoughton, 1977), 164.

33. Carpenter, *The Intermediate Sex,* 104.

34. Honey, *Tom Brown's Universe,* 190.

35. Gathorne-Hardy, *The Public School Phenomenon,* 164.

36. Honey, *Tom Brown's Universe,* 178–185.

37. Carroll Smith-Rosenberg, "Sex as Symbol in Victorian Purity: An Ethnohistorical Analysis of Jacksonian America," *The American Journal of Sociology,* 84, Supplement: Turning Points: Historical and Sociological Essays on the Family (1978), S212-S247.

38. William Alcott, *The Young Man's Guide* (Boston: Marvin, 1833), "Section III. Diseases of Licentiousness," which also is available online at http://www.nimbus.org/ElectronicTexts/YgMnsGde.1836.html.

39. Quoted in Smith-Rosenberg, "Sex as Symbol," S233.

40. Ibid., S226-S227. Also, Vern Bullough and Martha Voght present the argument that the term commonly employed during the mid-1800s for masturbation was "onanism," which also included same-sex sexual activities and everything else short of heterosexual intercourse. See "Homosexuality and Its Confusion with the 'Secret Sin' in Pre-Freudian America," *Journal of the History of Medicine and Allied Sciences* 28, 2 (1973): 143–155.

41. Edward Stevenson, "The Intersexes," in *Gay/Lesbian Almanac: A New Documentary,* ed. Jonathan Ned Katz (New York: Harper & Row, Publishers, 1983), 326–332, especially 329.

42. Amit R. Paley, "The Secret Court of 1920," *The Harvard Crimson,* 21 November 2002.

43. Harbeck, *Gay and Lesbian Educators,* 171–172; and David S. Reynolds, *Walt Whitman's America: A Cultural Biography* (New York: Alfred A. Knopf, 1995), 70–72.

44. Gary Scharnhorst and Jack Bales, *The Lost Life of Horatio Alger, Jr.* (Bloomington: Indiana University Press, 1985), 1–3; Tom Cowan, "Horatio Alger Jr.," in *Gay Men and Women Who Enriched the World* (Los Angeles: Alyson Publications, 1996), 80–86; and Jonathan Katz, "1866: Unitarian Church, Brewster, Massachusetts; Horatio Alger Accused," in *Gay American History: Lesbians & Gay Men in the U.S.A.,* revised edition (New York: Meridian, 1992), 33–34.

45. Sherwood Anderson, "Hands," *Winesburg, Ohio* (New York: The Modern Library, 1919), 9–12.

46. David Tyack and Elisabeth Hansot, *Learning Together: A History of Public Education in American Schools* (New York: Russell Sage Foundation, 1991), 166.

47. Quoted in Woody, *A History of Women's Education,* 265. Here, Woody notes that "extremely few articles in favor of coeducation failed to mention the purifying influence as an argument."

48. Constance Long, "A Sign of the Times for Those Who Can Read Portents," in *Gay/Lesbian Almanac: A New Documentary,* ed. Jonathan Ned Katz (New York: Harper & Row, Publishers, 1983), 387.

49. Willard Waller, *The Sociology of Teaching* (New York: John Wiley & Sons, 1932), 140.

50. For example, Karen Graves documents how high schools in St. Louis shifted their curricula so that, by the 1930s, females typically enrolled in a distinct set of courses designed to make them "domesticated citizens." See *Girls' Schooling during the Progressive Era: From Female Scholar to Domesticated Citizen* (New York: Garland Publishing, 1998). Also, David Tyack and Elisabeth Hansot offer a groundbreaking analysis of this phenomenon in "Differentiating the High School: The 'Woman Question,'" in *Learning Together,* 201–242.

Chapter 3

1. John K. Folger and Charles B. Nam, *Education of the American Population: A 1960 Census Monograph,* U.S. Bureau of the Census (Washington, DC: U.S. Government Printing Office, 1967), 81.

2. Kathleen Hickok, "The Spinster in Victoria's England: Changing Attitudes in Popular Poetry by Women," *Journal of Popular Culture* 15, 3 (1981): 120.

3. Margaret Mead, *Male and Female: A Study of the Sexes in a Changing World* (New York: Mentor Books, 1962), 225.

4. Harriet Elizabeth Paine (pseudonym: Eliza Chester), *The Unmarried Woman* (New York: Dodd, Mead and Company, 1892), 2.

5. Paine, *The Unmarried Woman,* 107–108. In a similar vein, Geraldine Clifford quotes Benjamin Ide Wheeler, president of the University of California, who tells women students in 1904: "You may have the same studies as the men, but you put them to different use. You are not here with the ambition to be school teachers or old maids; but you are here for the preparation of marriage and motherhood. This education should tend to make you more serviceable as wives and mothers." Benjamin Ide Wheeler, *The Daily Californian,* September 1, 1904 (p. 9), quoted in Geraldine Jonçich Clifford, "Gender Expectations and American Teachers," *Teacher Education Quarterly* 14, 2 (1987): 6–16. Also see Christina Simmons, "Companionate Marriage and the Lesbian Threat," *Frontiers* 4, 3 (1979): 54–59, for a discussion of the rise of marriages based on romantic love rather than convenience or arrangement by families.

6. "The Abandoned Spinster: By One of the Sisterhood," *The Atlantic Monthly,* January 1922, 80–84.

7. Ruth Freeman and Patricia Klaus, "Blessed or Not? The New Spinster in

England and the United States in the Late Nineteenth and Early Twentieth Centuries," *Journal of Family History* 9, 4 (1984): 395.

8. Around the turn of the century there was no clear consensus on an appropriate term to describe single women. Once single woman wrote: "In the eyes of the world, we lack entity. We do not even have a name. 'Old maid' is outlawed by connotation, 'spinster' sounds bookish and a little affected, 'maiden lady' belongs to an earlier day, 'unmarried woman' is roundabout, 'bachelor girl' is silly. We need the recognition of a fair title." Anonymous, "A Spinster I," *Atlantic Monthly*, May 1934, 542–543. Also see Susan Koppelman, *Old Maids: Short Stories by Nineteenth Century US Women Writers* (Boston: Pandora Press, 1984), 3.

9. Paine, *The Unmarried Woman*, 50.

10. Spencer J. Maxcy, "The Teacherage in American Rural Education," *The Journal of General Education* 30, 4 (1979): 271; and Marta Danylewycz, Beth Light, and Allison Prentice, "The Evolution of the Sexual Division of Labor in Teaching: Nineteenth Century Ontario and Quebec Case Study," in *Women and Education: A Canadian Perspective*, eds. Jane S. Gaskell and Arlene Tigar McLaren (Calgary, Alberta: Detselig Enterprises Ltd., 1987), 51.

11. Ibid., 51–53.

12. John W. Chalmers, "Do You Remember the Teacherage?" *Alberta History* 39, 3 (1991): 26–28.

13. Paula M. Bauman, "Single Women Homesteaders in Wyoming 1880–1930," *Annals of Wyoming* 58, 1 (1986): 39–53.

14. Philip L. Gerber, editor, *The Homesteading Letters of Elizabeth Corey, 1909-1919* (Iowa City: University of Iowa Press, 1990), xi–xviii. For a general discussion of the experiences of early women teachers in the Midwest, see Mary Hurlbut Cordier, *Schoolwomen of the Prairies and Plains: Personal Narratives From Iowa, Kansas, and Nebraska, 1860s-1920s* (Albuquerque: The University of New Mexico Press, 1992).

15. Dick D'Easum, *Dowager of Discipline: The Life of Dean of Women Permeal French* (Moscow: University Press of Idaho, 1981), 40–47.

16. J. C. Muerman, *The District Owned or Controlled Teacher's Home*, Bulletin No. 16. (Washington, DC: Government Printing Office, 1922).

17. Edith A. Lathrop, "Many Rural Districts Provide Comfortable Homes for Teachers," *School Life* 11, 3 (1925): 47–49.

18. Josephine Corliss Preston, "The Nation, Our Field," *Addresses and Proceedings of the National Education Association, 1920* (Washington, DC: NEA, 1920), 35–39; and Mrs. W. S. Griswold, "The Rural School's Friend," *The Woman Citizen*, 16 June 1923: 10; and Maxcy, "The Teacherage." Preston was elected president of the NEA in 1920.

19. Griswold, "Rural School's Friend," 10.

20. "Teacherages in Texas," *School and Society* 31, 805 (1930): 731.

21. Ronald E. Butchart, "The Frontier Teacher: Arizona, 1875–1925," *Journal of the West* 16, 3 (1977): 57.

22. Richard F. Hayes, "Standards of Living of Single Women Public-School

Teachers in New York State," Abstract of Dissertation, New York University (1935), 3, 5.

23. Griswold, "The Rural School's Friend," 10; and Maxcy, "The Teacherage," 267–274.

24. Edith A. Lathrop, "Many Rural Districts Provide Comfortable Homes for Teachers," *School Life* 11, 3 (1925): 47–49.

25. George Ellington, *Women of New York, or the Under-World of the Great City* (New York: New York Book Company, 1869), 640–641.

26. Joanne Meyerowitz's groundbreaking work, *Women Adrift: Independent Wage Earners in Chicago, 1880–1930* (Chicago: University of Chicago Press, 1988), details the rapid shift in urban accommodations available to single women around the turn of the century—and consequently, a shift in their lifestyles as well.

27. Helen Sard Hughes, "Can Women Make Good?" *School and Society* 2, 36 (1915): 342–343.

28. Freeman and Klaus, "Blessed or Not?" 401–407; and Richard Harris, "The End Justified the Means: Boarding and Rooming in a City of Homes, 1890–1951," *Journal of Social History* 26, 2 (1992): 331–358.

29. "A Spinster I," *Atlantic Monthly,* May 1934, 542.

30. Paine, *The Unmarried Woman,* 147.

31. Hazel Davis and Richard R. Foster, "Teacher Personnel—II. Economic and Social Status," in *Encyclopedia of Educational Research,* ed. Walter S. Monroe (New York: Macmillan Company, 1950), 1417.

32. Hughes, "Can Women Make Good?" 342.

33. Frances Donovan, *The School Ma'am* (New York: Frederick A. Stokes Co., 1938), 228.

34. Paine, *The Unmarried Woman.*

35. Ibid., 163–164.

36. Susan B. Anthony and Ida Harper, eds., *History of Woman Suffrage,* 4 (1900; repr. Salem, NH: Ayer, 1985), 1043–1044.

37. Ibid., 1071–1072.

38. Estelle Freedman, "Separatism As Strategy: Female Institution Building and American Feminism, 1870–1930," *Feminist Studies* 5, 3 (1979): 512–529.

39. Ibid., 513.

40. May Wright Sewall, "Woman's Work in Education," *Proceedings of the National Educational Association, 1884* (Boston: J. E. Farwell & Co., 1885), 155; Alice S. Blackwell, "Do Teachers Need the Ballot?" in *Selected Articles on Woman Suffrage,* 2nd and revised edition, ed. Edith M. Phelps (Minneapolis, MN: H. W. Wilson, 1912), 74–82; and Mary Sumner Boyd, "The Woman Educator and the Vote," in *The Woman Suffrage Yearbook, 1917* (New York: National Woman Suffrage Publishing Company, 1917), 165–167.

41. Frances M. Bjrkman and Annie G. Porritt, eds., "The Blue Book," *Woman Suffrage History, Arguments, and Results* (New York: National Woman Suffrage Publishing, 1917), 30–40.

42. Patricia Smith Butcher, "Education for Equality: Women's Rights Periodicals

and Women's Higher Education, 1949–1920," *History of Higher Education Annual* 6 (1986): 63–74.

43. Kathleen Barry, *Susan B. Anthony: A Biography of a Singular Feminist* (New York: Ballantine, 1988), 39–45; and Louise Rosenfield Noun, "Carrie Lane Chapman Catt and her Mason city Experience," *Palimpsest* 74, 3 (1993): 130–144.

44. Paul H. Mattingly, *The Classless Profession: American Schoolmen in the Nineteenth Century* (New York: New York University Press, 1975); and Leslie Butler, *The Michigan Schoolmasters' Club: A Story of the First Seven Decades, 1886–1957* (Ann Arbor: University of Michigan, 1958).

45. Mattingly, *The Classless Profession,* 110–111; "Constitution of the NTA," *Proceedings of the National Teachers Association* (1857), 311–312; and Willard Ellsbree, *The American Teacher: Evolution of a Profession in a Democracy* (New York: American Book Company, 1939), 254–255.

46. Carter Alexander, *Some Present Aspects of the Work of Teachers' Voluntary Associations in the United States,* Contributions to Education, No. 36 (New York: Teachers College, 1910), 80–83. These organizations include: Boston Lady Teachers' Association; Boston Teachers' Club; Boston Master's Assistants' Club; Canton, OH Teachers' Club; Cincinnati Women Teachers' Club; Chicago: Ella Flagg Young Club (Principals), Chicago Teachers' Federation; New York: Interboro Association, Women Principals' Association; San Jose, CA: Schoolwomen's Club; Somerville, MA: Woman Teachers' Club; Springfield, MA: Teachers' Club; Toledo, OH: Schoolmistresses' Club; Jersey City Teachers' Club; Jersey City Primary Principals' Association; Patterson, NJ: Public Kindergarten Association; Philadelphia Teachers' Club; Providence, RI: Rhode Island Kindergarten League, Sarah E. Doyle Club; Savannah Teachers' Mutual Benefit Association; Indianapolis: Federation of Teachers; Hartford, CT: Grade Teachers' Club; Houston, TX: Story Tellers' League; Memphis: Story Tellers' League; Pittsburgh Teachers' Art Club; Denver: Women's Educational Club of Colorado; Savannah Kindergarten Club.

47. Ibid., 80.

48. See Kate Rousmaniere's brilliant forthcoming biography of Margaret Haley, *Citizen Teacher: Margaret Haley and the Origin of Teacher Activism.*

49. Alexander, *Some Present Aspects,* 77; Joan K. Smith, *Ella Flagg Young: Portrait of a Leader* (Ames, IA: Educational Studies Press, 1979), 158–159.

50. Carroll Smith-Rosenberg suggests that during the nineteenth century, women enjoyed deep, same-sex friendships that ranged from "the supportive love of sisters, through the enthusiasms of adolescent girls, to sensual avowals of love by mature women" and were woven into the layers of homosocial networks in which they lived. Further, this was a time that "permitted a wide latitude of emotions and sexual feelings" that stretched between "committed heterosexuality" and "uncompromising homosexuality." "The Female World of Love and Ritual: Relations between Women in Nineteenth-Century America," in *Disorderly Conduct: Visions of Gender in*

Victorian America (New York: Oxford University Press, 1985), 53–76. It was in this context that turn-of-the-century women teachers came of age.

51. Lillian Faderman, "Nineteenth-Century Boston Marriage as a Possible Lesson for Today," in *Boston Marriages: Romantic but Asexual Relationships among Contemporary Lesbians,* eds. Esther D. Rothblum and Kathleen A. Brehony (Amherst: The University of Massachusetts Press, 1993), 29–42. Also see Lillian Faderman, *To Believe in Women: What Lesbians Have Done for America—A History* (Boston: Houghton Mifflin, 1999). In her important piece, "'Imagine My Surprise': Women's Relationships in Mid-Twentieth Century America," Leila J. Rupp argues that caution is in order when trying to make sense of the close relationships of women during the early and mid-twentieth century. She suggests that while the significance of such relationships is clear, modern categories of sexual orientation should not be imposed on them. Essentially, it may not be accurate to call such women lesbians in the contemporary sense of the label. In *Hidden from History: Reclaiming the Gay & Lesbian Past,* eds., Martin Bauml Duberman, Martha Vicinus, and George Chauncey (New York: New American Library, 1989), 395–410. On the other hand, it is important to recognize that sexual activity may well have been part of some such relationships, whether or not these women identified as lesbians.

52. Ronald E. Butchart, "Mission Matters: Mount Holyoke, Oberlin, and the Schooling of Southern Blacks, 1861–1917," *History of Education Quarterly* 42, 1 (2002): 5–6.

53. Smith, *Ella Flagg Young,* 28–36; John T. McManis, *Ella Flagg Young and a Half-Century of the Chicago Public Schools* (Chicago: A. C. McClurg & Co., 1916), 56–72; and Rosemary V. Donatelli, "The Contributions of Ella Flagg Young to the Educational Enterprise," Doctoral dissertation, University of Chicago (1971), 101–102.

54. Smith, *Ella Flagg Young,* 231.

55. Blanche Wiesen Cook, "Female Support Networks and Political Activism: Lillian Wald, Crystal Eastman, Emma Goldman," *Chrysalis* (1977): 43–61, especially 48.

56. Debbie Mauldin Cottrell, *Pioneer Woman Educator: The Progressive Spirit of Annie Webb Blanton* (College Station: Texas A&M University Press, 1993), 24–25.

57. Cottrell, *Pioneer Woman Educator,* 3–41, especially 23–25.

Chapter 4

1. Department of Education, Center for Education Statistics; Barbara Miller Solomon, *In the Company of Educated Women* (New Haven: Yale University Press, 1985).

2. Susan B. Anthony and Ida Husted Harper, eds., *The History of Woman Suffrage,* Vol. 4 (1920; repr. Salem, NH: Ayer, 1985), 1042–1044.

3. *The Statistical History of the United States from Colonial Times to the Present* (Stamford, CT: Fairfield Publishers, 1965), 208; John K. Folger and Charles B. Nam, *Education of the American Population: A 1960 Monograph* (Washington, DC: U.S. Bureau of the Census, 1967), 81. In 1930, census reports indicated that of the 5,734,825 single women in the general workforce, 660,754 of them, or 11.5 percent, were teachers. Most other single women were employed in areas that did not require higher or specialized education. Frances Donovan, *The School Ma'am* (New York: Frederick A. Stokes Company, 1938), 32.

4. "Game of Old Maid," http://www.ahs.uwaterloo.ca/~museum/vexhibit/cardgames/table3/omaid.html (07/05/02).

5. Carroll Smith-Rosenberg offers a nuanced analysis of this shift in regard for the "new woman" in "The New Woman as Androgyne: Social Disorder and Gender Crisis, 1870–1936," in *Disorderly Conduct: Visions of Gender in Victorian America* (New York: Oxford University Press, 1985), 245–296.

6. Margaret Culkin Banning, "The Plight of the Spinster," *Harpers Monthly Magazine*, June 1929, 88.

7. Solomon, *In the Company*.

8. "Colorado," *Journal of Education* 39 (May 31, 1894): 348; "Colorado School Election," *Journal of Education* 39 (May 17, 1894): 312; *The Woman Suffrage Yearbook, 1917*, 165; Helen Laura Sumner Woodbury, *Equal Suffrage* (New York: Collegiate Equal Suffrage League, 1909), 122–146; and Joseph G. Brown, *The History of Equal Suffrage in Colorado, 1868–1898* (Denver: News Job Printing, 1898), 16–52.

9. Jackie M. Blount, *Destined to Rule the Schools: Women and the Superintendency, 1873–1995* (Albany: SUNY Press, 1998), 81–87.

10. Linda Gordon, *Pitied but not Entitled: Single Mothers and the History of Welfare, 1890–1935* (New York: Free Press, 1994); and Sheila Jeffreys, *The Spinster and Her Enemies* (London: Spinifex Press, 1997), 91–92.

11. Cicely Hamilton, *Marriage as a Trade*, quoted in Jeffreys, *The Spinster*, 93.

12. Edward Carpenter, *The Intermediate Sex: A Study of Some Transitional Types of Men and Women* (New York: Mitchell Kennerley, 1912), 72–73.

13. Blount, *Destined to Rule the Schools*.

14. Trisha Franzen, *Spinsters and Lesbians: Independent Womanhood in the United States* (New York: New York University Press, 1996), 4–6.

15. Dorothy Yost Deegan cites this study by Hergt and Shannon in *The Stereotype of the Single Woman in American Novels: A Social Study with Implications for the Education of Women* (New York: King's Crown Press, 1951), 19. The study specifically found that 44 percent of women 70 year old or older remained single as did 48 percent of women between 60 and 69, 41 percent of women aged 50–59, 37 percent of women between 40–49, and 30 percent of women under 40. Overall, about 40 percent of the eminent women listed remained single.

16. Harry D. Kitson and Lucille Kirtley, "Educational Research and Statistics: The Vocational Changes of One Thousand Eminent American Women," *School and Society* 19, 474 (1924): 112.

17. J. H. Doyle, "The Phi Beta Kappa Tempest." *Education* 41 (October 1921): 86–94.
18. Ibid.
19. Pat Griffin, *Strong Women, Deep Closets: Lesbians and Homophobia in Sport* (Champaign, IL: Human Kinetics, 1998), 35; and Susan E. Cayleff, *Babe: The Life and Legend of Babe Didrickson Zaharias* (Urbana: University of Illinois Press, 1995).
20. G. Stanley Hall, *Adolescence: Its Psychology and Its Relations to Physiology, Anthropology, Sociology, Sex, Crime, Religion and Education,* Vol. 2 (New York: Appleton, 1904), 633.
21. Ibid., 622; and Lesley A. Diehl, "The Paradox of G. Stanley Hall: Foe of Co-education and Educator of Women," *American Psychologist* 41, 8 (1986): 872.
22. Ibid., 872. Interestingly, fourteen years after Hall's landmark work was published, Willard Ellsbree, the noted education scholar, explained that women truly had come to use elementary teaching as preparation for marriage and motherhood, much as Hall had proposed. However, the same did not hold for high school teaching. Ellsbree explained that teachers of young children were much more likely to leave teaching for marriage than their high school counterparts. He contended that high school teaching fostered spinsterhood and that fewer women high school teachers married because of "the effect of college education," usually a prerequisite for the work. He argued that college-educated women's "greater desire for independence of every sort coupled with higher standards for the opposite sex tend to lower the proportion of marriages among this group. Moreover, since salaries are uniformly higher in the high school than in either the grades or the kindergarten, the high school teacher sacrifices more than the others in giving up her job." See *Teacher Turnover in the Cities and Villages of New York State,* Contributions to Education, No. 300 (New York: Teachers College, 1928), 31–32.
23. Thomas Percival Beyer, "Creative Evolution and the Woman Question," *Educational Review* (January 1914): 25–27.
24. Patricia Smith Butcher, "Education for Equality: Women's Rights Periodicals and Women's Higher Education, 1849–1920," *History of Higher Education Annual* 6 (1986): 73–74.
25. Ibid., 63–79.
26. Ibid.
27. Charles Franklin Emerick, "College Women and Race Suicide," *Political Science Quarterly* 24, 2 (1909): 269–283.
28. Henry Armstrong, "Report," *Reports of the Mosely Educational Commission to the United States* (London: Co-operative Printing Society Limited, 1903; repr. New York: Arno Press & The New York Times, 1969), 13.
29. G. Stanley Hall and Theodate L. Smith, "Marriage and Fecundity of College Men and Women," *Pedagogical Seminary* 10, 3 (1903): 309–310.
30. Banning, "The Plight of the Spinster," 93.
31. Havelock Ellis, *Sexual Inversion in Women* (1895); Lillian Faderman, "The

Morbidification of Love between Women by 19th-Century Sexologists," *Journal of Homosexuality* 4, 1 (1978): 78. Faderman argues that sexologists caused the morbidification of intimate relationships between women over these years. However, George Chauncey cautions that although medical conceptions of gender and then sexuality did play a role in stigmatizing persons who engaged in same-sex sexual activity, the medical profession should not be granted such great responsibility for the larger public shift in perception. Rather, he contends that the work of the "the published materials of the early sexologists are interesting and illuminating—mainly because they might well be a reflection of society, rather than a major influence on social thought." See "From Sexual Inversion to Homosexuality: The Changing Medical Conceptualization of Female 'Deviance,'" *Salmagundi* 58–59 (Fall/Winter 1983): 114–116.

32. Ibid., 141.
33. Jeffries, *The Spinster,* 155–156.
34. Nathan G. Hale, *The Rise and Crisis of Psychoanalysis in the United States: Freud and the Americans, 1917-1985* (New York: Oxford University Press, 1995), 3–9.
35. Jennifer Terry, *An American Obsession: Science, Medicine, and Homosexuality in Modern Society* (Chicago: University of Chicago Press, 1999).
36. Anonymous, "A Spinster I," *Atlantic Monthly,* May 1934, 542–543.
37. Ellen Fitzpatrick, "Introduction," in *Katharine Bement Davis, Early Twentieth-Century American Women, and the Study of Sex Behavior,* editor Ellen Fitzpatrick (New York: Garland Publishing, Inc., 1987), 1–5.
38. Vern L. Bullough, "Katharine Bement Davis, Sex Research, and the Rockefeller Foundation," *Bulletin of the History of Medicine* 62 (Spring 1988): 78–79.
39. Quoted in Fitzpatrick, "Introduction," 1–5.
40. Katharine Bement Davis, *Factors in the Sex Life of Twenty-Two Hundred Women* (1929; reprint, New York: Arno Press and New York Times, 1972), 247, 263.
41. Deegan, *The Stereotype,* 13–14.
42. Ibid.
43. Ibid.
44. Katharine Bement Davis, "Why They Failed to Marry," *Harper's,* March 1928, 466–467.
45. James H. Jones, *Alfred C. Kinsey: A Public/Private Life* (New York: W. W. Norton, 1997), 67.
46. O. Edward Janney, *The Making of a Man: The Physiology and Hygiene of Sex for High School Boys, Their Parents and Teachers* (Baltimore, MD: Lord Baltimore Press, 1914).
47. Lawrence Augustus Averill, *Mental Hygiene for the Classroom Teacher* (New York: Pitman Publishing Corp., 1939), 10–14.
48. Banning, "The Plight of the Spinster," 89.
49. Jonathan Katz, ed., "1926-27: *New York Times;* The Reaction to The

Captive," in *Gay American History: Lesbians & Gay Men in the U.S.A.*, revised edition (New York: Meridian, 1992), 82–91.

50. Davis, "Why They Failed to Marry," 466–467.

51. "People v. Friede: City Magistrate's Court of New York City (1929)," in *We Are Everywhere: A Historical Sourcebook for Gay and Lesbian Politics*, eds. Mark Blasius and Shane Phelan (New York: Routledge, 1997), 218–220.

52. Radclyffe Hall, *The Well of Loneliness* (1928; repr. New York: Doubleday, 1990). Also, see Esther Newton, "The Mythic Mannish Lesbian: Radclyffe Hall and the New Woman," in *Hidden from History: Reclaiming the Gay and Lesbian Past*, eds., Martin Bauml Duberman, Martha Vicinus, and George Chauncey (New York: New American Library, 1989), 281–293.

53. Boze Hadleigh, *The Lavender Screen—The Gay and Lesbian Films: Their Stars, Makers, Characters, and Critics* (New York: Citadel Press, 1993), 17–21; Andrea Weiss, *Vampires & Violets: Lesbians in Film* (New York: Penguin Books, 1992), 8–11; and Kael is quoted in Hadleigh, *Lavender Screen*, 20–21. Also see Vito Russo, *The Celluloid Closet: Homosexuality in the Movies*, revised edition (New York: Quality Paperback Book Club, 1995), 56–58; and B. Ruby Rich, "From Repressive Tolerance to Erotic Liberation: Maedchen in Uniform," in *Out in Culture: Gay, Lesbian, and Queer Essays on Popular Culture*, eds. Corey K. Creekmur and Alexander Doty (Durham, NC: Duke University Press, 1995), 137–166.

54. Howard K. Beale, *Are American Teachers Free?* (New York: Charles Scribner's Sons, 1936), 384–385.

55. C. W. Bardeen, "The Monopolizing Woman Teacher," *Educational Review* 43 (January 1912): 32–34.

56. David Wilbur Peters, *The Status of the Married Woman Teacher*, Teachers College Contributions to Education, no. 603 (New York: Teachers College, 1934), 87.

57. S. P. Breckinridge, "The Activities of Women Outside the Home," *Recent Social Trends in the United States*, President's Research Committee on Social Trends, 709–750, Vol. 1 (New York: McGraw-Hill Book Company, 1933), 716.

58. "Marriage as Related to Eligibility," *NEA Research Bulletin* 20 (March 1942), 61.

59. Willard Waller, *The Veteran Comes Back* (New York: Dryden Press, 1944), 92–191.

60. For example, see Alice S. Barter, "The Status of Women in School Administration," *Education Digest* 25 (October 1959): 40.

61. "The Organized Teaching Profession," in *Education in the States: Nationwide Development since 1900*, ed. Edgar Fuller and Jim Pearson (Washington, DC: NEA, 1969), 667.

62. Leo M. Chamberlain and Leonard E. Meece, "Women and Men in the Teaching Profession," *Bulletin of the Bureau of School Service*, 9 (March 1937): 57.

63. As I pointed out in *Destined to Rule the Schools,* this reasoning effectively inverted the arguments that Catherine Beecher had made a century earlier to support women's entrance into teaching. She had maintained that teaching prepared single women for marriage and motherhood.

64. Folger and Nam, *Education of the American Population,* 81; Lynn Weinner, *From Working Girl to Working Mother* (Chapel Hill: University of North Carolina Press, 1985), 89; U.S. Department of Labor, Bureau of Labor Statistics, *Labor Force Statistics Derived from the Current Population Survey: A Data Book, Vol. 1* (September 1982), Bulletin 2096, table C-11; 1985: *BLS News Release,* USDL 85–381 (September 19, 1985), table 1; total from unpublished tabulations.

65. Willard Waller, *The Sociology of Teaching* (New York: John Wiley & Sons, 1932), 147–149.

Chapter 5

1. Jackie Blount, *Destined to Rule the Schools: Women and the Superintendency, 1873-1995* (Albany: SUNY Press, 1998).

2. George Chauncey argues in *Gay New York: Gender, Urban Culture, and the Making of the Gay Male World, 1890-1940* (New York: Basic Books, 1994) that a degree of openness, toleration, and visibility characterized gay male life in New York during the early decades of the century. This, he explains, changed during the second third of the century when repressive conditions forced gay men to cloak their activities and maintain separate communities. Nan Boyd similarly describes conditions in San Francisco following Prohibition where "tourist-based queer cultures mutated and exploded, shooting off in multiple directions" (5). Then, in reaction to this heightened visibility, laws changed, police staked out bars that catered to homosexual and/or transgender clientele, and other social sanctions compelled queer individuals to conceal their activities and organizations. See *Wide Open Town: A History of Queer San Francisco to 1965* (Berkeley: University of California Press, 2003).

3. Alfred C. Kinsey, Wardell B. Pomeroy, and Clyde E. Martin, *Sexual Behavior in the Human Male* (Philadelphia: W. B. Saunders Company, 1948), 621–622.

4. Leisa D. Meyer, *Creating GI Jane: Sexuality and Power in the Women's Army Corps during World War II* (New York: Columbia University Press, 1996), 148–178. This fascinating volume brilliantly analyzes the intersections of sexuality and gender in the experiences of women in the military.

5. John D'Emilio, "Capitalism and Gay Identity," in *The Lesbian and Gay Studies Reader,* eds., Henry Abelove, Michele Aina Barale, and David M. Halperin (New York: Routledge, 1993), 467–476.

6. John D'Emilio and Estelle B. Freedman, *Intimate Matters: A History of Sexuality in America,* 2nd edition (Chicago: University of Chicago Press, 1997), 288–289.

7. The seminal work on this phenomenon is John D'Emilio's *Sexual Politics, Sexual Communities: The Making of a Homosexual Minority in the United States, 1940-1970,* 2nd edition (Chicago: University of Chicago Press, 1998).

8. D'Emilio and Freedman, *Intimate Matters,* 290.

9. Ferdinand Lundberg and Marynia Farnham, *Modern Woman: The Lost Sex* (New York: Harper & Brothers, 1947), 364-365.

10. Blount, *Destined,* 181.

11. Ibid., 111-132.

12. Leonard, V. E., "No Man's Land," *American School Board Journal,* September 1946, 21-22.

13. L. A. Zeliff, "Bachelor or Married Man as Small-Town Superintendent?" *American School Board Journal,* September 1947, 53, 86.

14. D. Mundt, "How We Selected a Superintendent," *American School Board Journal,* April 1963, 13-14.

15. American Association of School Administrators, *Thirtieth Yearbook: The American School Superintendency* (Washington, DC: The Author, 1952), 287-288; C. Emily Feistritzer, *Profile of School Administrators in the United States* (Washington, DC: National Center for Education Information, 1988), 17. For data on marriage rates of men in the general population, see Bureau of the Census, *Statistical Abstract of the U.S.* (Washington, DC: Author, 1999), Table 1418, 873.

16. Regina Markell Morantz, "The Scientist As Sex Crusader: Alfred C. Kinsey and American Culture," *American Quarterly* 29 (1977): 563-564.

17. Alfred C. Kinsey, Wardell B. Pomeroy, Clyde E. Martin, and Paul H. Gebhard, *Sexual Behavior in the Human Female* (Philadelphia: W. B. Saunders Company, 1953), 446-447.

18. Ibid., 453-454.

19. Ibid., 460.

20. Ibid., 478.

21. Ibid., 477.

22. Ibid., 483.

23. Morantz, "The Scientist."

24. Allan Bérubé and John D'Emilio, "The Military and Lesbians during the McCarthy Years," *Signs: Journal of Women and Culture in Society* 9 (Summer 1984): 759-775; see also Allan Bérubé, *Coming Out under Fire: The History of Gay Men and Women in World War Two* (New York: Penguin, 1990).

25. Barbara Stephens, "Homosexuals in Uniform," *The Ladder,* June 1959, 17-20. Also, William Eskridge lists the number of U.S. military personnel dismissed for homosexuality from 1947 to 1998. *Gaylaw: Challenging the Apartheid of the Closet* (Cambridge, MA: Harvard University Press, 1999), 381-382.

26. U.S. Senate, 81st Congress 2nd Session, Committee on Expenditures in the Executive Departments Document #241, "Employment of Homosexuals and Other Sex Perverts in Government," reprinted in *Government Versus Homosexual,* editor Leslie Parr (New York: Arno Press, 1975), 4.

27. 81st Congress, 2nd Session, comments by Robert F. Rich (Representative from Pennsylvania), "Perverts in Federal Agencies Called Peril to United States Security," *Congressional Record* (Washington, DC: Government Printing Office, 1950), Appendix 7755.

28. "When Is an 'H' Not an 'H'?" in *About Time: Exploring the Gay Past,* ed. Martin Bauml Duberman (New York: Penguin Books USA, 1991), 157–158.

29. Ralph H. Major, "New Moral Menace to Our Youth," *Coronet,* September 1950, 101.

30. Ibid., 102.

31. Ibid., 101.

32. Ibid., 102.

33. Ibid., 102–103.

34. Ibid., 107.

35. "Social-Sex Attitudes in Adolescence," Crawley Films for McGraw-Hill Book, Co. (1953), http://www.archive.org/movies/list_P-S.html. Rick Prelinger has performed the remarkable service of archiving and making available a wide variety of "ephemeral films," including many of the social guidance films produced for schools during the Cold War. To view some of these films, see http://www.archive.org/movies. Ken Smith has described and contextualized a number of such films in *Mental Hygiene: Classroom Films, 1945–1970* (New York: Blast Books, 1999). For his discussion of "Social-Sex Attitudes," see 207–208.

36. *The Blackboard Jungle,* produced by Metro-Goldwyn-Mayer, was nominated for four Academy Awards. Adam Golub, "'They Turned a School Into a Jungle!': Popular Culture and the Educational Crisis in the 1950s America," unpublished paper (April 2003). For a sample of such Cold War scholarship on adolescent deviance, see William Wattenberg, ed., *Social Deviancy among Youth* (Chicago: University of Chicago Press, 1966).

37. Estelle B. Freedman, "'Uncontrolled Desires': The Response to the Sexual Psychopath, 1920–1960," *Journal of American History* 74, 1 (1987): 83–106.

38. See footnote 1, Kinsey et al., *Sexual Behavior in the Human Female,* 447–448.

39. Kinsey et al., *Sexual Behavior in the Human Male,* 637–638.

40. Ibid.

41. Charles C. Hewitt, "On the Meaning of Effeminacy in Homosexual Men," *American Journal of Psychotherapy* 15, 4 (1961): 595.

42. Major Baisden, *The Dynamics of Homosexuality* (Sacramento, CA: Allied Research Society, 1975), 12–13.

43. Alfred A. Gross, *Strangers in Our Midst: Problems of the Homosexual in American Society* (Washington, DC: Public Affairs Press, 1962), 151.

44. John D'Emilio, *Sexual Politics,* 44.

45. Frank Caprio, *Female Homosexuality: A Psychodynamic Study of Lesbianism* (New York: The Citadel Press, 1954), 58.

46. Neil Miller, *Sex-Crime Panic: A Journey to the Paranoid Heart of the 1950s* (Los Angeles: Alyson Books, 2002).

47. Freedman, "'Uncontrolled Desires,'" 103.

48. Quoted in John Gerassi, *The Boys of Boise: Furor, Vice, and Folly in an American City* (New York: Macmillan, 1966), 15–17.

49. Ibid., 14.

50. Ibid., 34.

51. "Witch-Hunt in Boise, Idaho; An Interview with a Victim, 'They Lit a Match to a Bonfire'," in *Gay American History: Lesbians and Gay Men in the U.S.A., A Documentary History,* revised ed., ed. Jonathan Ned Katz (New York: Meridian, 1992), 109–119.

52. William N. Eskridge, "Privacy Jurisprudence and the Apartheid of the Closet, 1946–1961," *Florida State University Law Review* (Summer 1997): 703–840, especially 747–749.

53. Merrill Mushroom, "The Gay Kids and the Johns Committee: 1956," in *Telling Tales Out of School: Gays, Lesbians, and Bisexuals Revisit Their School Days,* ed. Kevin Jennings (Los Angeles: Alyson Publications Inc., 1998), 14.

54. Quoted in the Florida Legislative Investigation Committee, "Homosexuality and Citizenship in Florida" (1964), reprinted in *Government Versus Homosexuals,* editor Leslie Parr (New York: Arno Press, 1975), preface.

55. Florida Legislative Investigation Committee, "Homosexuality and Citizenship," 4.

56. Karen M. Harbeck, *Gay and Lesbian Educators: Personal Freedoms, Public Constraints* (Malden, MA: Amethyst Press and Productions, 1997), 182.

57. Ibid., 182–185.

58. R. O. Mitchell, *Report of the Florida Legislative Investigation Committee* (Tallahassee, FL: 1965), 8–9.

59. "1965–69: Sara Harris; The Puritan Jungle: A Homosexual 'is better off dead,'" in *Gay American History: Lesbians and Gay Men in the U.S.A., A Documentary History,* revised ed., ed. Jonathan Ned Katz (New York: Meridian, 1992), 123–125.

60. Hal Call, "Open Letter to the Florida Legislature's 'Johns Committee,'" *Mattachine Review* 10, 11 (1964): 5–8.

61. "Still Another List," *Nation,* 22 June 1964, 615.

62. Mushroom, "The Gay Kids," 14. James Sears has written a rich account of how these city and state investigations of supposed homosexual enclaves affected a number of individual women and men, including Merrill Mushroom. See the first three chapters of *Lonely Hunters: An Oral History of Lesbian and Gay Southern Life, 1948–1969* (Boulder, CO: Westview Press, 1997), 12–107.

63. Instead of teaching, Sarria polished his performance skills and became a celebrity drag queen who performed regularly at the Black Cat, a club famous for its homosexual and transgender clientele. His stunning wit and campy humor helped audiences understand their place in a larger homosexual

community and he prodded listeners to resist with slogans such as "United we stand, divided they arrest us one by one." Sarria is recounted now as one of the most important figures in pre-Stonewall gay San Francisco. Nan Boyd, *Wide Open Town: A History of Queer San Francisco to 1965* (Berkeley: University of California Press, 2003), 20–24, 57–61; and D'Emilio, *Sexual Politics,* 186–189.

64. Harbeck, *Gay and Lesbian Educators,* 188–200.
65. Harbeck offers a detailed legal and historical analysis of the Sarac case in *Gay and Lesbian Educators,* 188–200.
66. This quote is attributed to Reverend Robert W. Cromey in Del Martin and Phyllis Lyon, *Lesbian/Woman,* revised ed. (New York: Bantam Books, 1983), 200.
67. Quote from an interview conducted by Eric Marcus with an anonymous source. See Eric Marcus, *Making History: The Struggle for Gay and Lesbian Equal Rights, 1945–1990, An Oral History* (New York: HarperCollins Publishers, 1992), 157.
68. Ibid., 72–73.
69. S. G. Lewis, *Sunday's Women: Lesbian Life Today* (Boston: Beacon Press, 1979), 58–59.
70. Ibid., 88.
71. *The Children's Hour,* William Wyler, director-producer (Hollywood, CA: United Artists, 1961); Boze Hadleigh, "School Days: The Children's Hour and Therese and Isabelle," *The Lavender Screen: The Gay and Lesbian Films: Their Stars, Makers, Characters, and Critics* (New York: Citadel Press Book, 1993), 34–39. Lillian Hellman reportedly based her play on the real story of two Scottish school mistresses, Jane Pirie and Marianne Woods. Lillian Faderman recounts the full sequence of events in *Scotch Verdict: Miss Pirie and Miss Woods v. Dame Cumming Gordon* (New York: Columbia University Press, 1993).
72. Quoted in Lillian Faderman, *Odd Girls and Twilight Lovers: A History of Lesbian Life in Twentieth-Century America* (New York: Penguin, 1991), 156.
73. Domino, *The Ladder* 6, 5 (1962): 11. The first lesbian periodical was *Vice Versa,* published for nine months in Los Angeles in 1947 by "Lisa Ben," (scrambled letters of "lesbian"). See D'Emilio, *Sexual Politics,* 29–32.
74. *The Ladder* 13, 1&2 (1968): 40–42.
75. Eskridge, *Gaylaw,* 27–29, 338–341.
76. Margaret Mead explained: "Group living for men is only really tolerated in college dormitories, in armies, and in work-camps, highly patterned situations where either men are assumed to be too young to marry or their wives cannot accompany them. Men who keep house together have to fend off very heavy doubts as to their heterosexuality." Margaret Mead, *Male and Female: A Study of the Sexes in a Changing World* (New York: Mentor Books, 1962), 242–243.
77. "Mail Snooping," *New Republic,* 21 August 1965, 6–7; R. E. L. Masters, *The Homosexual Revolution* (New York: Belmont Books, 1962), 56–57.
78. "Homosexuality in America," *Life,* 19 June 1964, 66–67.

79. Irving Bieber, *Homosexuality: A Psychoanalytic Study of Male Homosexuals* (New York: Basic Books, 1962).

80. Peter Wyden and Barbara Wyden, who wrote *Growing Up Straight: What Every Thoughtful Parent Should Know About Homosexuality* (New York: Stein and Day, 1968), 33–34, explain, "We are happy to acknowledge that we would not have attempted the present book without guidance from Dr. Bieber and his team's study."

81. Bieber, *Homosexuality;* Ernest Havemann, "Homosexuality: Scientists Search for the Answers to a Touchy and Puzzling Question—Why?" *Life,* 26 June 1964, 76–80.

82. Vincent T. Lathbury, "Mothers and Sons: An Intimate Discussion," *Ladies' Home Journal,* February 1965, 43–45.

83. Lester David, "Our Son Was Different," *Good Housekeeping,* January 1966, 51, 113, 115, 120, 122–125.

84. Wyden and Wyden, *Growing Up Straight,* 18.

85. Ibid., 13, 19.

86. Ibid., 17.

87. Ibid., 19, 23.

88. Evelyn Hooker, "Parental Relations and Male Homosexuality in Patient and Nonpatient Samples," *Journal of Consulting and Clinical Psychology* 33, 2 (1969): 140–142.

89. George Kriegman, "Homosexuality and the Educator," *Journal of School Health* 39, 5 (1969): 306–310.

90. Ibid., 308–309.

91. Jeffrey P. Moran, *Teaching Sex: The Shaping of Adolescence in the 20th Century* (Cambridge: Harvard University Press, 2000), 175–176.

92. Smith, *Mental Hygiene,* 126–127. The film, *Boys Beware,* can be found online at http://www.archive.org/movies/prelinger.php.

93. Quoted in Moran, *Teaching Sex,* 175–176.

Chapter 6

1. John D'Emilio, *Sexual Politics, Sexual Communities: The Making of a Homosexual Minority in the United States, 1940-1970,* 2nd edition (Chicago: University of Chicago Press, 1998), 33, 57–58; Donald Webster Cory (Edward Sagarin), *The Homosexual in America: A Subjective Approach* (New York: Greenberg, 1951).

2. D'Emilio, *Sexual Politics,* 57–74.

3. Del Martin, "President's Message," *The Ladder,* October 1956, 6–7.

4. "Daughters of Bilitis—Purpose," *The Ladder,* October 1956, 4.

5. "Mattachine Breaks Through the Conspiracy of Silence," *The Ladder,* October 1959, 5.

6. Mark Thompson, "Introduction," in *Long Road to Freedom: The Advocate History of the Gay and Lesbian Movement,* Mark Thompson, ed. (New York: St. Martin's Press, 1994), xvii–xviii.

7. "Happy Birthday to Us," *The Los Angeles Advocate,* September 1967, 6.
8. Dick Leitsch, "Police Raid on N.Y. Club Sets Off First Gay Riot," *Los Angeles Advocate,* September 1969, 3, 11–12.
9. Lige and Jack, "N.Y. Gays: Will the Spark Die?" *Los Angeles Advocate,* September 1969, 3, 12; D'Emilio, *Sexual Politics,* 231–233; and Martin Duberman, *Stonewall* (New York: Dutton, 1993), 181–212.
10. Nancy Tucker, "New York City Has Largest Turnout, Longest Gay March," *The Advocate,* 22 July–4 August 1970, 1, 5.
11. "1200 Parade in Hollywood, Crowds Line Boulevard," *The Advocate,* 22 July–4 August 1970, 1, 6.
12. Karen Harbeck, *Gay and Lesbian Educators: Personal Freedoms, Public Constraints* (Maulden, MA: Amethyst Press, 1997), 213–220; "ACLU Defends Teacher," *The Advocate,* February 1968, 3; and Kenneth Ostrander, "The Teacher's Duty to Privacy: Court Rulings in Sexual Deviancy Cases," *Phi Delta Kappan,* September 1975, 21.
13. "State Can't Take Teacher's Credentials for Homosexual Act," *The Advocate,* January 1970, 3, 10.
14. Harbeck, *Gay and Lesbian Educators,* 235, 244.
15. "School Suspends Counselor after Appearance on TV," *The Advocate,* 20 January–2 February 1971, 1, 11.
16. "Homosexuals Acceptable in Poll," *The Advocate,* 5–18 August 1970, 3, 13–14.
17. "Fired Because of Rumor, Rural Teacher Fights Back," *The Advocate,* 21 June 1972, 1.
18. Harbeck, *Gay and Lesbian Educators,* 245–246.
19. "Fired Because of Rumor," 1.
20. Gregory Lewis, "Yearbooks Mutilated: Fired Teacher Rejects Settlement," *The Advocate,* 22 May 1974, 13.
21. "Fired Because of Rumor," *The Advocate,* 1; Lewis, "Yearbooks Mutilated," 13.
22. "U.S. Judge Says Teacher's Firing Unconstitutional," *The Advocate,* 28 February 1973, 2.
23. "U.S. Judge Says," *The Advocate,* 2.
24. Harbeck, *Gay and Lesbian Educators,* 244–248.
25. Lewis, "Yearbooks Mutilated," 13.
26. "Gay Teachers Organizing," *The Advocate,* 5 July 1972, 17.
27. "Gay Teacher Wins Fight against Mental Exam," *The Advocate,* 11 October 1972, 17.
28. "New Jersey Teacher Goes on Hunger Strike," *The Advocate,* 6 December 1972, 2.
29. *Gish v. Board of Education of Paramus,* 145 N.J. Super. 96 (1976), cited in Harbeck, *Gay and Lesbian Educators,* 266.
30. Harbeck, *Gay and Lesbian Educators,* 266–268.
31. Paul Shelly, Superintendent of Paramus Public Schools, "Charges Against John Gish" (1978), Eric Rofes's private collection.

32. "Gay Teacher Agrees to Test," *San Francisco Examiner,* 17 June 1979, n.p.
33. Harbeck, *Gay and Lesbian Educators,* 267–268.
34. Ibid., 239–240.
35. "Teaching Ticket Held Off for Penn State Gay Grad," *The Advocate,* August 1972, 14.
36. "Gay Wins Credential to Teach," *The Advocate,* 11 October 1972, 1, 18.
37. "Joe's War Starts Over," *The Advocate,* 25 October 1972, 2.
38. Harbeck, *Gay and Lesbian Educators,* 236–237.
39. "D. C. School Board Bans Gay Bias," *The Advocate,* 21 June 1972, 3, 11.
40. "Acanfora Files Suit Over Job," *The Advocate,* 22 November 1972, 2, 13.
41. "Only Supreme Court Left: Acanfora Loses Another Bout," *The Advocate,* 13 March 1974, 9.
42. "Acanforas on TV: 'I Loved You Then, I Love You Now,'" *The Advocate,* 22 November 1972, 13, 40.
43. "Acanfora Decision May Help Teachers," *The Advocate,* 10 April 1974, 19; "Lower Court Decision Stands: Court Refusal to Hear Acanfora Appeal May Be Hidden Victory," *The Advocate,* 20 November 1974, 20; Kenneth Ostrander, "The Teacher's Duty to Privacy: Court Rulings in Sexual Deviancy Cases," *Phi Delta Kappan,* September 1975, 20–22. Karen Harbeck describes this case fully in *Gay and Lesbian Educators,* 248–257.
44. "Gay Teacher Loses Appeal to High Court," *San Francisco Chronicle,* 4 October 1977, 1, 24.
45. "Schools and School Districts: Admission of Status as a Homosexual by Teacher Held Sufficient Cause for Dismissal on the Basis of Immorality, Gaylord V. Tacoma School District No. 10, Wash. 2d, 559 P.2d 1340, Cert. Denied, 45 U.S.L.W. 3220 (1977)," *Journal of Family Law, University of Louisville School of Law* (1977–78): 129–134.
46. Grace and Fred Hechinger, "Should Homosexuals Be Allowed to Teach?" *McCall's,* March 1978, 100, 160–162.
47. Harbeck, *Gay and Lesbian Educators,* 258–263. A legal writer for *Phi Delta Kappan* argued that the Supreme Court's decision was problematic because it did not sufficiently resolve what "immorality" was. Thomas Flygare contended that even a heterosexual male who admitted attraction to women could be targeted for lewd intent. Because the decision did not sufficiently support this possibility, he urged schools to proceed with caution. See Thomas Flygare, "Schools and the Law: Supreme Court Refuses to Hear Case of Discharged Homosexual Teacher," *Phi Delta Kappan* 59, 7 (1978): 482–483.
48. "Political News," *Cheery Chalkboard,* Gay Teachers of Los Angeles, April 1978, 5, Eric Rofes's private collection.
49. "Transsexual Sues to Get Job," *The Advocate,* 18 December 1974, 16; "Disability Award to Transsexual Teacher" [source unknown], February 1977; Anita C. Barnes, "The Sexual Continuum: Transsexual Prisoners," *New England Journal on Criminal and Civil Confinement,* Summer 1998, 622–623.
50. Associated Press, San Francisco, 26 January 1977; Associated Press, San

Francisco, 22 May, 1980; and "Sex Change Case: State Upholds Firing of East Bay Teacher" [source unknown], January 1980.

51. "Teachers Favor Freedom for Gays," *The Advocate*, March 1970, 10.

52. Harbeck, *Gay and Lesbian Educators*, 236.

53. "Fired Sex-Ed Teacher Hired Back," *The Advocate*, 23 June–6 July 1971.

54. "Sick No More," *The Advocate*, 16 January 1974, 1.

55. "'Big Brother' Stirring in Missouri," *The Advocate*, 13 March 1974, 1.

56. "Job Protection for Gays: Teacher Union Votes Rights Stand," *The Advocate*, 28 August 1974, 3.

57. David Aiken, "Boy Raped on TV Show Stirs Protest," *The Advocate*, 11 September 1974, 10.

58. "Movement Gears for Action: Welby's 'Outrage' Set; Gay Outrage Grows," *The Advocate*, 25 September 1974, 3, 10.

59. Ibid.

60. "Network Squirms as Sponsors Flee 'Welby' Episode," *The Advocate*, 23 October 1974, 2, 30.

61. "Gay Giant Seen As 'Welby' Legacy," *The Advocate*, 6 November 1974, 2.

62. Feldman eventually became president of the AFT in 1997.

63. Marc Rubin, "History of the Gay Teachers Association," *Gay Teachers Association Newsletter*, January 1978, 1–4, Eric Rofes's private collection.

64. Leonard Levitt, "Homosexual Teachers Are Posing a Quandary in the City's Schools," *New York Post*, 9 July 1979, 8.

65. Rubin, "History," 1–4.

66. Ibid.

67. Letter from Frank Arricale to Meryl Friedman (January 24, 1975), Eric Rofes's private collection. This letter also was discussed in Meryl C. Friedman, "Lesbian as Teacher, Teacher as Lesbian," *Our Right to Love: A Lesbian Resource Book*, editor Ginny Vida (Englewood Cliffs, NJ: Prentice Hall, Inc., 1978), 157–164. The letter garnered the attention of *The Advocate*, which hailed it as an important victory for teachers. See "NY Gay Teachers Have 1–1 Season," *The Advocate*, 2 June 1976, 11.

68. Rubin, "History," 1–4.

69. "NY Gay Teachers," 11.

70. Rubin, "History," 1–4.

71. Ibid.

72. David Lamble, "10th Anniversary: Gay Teachers Struggle for Right to Teach; Take on the City's School Board," *Coming Up!*, June 1985, 5–6.

73. Flier for "Mass Gay Rights Demonstration" for Gay Teachers and Other Schoolworkers," for June 17, 1975, Board of Education meeting, June Mazer Collection.

74. Lamble, "10th Anniversary," 5–6.

75. Ibid.; "School Board Approves A Gay Anti-Bias Policy," *San Francisco Chronicle*, 18 June 1975, n.p.; and Jim Wood, "Gay, Gifted Yet Closeted in City's Classrooms," *San Francisco Examiner*, 12 June 1975, n.p.

76. Lamble, "10th Anniversary," 5–6.

77. "School Board Approves a Gay Anti-Bias Policy."

78. "Who We Are," *Gay Teachers and Schoolworkers Coalition,* August/September 1977, 1, Eric Rofes's private collection.
79. "Apple Banner Energy Transformed," *Gay Teachers and School Workers Coalition,* August/September 1977, 2, located in "Briggs" file, June Mazer Collection.
80. "Minutes of June 17, 1976, Meeting," *Gay Teachers of Los Angeles,* 26 June 1976, Eric Rofes's private collection.
81. "Minutes of July 22, 1976, Meeting," *Gay Teachers of Los Angeles,* 24 August 1976, Eric Rofes's private collection.
82. "Minutes of September 30, 1976, Meeting," *Gay Teachers of Los Angeles,* Eric Rofes's private collection.
83. "Next Week the World," *Gay Teachers of Los Angeles Newsletter,* 11 February 1977, 2, Eric Rofes's private collection.
84. "United Teachers of Los Angeles," *Gay Teachers of Los Angeles Newsletter,* 15 March 1977, 2, Eric Rofes's private collection.
85. "United Teachers of Los Angeles," *Gay Teachers of Los Angeles Newsletter,* 11 April 1977, 2, Eric Rofes's private collection.
86. "The Gay Pride Parade," *Cheery Chalkboard,* Gay Teachers of Los Angeles, July 1977, 2, Eric Rofes's private collection.
87. "Putting the Squeeze on Bryant," *Gay Teachers of Los Angeles Newsletter,* 15 March 1977, 2, Eric Rofes's private collection.
88. "Political News," *Cheery Chalkboard,* Gay Teachers of Los Angeles, July 1978, 3, Eric Rofes's private collection.
89. Dudley Clendinen and Adam Nagourney, *Out for Good: The Struggle to Build a Gay Rights Movement in America* (New York: Simon & Schuster, 1999), 293–295.
90. Ibid., 295.
91. Anita Bryant, *The Anita Bryant Story: The Survival of Our Nation's Families and the Threat of Militant Homosexuality* (Old Tappan, NJ: Fleming H. Revell Company, 1977), 13–15.
92. Clendinen and Nagourney, *Out for Good,* 295–299.
93. Bryant, *The Anita Bryant Story,* 41–44.
94. Ibid., 53.
95. Ibid., 114–115.
96. "Anita's Circle," *Time,* 2 May 1977, 76.
97. "Bryant Rants . . . No Sunshine for Gays in Florida," *Lesbian Tide,* May/June 1977, 16–17.
98. Clendinen and Nagourney, *Out for Good,* 303.
99. Ralph Blair, *Holier-Than-Thou, Hocus-Pocus & Homosexuality* (New York: HCCC, Inc., 1977), 37–38.
100. Martin Bauml Duberman, "The Anita Bryant Brigade," *About Time: Exploring the Gay Past* (New York: A Seahorse Book, 1986), 297–308.
101. "Queen Anita Loses Parade," *Lesbian Tide,* January/February 1978, 21.
102. Clendinen and Nagourney, *Out for Good,* 308–11.
103. "65% in Poll Oppose Gays as Teachers," *Los Angeles Times,* 17 July 1977, sec. 1, p. 27.

Chapter 7

1. Dudley Clendinen and Adam Nagourney, *Out for Good: The Struggle to Build a Gay Rights Movement in America* (New York: Simon & Schuster, 1999), 365; and Randy Shits, *The Mayor of Castro Street: The Life and Times of Harvey Milk* (New York: St. Martin's Press, 1982), 153–158.
2. "Why Is Gay Law Needed, Anyway?" *Los Angeles Times,* 12 June 1977, sec. 5, 5.
3. "Briggs Does His Thing Amid Jeers of the Gays," *San Francisco Examiner,* 15 June 1977, n.p.
4. Philip Hager, "Gay Teachers: Both Sides Look to High Court," *Boston Globe,* 29 August 1977, n.p.
5. "Introduction," *Gay Teachers Association Newsletter,* February 1978, 1, Eric Rofes's private collection.
6. Jeanne Cordova, "Teachers May Face Initiative," *Lesbian Tide,* September/October 1977, 13, 35.
7. "Gay's Fast Raises $100,000," *San Francisco Examiner,* 22 September 1977, n.p.
8. "Briggs Goes Bananas," *Gay Teachers and School Workers Coalition,* August/September 1977, 1, "Briggs" file, June Mazer Collection.
9. Diana Kurland, "Gay Teachers and School Workers Coalition," *Plexus,* September 1977, 5.
10. Don Liles, AFT, "The Briggs Initiative: Shades of Joe McCarthy," June Mazer Collection, 1977, "Schools—Proposition 6" file.
11. Amber Hollibaugh, one of the most active and articulate LGBT organizers during the Briggs Initiative battle, reflected on the meaning of these months in a brilliant interview published in her book, *My Dangerous Desires: A Queer Girl Dreaming Her Way Home* (Durham, NC: Duke University Press, 2000), 43–61. Here, she explains the union undercurrents of the initiative.
12. "News from Our Friends," *Gay Teachers Association Newsletter,* September/October 1978, 6, Eric Rofes's private collection.
13. Hollibaugh, *My Dangerous Desires,* 43–61.
14. John Merrow, "Gay Sex in the Schools," *Parents' Magazine* 52, 9 (1977), 66, 100, 104, 106
15. Peter Schrag, "Education Now," *Saturday Review* 5, 4 (1977), 53–54.
16. Quoted in Anonymous, "A Homosexual Teacher's Argument and Plea," *Phi Delta Kappan,* October 1977, 94.
17. Max Rafferty, "Should Gays Teach School?" *Phi Delta Kappan,* October 1977, 91–92.
18. Ibid., 92.
19. For a discussion of how the California sodomy law was struck down, see William N. Eskridge, *Gaylaw: Challenging the Apartheid of the Closet* (Cambridge: Harvard University Press, 1999), 106–107.
20. Ellen Broidy, "A Personal Reflection: KNTV Interview," *Unlearning the Lie/*

Gay Teachers and School Workers Coalition, October/November 1977, 1, 3, "Briggs" file, June Mazer Collection.

21. Jeanne Cordova, "Teachers May Face Initiative," *Lesbian Tide,* September/October 1977, 13, 35.

22. "Teachers' Battle Looms," *Lesbian Tide,* November/December 1977, 13.

23. Marilyn Gode-von Aesch, "Statewide Network Fights Briggs Initiative," *Unlearning the Lie/Gay Teachers and School Workers Coalition,* April 1978, 3, " Briggs" file, June Mazer Collection.

24. Lin Duke, "California Goes on Orange Alert!" *Lesbian Tide,* November/December 1977, 13–14.

25. "The Briggs Initiative: Menace in California," *Gay Teachers Association Newsletter,* September/October 1978, 1–2, Eric Rofes's private collection.

26. Pat Donohue, "Initiative Measure to Be Submitted Directly to the Voters with Analysis," "Briggs" file, June Mazer Collection.

27. Jerry Burns, "Briggs Files Anti-Gay Initiative," *San Francisco Chronicle,* 2 May 1978, n.p.

28. David Goodstein, "Fighting the Briggs Brigade," *The Advocate,* June 1978, 6.

29. Grace and Fred Hechinger, "Should Homosexuals Be Allowed to Teach?" *McCall's,* March 1978, 100, 160–162.

30. "Media Notes: McCall's Article Examines the Issues," *Gay Teachers Association Newsletter,* March 1978, 3, Eric Rofes's private collection.

31. Michael Trent, "On Being a Gay Teacher: My Problem—and Yours," *Psychology Today* 11, 11 (1978): 136.

32. "Teens Say 'No' to Anti-Gay Discrimination," *Gay Teachers Association Newsletter,* September/October 1978, 5, Eric Rofes's private collection.

33. "Dignifying Rumor and Innuendo," *Los Angeles Times,* 21 August 1978, sec. 2, 6.

34. Lesbian Schoolworkers, "Announcement of Demonstration by Lesbian Schoolworkers Group" (1978), "Briggs" file, June Mazer Collection.

35. Poe Asher, "Toe-to-Toe, Tête-à-Tête with Briggs," *Unlearning the Lie/Coalition of Gay and Lesbian Schoolworkers and Teachers,* April 1978, 1, "Briggs" file, June Mazer Collection.

36. Anita Bryant, "Fundraising/Survey Letter for Anita Bryant Ministries," "Briggs" file, June Mazer Collection.

37. Jerry Fuchs, "Briggs Targets America's Latest Scapegoats," *Santa Cruz Independent,* 31 August–6 September 1978, n.p.

38. Mark Thompson, ed., *Long Road to Freedom: The Advocate History of the Gay and Lesbian Movement* (New York: St. Martin's Press, 1994), 149.

39. Jeanne Cordova, "Hollywood, Reagan Turn Out Against Briggs," *Lesbian Tide,* November/December 1978, 12–16.

40. Penelope McMillan, "Fear Stalks No-On-6 Drive," *Los Angeles Times,* 15 September 1978, sec. 1, 1, 26; Melinda Beck, Martin Kasindorm, and Michael Reese, "Gay Teachers," *Newsweek,* 2 October 1978, 56.

41. Karen Harbeck, *Gay and Lesbian Educators: Personal Freedoms, Public Constraints* (Maulden, MA: Amethyst Press, 1997), 241.

42. "Riles Sees No Need for Prop. 6," *Los Angeles Times,* 7 September 1978, sec. 2, 8.
43. Beck, Kasindorm, and Reese, "Gay Teachers," 56.
44. "To Class or to Court? Teachers on the Line," *Lesbian Tide,* September/October 1978, 14; and Jeanne Cordova, "Hollywood, Reagan Turn Out Against Briggs."
45. "S.F. Archbishop Opposes Passage of Proposition 6," *Los Angeles Times,* 12 October 1978, sec. 1, 28.
46. Jack McCurdy, "School Board Unanimously Opposes Prop. 6," *Los Angeles Times,* 19 October 1978, 1, 22.
47. Cordova, "Hollywood, Reagan."
48. George Skelton, "Voters' Opposition to Props. 5 and 6 Growing," *Los Angeles Times,* 1 November 1978, n.p.
49. Cindy Riggs, "Sexist Bias Distorts Prop 6 Campaign," *Sonoma SCLGA,* October 1978, n.p.
50. Shilts, *The Mayor of Castro Street,* 229–231.
51. Ivan Sharpe, "A Gay Teacher Comes Out to Fight Briggs." *San Francisco Chronicle,* 25 June 1978, n.p.
52. Doyle McManus, "Briggs Debates Gay Teacher," *Los Angeles Times,* 26 October 1978, sec. 1, 3.
53. "A California Travesty," *The New Republic,* 28 October 1978, 81.
54. Jack Cheevers, "Gay Teacher Issue Divides California," *The Boston Globe,* 31 October 1978, 44.
55. Cordova, "Hollywood, Reagan."
56. March Fong Eu, Secretary of State, CA, "California Voters Pamphlet, General Election, November 7, 1978," "Briggs" file, June Mazer Collection.
57. "How Sweet It Is!" *Lesbian Tide,* January/February 1979, 10–12.
58. Ibid.
59. Lionel Schaen, Vice President and General Manager, KHJ-TV Editorial Comment (November 20–22, 1978), "Briggs" file, June Mazer Collection.
60. Joseph R. Gusfield, "Proposition 6: Political Ceremony in California," *The Nation,* 9 December 1978, 633–635.
61. Hollibaugh, *My Dangerous Desires,* 43–61.
62. Ivan Sharpe, "Celebrated Healdsburg Gay Finds Happiness," *San Francisco Examiner,* 9 April 1979, 1, 5.
63. Associated Press, Domestic News, San Francisco, "Teacher Wins Defamation Settlement," 2 September 1982. Berner subsequently taught English in Japan for several years. After suffering with AIDS and providing AIDS counseling for others, he died on January 25, 1995, in Tokyo. Kyodo News Service, Tokyo, "U.S. AIDS Sufferer Berner Dies," 25 January 1995.
64. Shilts, *The Mayor of Castro Street,* 265–281.
65. Ibid., 299–323.
66. Kathy McManus and Dan Leighton, "Brigg's Double Life Under Scrutiny," *New West,* 2 July 1979, 5.
67. "Farewell to Briggs," *Los Angeles Times,* Update, 13 November 1981, n.p.

Chapter 8

1. Eric Rofes, *Socrates, Plato, and Guys Like Me* (Boston: Alyson, 1985), 31–32.

2. Ibid., 63–68.

3. Ibid., 104–105.

4. David Lamble, "10th Anniversary: Gay Teachers Struggle for Right to Teach; Take on the City's School Board," *Coming Up!*, June 1985, 5–6; Arthur Lubow, Lucy Howard, and Lisa Dougherty, "The Homosexual Teacher," *Newsweek*, 18 December 1978, 5; Jim Wood, "Gay, Gifted, Yet Closeted in City's Classrooms," *San Francisco Examiner*, 12 June 1975, n.p.; Dan Woog, *School's Out: The Impact of Gay and Lesbian Issues on America's Schools* (Boston: Alyson Publications, Inc., 1995), 69–73; Rachel Gordon, "Ammiano Pines for Room 200," *San Francisco Chronicle*, 20 February 2003, A15.

5. Kellie McGarrh, "Hangin' in Tough: The Life of Superintendent Mildred E. Doyle, 1904–1989," Dissertation completed at the University of Tennessee, Knoxville (August 1995), 121–122. McGarrh's dissertation was published posthumously as Clinton B. Allison, ed., *Kellie McGarrh's Hangin' in Tough: Mildred E. Doyle, School Superintendent* (New York: Peter Lang, 2000). See p. 84 for McGarrh's description of Doyle's reelection campaign experience.

6. "Dallas' Gay Teachers Have Rights," *The Advocate*, 11 January 1978, n.p.

7. Arthur Lubow, Lucy Howard, and Lisa Dougherty, "The Homosexual Teacher," *Newsweek*, 18 December 1978, n.p.

8. "Sallie Herson Reinstated," *Gay Teachers Association Newsletter*, March 1978, 3, Eric Rofes's private collection.

9. George Esper, "When It Comes to Divorce, They Wrote the Book," Associated Press, 6 April 1981.

10. There have been other accounts published such as John Warburton's book detailing his experience of losing his teaching position in England: *Open and Positive: An Account of How John Warburton Came Out at School and the Consequences* (London: Gay Teachers' Group, 1978). More recently, several anthologies have documented brief stories of LGBT teachers' experiences—such as Kevin Jennings, *One Teacher in 10: Gay and Lesbian Educators Tell Their Stories* (Los Angeles: Alyson, 1994) and Carolyn Sidaway, Ellen Louise Hart, M. Eugenia Rosa, Sarah-Hope Parmeter, and Anza Stein, *The Lesbian in Front of the Classroom: Writings by Lesbian Teachers* (Santa Cruz, CA: McNaughton and Gunn, 1988). (My thanks to Chris Ohana for bringing this collection to my attention.) Dan Woog weaves stories of many LGBT educators/leaders into his fine narrative on recent LGBT school worker activism: *School's Out: The Impact of Gay and Lesbian Issues on America's Schools* (Boston: Alyson, 1995).

11. "Oklahoma's Helm Slates Anti-Gay Teacher's Bill," *Gaysweek*, 30 January 1978, n.p.

12. "Students and Teachers Win Some, Lose Some," *The Advocate,* 22 March 1978, n.p.; Jeanne Cordova, "Eugene, Wichita Go to Polls," *Lesbian Tide,* May/June 1978, 12–13.

13. Aric Press and Ann McDaniel, "The Afterhours Question," *Newsweek,* 21 January 1985, 68.

14. Linda Greenhouse, "Vote Upholds Teachers on Homosexual Rights," *The New York Times,* 27 March 1985, n.p; and Edie Dixon, "Supreme Court: Gay Teachers OK," *off our backs,* May 1985, 8; *Board of Education of Oklahoma City v. National Gay Task Force,* No. 83–2030, Supreme Court of the United States, 470 U.S. 903.

15. Coalition for Human Rights, "Verbatim Transcripts: The Family Protection Act Conference & Workshop, Held November 14, 1981," "Family Protection Act" folder, June Mazer Collection.

16. Dudley Clendinen and Adam Nagourney, *Out for Good: The Struggle to Build a Gay Rights Movement in America* (New York: Simon & Schuster, 1999), 508–509. For a careful analysis of the education politics of the Reagan administration and its close relationship to religious conservatives, see Catherine A. Lugg, *For God and Country: Conservatism and American School Policy* (New York: Peter Lang, 2000).

17. "GTA Responds to AFT Article," *Gay Teachers Association Newsletter,* November 1978, 3–4, Eric Rofes's private collection.

18. George Alan Rekers, *Shaping Your Child's Sexual Identity* (Grand Rapids, MI: Baker Book House, 1982); and *Growing Up Straight: What Families Should Know About Homosexuality* (Chicago: Moody Press, 1982).

19. Rekers claimed that members of the "homosexual liberation movement" had unfairly co-opted the word "gay" to describe themselves. Therefore he used the word "homosexual" throughout both volumes. By this time, LGBT activists tended to refrain from using the word "homosexual" because increasingly it had become a derogatory label used mainly by conservatives.

20. Rekers, *Shaping,* 3, 6–7.

21. Ibid., 13.

22. Ibid., 141–142, 148.

23. Ibid., 158–159.

24. Ibid., 166–167.

25. Rekers, *Growing Up Straight,* 35–36.

26. National Gay and Lesbian Task Force, "NGLTF Statement on Gender Identity Disorder and Transgender People" (Washington, DC: NGLTF, December 11, 1996).

27. See, for example, "The Essential Characteristics of the Father's Role for Child Adjustment and Family Strength," a paper Rekers presented at a Congressional Hearing before the Select Committee on Children, Youth and Families, United States House of Representatives (Washington, DC, February 25, 1986), ERIC Document 275403. Also, for a more thorough treatment of gender identity disorder and Rekers's role in its creation, see Phyllis Burke, *Gender Shock: Exploding the Myths of Male and Female* (New York: Anchor Books, 1996).

28. Paula Krebs, "To Teach—Or Not to Teach: Rumor Can Get You Fired in West Virginia," *off our backs,* January 1985, 5.

29. Krebs, "To Teach," 5; and *Linda J. Conway v. Hampshire County Board of Education,* No. 16540, Supreme Court of Appeals of West Virginia, 177 W. Va. 451; 352 S.E.2nd 739; 1986 W. Va. LEXIS 580 (Filed December 19, 1986).

30. Lawrence K. Altman, "Rare Cancer Seen in 41 Homosexuals," *New York Times,* 3 July 1981, A20, col. 1.

31. Randy Shilts, *And the Band Played On: Politics, People, and the AIDS Epidemic* (New York: Penguin Books, 1988). Among the gay teachers lost to AIDS are Rob Berle, a leader of the Bay Area Gay Teachers and Schoolworkers Coalition; Joe Zogby, a leader in the New York Gay Teachers Association; Larry Berner, who had debated John Briggs on several occasions; and Bill Beneville, one of the founders of the Boston Area Gay and Lesbian Schoolworkers.

32. Larry Kramer, "1,112 and Counting," *New York Native,* 14 March 1983, 1. Also see Michael Specter, "Larry Kramer, The Man Who Warned American about AIDS, Can't Stop Fighting Hard—and Loudly," *The New Yorker,* 13 May 2002, 56.

33. Thomas Morgan, "Mainstream Strategy for AIDS Group," *New York Times,* 22 July 1988, B2, col. 2.

34. Judy Keen and Desda Moss, "Ryan Inspired Dignity for All AIDS Patients," *USA Today,* 3 April 1990, 1A; and "Youth with AIDS Is Greeted Warmly at New High School," *Los Angeles Times,* 1 September 1987, A20, col. 3.

35. National Education Association, *Proceedings of the Sixty-Fifth Representative Assembly* (Washington, DC: National Education Association, 1986), 333–334, 338–339. Interestingly, Eric Rofes served as the Southern California co-chair of the "No on LaRouche" campaign, in his capacity at the time as director of the Los Angeles Gay and Lesbian Community Services Center.

36. National Education Association, *Proceedings of the Sixty-Sixth Representative Assembly* (Washington, DC: National Education Association, 1987), 217.

37. Ibid., 218–220.

38. National Education Association, *Proceedings of the Sixty-Seventh Representative Assembly* (Washington, DC: National Education Association, July 4–7, 1988), 227–233.

39. Ibid., 227–233. As a member of the North Carolina delegation, I proudly stood several rows behind Gladys Graves on this vote.

40. Corinne Lightweaver, "Sheldon Assaults Project 10," *Frontiers,* 21 September–5 October 1988, 7.

41. Patricia Ward Biederman, "Will Continue Work with Homosexuals, School Advisor Says," *Los Angeles Times,* 17 March 1988, 1, 17; Joyce Murdoch, "Young, Hurt and Homosexual," *International Herald Tribune,* 25 October 1988, 3; Dell Richards, "Gay Teens in L.A. Helped by Model School Program," *Bay Area Reporter,* 24 November 1988, 14; Pamela Klein, "Homophobia 101," *Los Angeles Weekly,* 9 December 1988, 8; and Craig Wilson, "Teacher Takes Homophobia to Task," *USA Today,* 12 February 1991, 4D.

42. "Department of Health and Human Services Report Calls for Action Against Lesbian/Gay Youth Suicide," press release of the NGLTF (August 10, 1989), "Youth Suicide" folder, June Mazer Collection.

43. Paul Gibson, "Gay Male and Lesbian Youth Suicide," *Report of the Secretary's Task Force on Youth Suicide,* Vol. 3 (Washington, DC: U.S. Department of Health and Human Services, 1989), 110.

44. Gary Remafedi, "Male Homosexuality: The Adolescent's Perspective," Unpublished report of the Adolescent Health Program, University of Minnesota (1985); and Gary Remafedi, James Farrow, and Robert W. Deisher, "Risk Factors for Attempted Suicide in Gay and Bisexual Youth," *Pediatrics* 87, 6 (1991): 869–875.

45. Letter from Representative William Dannemeyer to James O. Mason, Assistant Secretary for Health and Human Services (August 9, 1989), "Youth Suicide" folder, June Mazer Collection.

46. Letter from Representative William Dannemeyer to President George Bush (September 7, 1989), "Youth Suicide" folder, June Mazer Collection.

47. Letter from Urvashi Vaid, Executive Director of National Gay and Lesbian Task Forced, to President George Bush (September 11, 1989), "Youth Suicide" folder, June Mazer Collection.

48. Letter from Dr. Louis Sullivan, Secretary of Health and Human Services, to Representative William Dannemeyer (October 13, 1989), "Youth Suicide" folder, June Mazer Collection.

49. Letter from Urvashi Vaid, Executive Director of the National Gay and Lesbian Task Force, to Louis Sullivan, Secretary of Health and Human Services (October 23, 1989), "Youth Suicide" folder, June Mazer Collection.

50. Letter from Urvashi Vaid, Executive Director of the National Gay and Lesbian Task Force, to Louis Sullivan, Secretary of Health and Human Services (March 13, 1990), "Youth Suicide" folder, June Mazer Collection; and Letter from Urvashi Vaid, Executive Director of the National Gay and Lesbian Task Force, to Louis Sullivan, Secretary of Health and Human Services (June 1, 1991), "Youth Suicide" folder, June Mazer Collection.

51. Susan Okie, "Sullivan Cold-Shoulders Suicide Report," *Washington Post,* 13 January 1990, A5.

52. Shira Maguen, "Teen Suicide: The Government's Cover-up and America's Lost Children," *The Advocate,* September 1991, 40–47. Catherine Lugg contextualizes many of the political battles of the 1980s in which religious conservatives, LGBT rights activists, and schools intersected. See "The Religious Right and Public Education: The Paranoid Politics of Homophobia," *Educational Policy* 12, 3 (1998): 267–283.

53. Chance Claar, "Put Queer Youth in Their Place—United with All Gays and Lesbians," *The Advocate,* September 1991, 96.

54. Ibid.

55. Karen Diegmueller, "Massachusetts Approves Bill Outlawing Bias Against Gay Students," *Education Week,* 15 December 1993.

56. Jessica Portner, "Creating a Safe Place," *Education Week,* 2 March 1994.

57. Gavin Daly, "Students Rally for Gay/Straight March," *Boston Globe,* 21 May 1995, 34.

58. Matthew Brown, "Utah Board Faced All-or-None Decision; School Clubs Killed by Anti-Gay Move," *Chicago Sun-Times,* 22 February 1996, 14; James Brooke, "To Be Young, Gay and Going to High School in Utah," *New York Times,* 28 February 1996, B8, col. 1.

59. Karen Diegmueller, "Salt Lake City Prepares List of Banned Clubs," *Education Week,* 1 May 1996.

60. Ben Fulton, "It's a Bash," *Weekly Wire,* 10 November 1997, http://weekly wire.com/ww/11-10-97/slc_story.html.

61. Linda Jacobson, "Gay Student to Get Nearly $1 Million in Settlement," *Education Week,* 27 November 1996. Also see Catherine Lugg's interesting analysis of this case in "Sissies, Faggots, Lezzies, and Dykes: Gender, Sexual Orientation, and a New Politics of Education?" *Educational Administration Quarterly* 39, 1 (2003): 95–134, especially 113–114.

62. "Gay Student Attacked Twice in School Year," *New York Times,* 15 February 1999, A14, col. 5.

63. Scott S. Greenberger, "Gay Alliance Taking Hold in Schools," *Boston Globe,* 15 April 2001, B5.

64. Greenberger, "Gay Alliance," B5.

65. Dan Woog, *School's Out: The Impact of Gay and Lesbian Issues on America's Schools* (Boston: Alyson, 1995), 299–305; Kevin Jennings, "I Remember," in *One Teacher in 10: Gay and Lesbian Educators Tell Their Stories,* ed. Kevin Jennings (Los Angeles: Alyson, 1994), 19–28.

66. Letter from Ben Backus, Outgoing President, East Bay Chapter of Bay Area Network of Gay and Lesbian Educators, to East Bay BANGLE members, February 21, 1995, Eric Rofes's private collection.

67. Lugg, "Sissies, Faggots," 116–123.

68. Elaine Herscher, "Even in the Bay Area, Gay Teachers Are Taking a Risk," *San Francisco Chronicle,* 11 March 1998, A13.

69. "Report of the NEA Task Force on Sexual Orientation" (Washington, DC: NEA, 2002), http://www.nea.org/issues/diversity/orientation/02taskforce.html.

Epilogue

1. NEA, *Status of the American Public School Teacher, 2000–2001* (Washington, DC: NEA, 2003), 90. Also available online at http://www.nea.org/edstats/images/status.pdf.

2. Jackie M. Blount, *Destined to Rule the Schools: Women and the Superintendency, 1873–1995* (Albany: SUNY Press, 1998), 181.

3. Thomas Glass, Lars Björk, and Cryss Brunner, *The Study of the American School Superintendency, 2000* (Arlington, VA: AASA, 2000), 15.

4. Glass, Björk, and Brunner, *The Study,* 22; and Bureau of the Census, *Statis-*

tical Abstract of the U.S. (Washington, DC: Author, 1999), Table 1418, 873. This census data also is available online at: http://www.census.gov/prod/99pubs/99statab/sec31.pdf.

5. NEA, *Status*, 91.

6. Amicus brief, *John Geddes Lawrence and Tyrone Garner v. State of Texas,* Supreme Court no. 02–102. This document can be found online: http://www.ngltf.org/downloads/LawrenceFinal.pdf.

7. The National Gay and Lesbian Task Force maintains a current map of states with laws that protect against discrimination on account of sexual orientation and gender identity: http://www.ngltf.org/downloads/civilrightsmap.pdf.

8. Extensive current information regarding gay/straight alliances is available at: http://www.glsen.org/templates/issues/index.html?subject=3.

9. Evelyn Nieves, "After Sex Change, Teacher Is Barred from School," *New York Times,* 27 September 1999, A12.

10. Joe Mahoney, "Male Art Teacher's Now a She," *New York Daily News,* 16 June 2001, 4.

11. Art Golab, "Sex Change Ignites Debate," *Chicago Sun-Times,* 29 August 2001, 12.

12. When an elementary principal in Minnesota came out in 2002, a spokesperson for the National Association of Elementary Teachers explained, "This kind of thing has not come up before, to my knowledge. We don't have any services for gay principals, but we have had some requests. We know there are gay principals, but I'm not aware of one addressing the community like this." John Tevlin, "Principal Follows TV Rosie's Path; A Letter from the Maple Grove Educator to Families Explains That He Is Gay; Parent Reaction Was Divided," *Minneapolis Star Tribune,* 6 June 2002, 2B.

Index